ROLAND GELATT, distinguished editor and music critic, was born in Kansas City, Missouri, in 1920. Educated at Swarthmore College, he has been Associate Editor of *Musical Digest* magazine, Feature Editor of *Saturday Review,* and Editor-in-Chief of *High Fidelity* from 1958 to the present.

Music Makers

Da Capo Press Music Reprint Series

GENERAL EDITOR

FREDERICK FREEDMAN

VASSAR COLLEGE

Music Makers

Some Outstanding Musical Performers of Our Day

By Roland Gelatt

DA CAPO PRESS • NEW YORK • 1972

Library of Congress Cataloging in Publication Data

Gelatt, Roland, 1920-
Music makers.

(Da Capo Press music reprint series)
1. Musicians. I. Title.
ML394.G4 1972 780'.922 72-2334
ISBN 0-306-70519-2

This Da Capo Press edition of *Music Makers* is an unabridged republication of the first edition published in New York in 1953. It is reprinted by special arrangement with Alfred A. Knopf, Inc.

Published by Da Capo Press, Inc.
A Subsidiary of Plenum Publishing Corporation
227 West 17th Street, New York, New York 10011

Manufactured in the United States of America

Music-Makers

Roland Gelatt

Music Makers

Some

Outstanding

Musical

Performers

of Our Day

New York

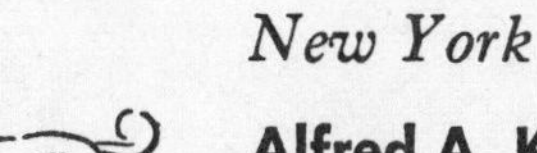

Alfred A. Knopf

1953

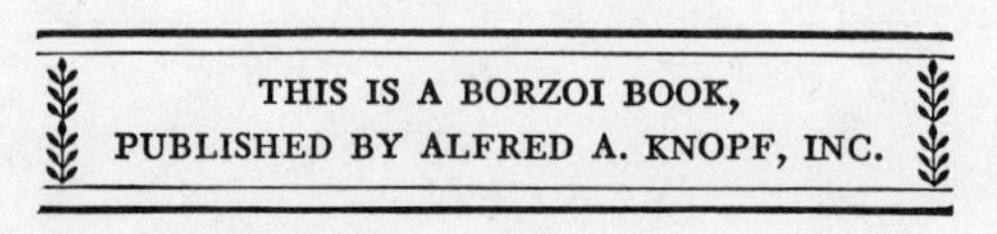

L. C. catalog card number: 51–11983

FIRST EDITION

Dedicated to the memory of my father

Arthur A. Gelatt 1894–1952

The idea can be written down, the form can be outlined, but the performer's feeling cannot be transfixed.

HECTOR BERLIOZ

Foreword

GALLERIES, whether they be of musicians or paintings, have this in common: nobody is altogether satisfied with the choice of contents; everybody is sure to find seemingly inexplicable omissions. And inevitably so, for a gallery must of necessity reflect the tastes and enthusiasms of the collector. This gallery of musicians is no exception. It offers no exhaustive who's who of contemporary performers, but rather an individual selection of musicians who have interested me over the years and whose careers have seemed to me susceptible of informed comment. I should not like to give the impression that these are the only musicians whom I admire or whose accomplishments I think worthy of analysis. But a gallery has only so much room, and the bounds must be set somewhere.

Acknowledgments

MY THANKS go first of all to the musicians discussed in the following pages, who interrupted busy schedules that I might quiz them about their careers and their art. Without this valued co-operation the book would have been impossible. For general and specific suggestions I am particularly indebted to Diran Alexanian, Jacques Barzun, Arthur Berger, Esther Gelatt, and Irving Kolodin. Finally, I wish to express my thanks to Norman Cousins and the staff of *The Saturday Review* for their indulgence when the demands of this book conflicted with those of the magazine.

ROLAND GELATT

Contents

III. *A Violinist, a Cellist, and a String Quartet*

IV. *A Clarinetist and a Guitarist*

V. *Pianists and a Harpsichordist*

Illustrations (*following page 110*)

1. Conductors

☼ Ernest *Ansermet*

ANY consideration of Ernest Ansermet must begin with Switzerland, French-speaking Switzerland, and the orchestra he created there. The Orchestre de la Suisse Romande, organized by Ansermet in 1918, has risen to be accounted one of the ranking ensembles of the world, giving the city of Geneva symphonic parity with New York, London, or Paris. This eminence of Switzerland in the world of music is of recent date. Prior to 1914, French-speaking Switzerland (the Suisse Romande) supported three small orchestras, none of them laying any claim to international distinction. That the best of the three belonged to Montreux could be traced in part to the qualities of its young conductor, Ernest Ansermet, in part to its healthy financial backing, which derived from a municipally operated gambling casino. In Lausanne there was another orchestra, supported by one affluent patron. The third was in Geneva, the orchestra from the opera house, whose members forsook their usual stint of Massenet and Gounod twice each month to give symphonic concerts under the direction of Bernhard Stavenhagen.

The outbreak of war in 1914 brought about the collapse of this orchestral phalanx. Montreux's international population fled, the roulette wheels spun no more, and the orchestra broke up. Lausanne's Mæcenas, suffering an attack of wartime jitters, declined to underwrite his ensemble any longer. And in Geneva, where the conductor Stavenhagen had died suddenly, the opera company decided to dispense henceforth with its semimonthly concerts.

A partial cure for the musical blight was found when members of the Geneva opera orchestra voted to continue giving concerts on their own, with Ansermet as conductor. Nevertheless, the situation had little to recommend it. The opera orchestra was of mediocre quality, and to bring the ensemble to symphonic proportions for these concerts its ranks were swelled by some thirty even less-favored players. In addition, Geneva's opera company, grinding out the same moribund repertory year in and year out, found its popularity diminishing. Ansermet foresaw the company's demise, and with it the virtual extinction of music in the Suisse Romande—an unhappy prospect that gave impetus to his campaign for a permanent symphony orchestra that could serve as the dominant musical institution of all French Switzerland.

Energetic proselytizing carried Ansermet's plan into operation. The Orchestre de la Suisse Romande was formed in 1918, and in the years since has put Switzerland on the musical map. Its membership is polyglot, though with a strong leaning toward French training and tradition. The orchestra as known to record-collectors throughout the world numbers ninety-two members. Yet more often than not the ninety-two-member Suisse Romande is split into a pair of forty-six-member groups, one of which performs in the pit of the revitalized Geneva opera house, while the other works as a studio ensemble for the powerful French Swiss broadcasting station. Such an arrangement keeps the orchestra men busy on a year-round schedule and provides radio and opera performances of a quality unequaled in cities many times the size of Geneva.

This Swiss city has the cultural background and enthusiasm to desire good music and the wealth to pay for what it wants. What is more, it has Ernest Ansermet. Without him, Geneva's musical standing might well be no more exalted than that of Rouen or Mainz or Peoria. For in Ansermet Geneva found no ordinary provincial time-beater, but a personality of decided influence on twentieth-century musical culture, both as champion and authoritative interpreter of modern music and as an orchestral tactician of the highest rank.

Ernest Ansermet was born on November 11, 1883, in Vevey, a small town near Montreux. In his teens he studied piano, violin, and harmony with local musicians while attending school at Vevey and, later, Lausanne. He wrote music, played in a small orchestra, and sang in a chorus. Yet at this juncture music figured in his life only as a diversion. Ostensibly a mathematics student, he had long dreamed of a stage career. He auditioned for many parts, never successfully. At twenty-two, in order to earn a living, he became a mathematics teacher at Lausanne's École Normale. We discover him a year later, the very model of a serious young mathematician, taking courses at the Sorbonne and returning to Switzerland as instructor in the Gymnase de Lausanne.

Already married and a father, Ansermet seemed safely ensconced in academic routine. But more and more the desire to serve music grew upon him. He diverted every spare hour to musical study, under the successive guidance of André Gédalge, Otto Barblan, and Ernest Bloch. At one point he temporarily abandoned job and family in order to attend the rehearsals of Artur Nikisch in Berlin. Finally, in 1911, an opportunity came his way. Francisco de Lacerda, erstwhile conductor of Montreux's Kursaal Orchestra, resigned his post, and Ansermet took over. When World War I put an end to the Montreux orchestra, Ansermet moved to Geneva to begin laying foundations for the Orchestre de la Suisse Romande. Meanwhile he had made the acquaintance of Stravinsky and Diaghilev, with consequences of profit to all three. In 1916 he made his first appearance as conductor for Diaghilev's Ballet Russe. Thereafter, until the impresario's death in 1929, Ansermet divided his time between symphony and ballet, with winters spent in Geneva and adjoining territory, and spring and summer on the grand tour with Diaghilev. Monte Carlo, Paris, and London served as focal points for excursions that sometimes went as far afield as Buenos Aires and New York.

American audiences first heard Ansermet in 1916 during a visit of the Ballet Russe. Twenty years elapsed before we saw him again, conducting at the Ravinia Festival and Hollywood Bowl during the summers of 1936 and 1937. Even at that late date his name was familiar in America only to musical *cognoscenti*. Specialists in the contemporary idiom knew him as the *exécutant attitré* of Stravinsky and Honegger; European travelers occasionally brought back reports of his absorbing Geneva programs, his luminous performances of Ravel and Debussy; but for most music-lovers on this side of the Atlantic Ansermet's renown lagged far behind that of his more highly publicized confreres. A single set of phonograph records changed this situation almost overnight, when in 1946 his recording of *Petrouchka*, for English Decca, was released in this country. Although launched with little fanfare, it soon created its own. Listeners marveled alike at the fidelity of Decca's newly perfected "ffrr" sound and at Ansermet's dazzling interpretation. Hard on the heels of *Petrouchka* came his recordings of *The Firebird* and the *Symphony of Psalms*, Ravel's *La Valse* and *Shéhérazade*, Debussy's *La Mer* and *Images pour Orchestre*, symphonies by Haydn and Mozart, Rimsky-Korsakoff's *Scheherazade*, and the Mussorgsky-Ravel *Pictures at an Exhibition*. These recordings clearly established

Ansermet among the great musicians of our day, and when he came to this country as guest conductor of the NBC Symphony Orchestra in 1947 his fame was no longer restricted to musical sophisticates and Continental travelers.

Ansermet's programs in his postwar American appearances with the NBC, Philadelphia, and Boston orchestras have been built largely around twentieth-century music. One who propagandizes thus vigorously must be a staunch adherent—or so most of us assumed. But here we encounter a paradox: this conductor who has been so identified with contemporary music is one of its severest critics.

In evaluating contemporary music, Ansermet makes clear from the start that for him form and content are indivisible. It is this conviction that leads him to consider anew the old notion of *ethos*. By *ethos* he means, as Aristotle meant, the innate element in character which determines human motivation. Ansermet describes it as "the sign of man and his nobility," and he is careful to emphasize that *ethos* is not to be confused with specific moral or ethical values. "The *ethos*," Ansermet believes, "is the only value we can recognize in music." If a composer makes a game of his art, elaborating his forms by an act of will (as when he tries to reconstitute merely by their outer signs forms already known), *ethos* vanishes, and human significance with it. Here is what Ansermet finds, to his dismay, in so much contemporary music. "The composer of today," he says, "confuses the canvas with the picture, and this is very serious. The world of sentiment that Western music once expressed seems to be dumbstruck, unproductive, paralyzed. There no longer seems to work in man that integration of his emotional life which once caused Pascal to speak of 'the intelligence of the heart.' "

Creative activity has lost its urgency. The composer considers himself an artisan. "Erroneous pretension," comments Ansermet. "In music the artisan comes *after* the artist, not before." As the creative drive failed, art could assume some steadfastness of purpose only by dogmatism and formalism. To Ansermet, Arnold Schönberg typified this tendency at its most acute. It is true, he concedes, that Schönberg's music shows extraordinary richness of structure. He recalls an article by Alban Berg on Schönberg's D minor Quartet, in which the younger composer acclaimed the labyrinthine marvels of his master's score. To which Ansermet remarks: "If significance depended on structural complexity, many classical works would seem poor indeed; however, the first theme of Mozart's G minor Symphony, in all its simplicity, strikes me as far more satisfying than the beginning measures of Schönberg's quartet. It is true that the significance of music resides in the quality of its structure, but the most erudite structure is not necessarily satisfying; formal activity in music does not consist of throwing together everything in sight, but in achieving structures perceptible to the heart. The Schönbergians by making structure itself their musical objective, and by eliminating the feeling of cadence, have robbed their music of expression; what remains is dead theory." Thus, he feels that Schönberg's achievements, important as they are, have been accomplished at the price of abandoning *ethos*.

Igor Stravinsky, the other outstanding figure of modern music, presents a somewhat different problem. Ansermet would not pair Stravinsky with Schönberg as exemplifying the complete abandonment of *ethos*. "There are intimations of a certain *ethos* in Stravinsky's music," he admits, "but it tells you nothing about him. When you hear a Bach fugue, you know beyond any doubt that the man who wrote it was possessed of a strong religious faith. When you hear a Beethoven symphony, you feel the humanity and optimistic strength of its composer. But when you hear a work of Stravinsky's, you are at a loss to know what manner of man it was who set the notes down on paper." How explain this? Ansermet ascribes it to a certain indirectness in Stravinsky's expression. "He speaks to the listener as if by proxy; he does not give of himself." Of him Ansermet can speak as George Sampson did of Henry James: "There are faint and complex reverberations of human encounters, like a carillon of memories." And so, in Stravinsky's case also, Ansermet finds contemporary music wanting in that basic value of *ethos*.

With these two great composers of our time judged deficient in this respect, it is no wonder that Ansermet offers similar criticisms of many lesser men. A gloomy picture this, whose Spenglerian overtones Ansermet will not deny. Nevertheless, he sees some breaks in the pattern. Hindemith, Malipiero, Martinu, Honegger, and Britten often seem to turn in what he considers an encouraging direction. Most of all Bartók, whom Ansermet views as a symbol of our time. "The work of Béla Bartók," he says, "mirrors the shock we have undergone, as if he had felt everything, put everything to the test, taken everything upon himself in order to surmount a situation even more difficult for him than for others. Beginning in the inauthentic, in imitation of Brahms, Strauss, and Reger, he proceeded successively through the revelations of Debussy, the agitation of his experiences with Schönberg and Stravinsky, to a laborious introspection and the awareness of his artificial Hungarianism. Bartók was one of those who 'groans while he searches,' though he always managed a smile; but he found himself, and his last works are the most beautiful tokens of hope that the music of our time has produced."

This summary of Ansermet's attitude toward contemporary music is sketchy in the extreme. It oversimplifies, disregards many links in the argument, neglects the examples that buttress opinion, makes his opinions seem inordinately extreme. To do justice to him would require a book in itself, and happily the conductor is writing one. Yet even this admittedly inadequate abstract of his opinions will demonstrate that he is not one of those whose heart belongs to every contemporary note.

By this time one will be prompted to ask, as I did, why this conductor chooses to conduct music for which he entertains such tepid regard. The answer is to be found in Ansermet's conception of the conductor's province. To him, it is a cultural duty to accord new music a hearing, to give audiences an opportunity for judgment. In his words, it is necessary for the conductor "to make known the document." Personal predilections have no bearing on the matter. Ansermet often conducts music that he would never perform merely for his own pleasure. "But," he adds significantly, "I never conduct a work unless I am convinced of its value. Though I may not *like* it subjectively, I must *admire* it objectively." Pressed for an example, Ansermet volunteered Ernest Bloch's *Concerto symphonique* for piano and orchestra, which he introduced in 1950 to audiences in Europe and America. Bloch's prolixity of expression does not lie closest to this conductor's heart, but that does not prevent him from performing a work in which objectively he finds much to commend. Here we can turn with advantage to Sainte-Beuve:

> One is not the only person in the world, nor can one claim to be the universal model; opinion may follow other forms of beauty besides that which appeals to the critic as being the nearest to his ideal. These other forms have the right to exist; and to enter into understanding of them it is necessary that the critic shall put himself to one side and even think against his own grain.

Substitute "conductor" for "critic" and we are in Ansermet's shoes. Like an actor with an ungrateful role, he does his best no matter what his opinion. Moreover, when immersed in rehearsal and performance, Ansermet finds himself under a momentary spell. He is persuaded for the nonce that the music at hand is of the highest quality. Only afterwards will he regain his critical point of view and perhaps lower his estimate.

For his own greatest pleasure Ansermet will choose Mozart and Haydn, Debussy and Ravel. His regard for Debussy amounts to a passion. "Why do they pay me to conduct his music?" he demands. "It is I who should pay for the privilege." The early Stravinsky of *The Firebird* and *Petrouchka* is another love. Indeed, for all his strictures, Ansermet has probably been more instrumental than any other conductor in bringing Stravinsky's works to public attention. Count among his first performances *L'Histoire du Soldat* (1918), *Renard* (1922), *Les Noces* (1923), the Capriccio for Piano and Orchestra (1929), the *Symphony of Psalms* (1930), and the Mass (1948). In the 1920's, says Ansermet, it was no easy matter to conduct Stravinsky's music, for orchestras accustomed to music with a regular beat could not easily cope with constantly changing time-signatures. "Stravinsky abolished the feeling of periodicity and destroyed the conductor's function as a time-beater. With him," Ansermet explains, "you have a speed but no more tempo." In order to conduct such music Ansermet was obliged to evolve an entirely new technique, one that without regular beats would give players the feeling of tempo. It was accomplished through "the quality and amplitude of gesture." All conductors have evolved similar techniques to cope with Stravinsky's scores. "The trouble is," objects Ansermet, "that this way of conducting has now permeated all music. Although right for Stravinsky, it is quite wrong for Mozart or Schumann. Stravinsky brought an exciting new resource to music. I regret to see musicians applying it to works where it is wholly inappropriate."

One hesitates to characterize a musician in the light of his biography. How obvious to say of Ansermet that he conducts with the calculation of a mathematician, that his interpretations are organized with the jeweled precision of a Swiss watch! Yet both descriptions are inescapable. One could instance Ansermet's recordings of *Petrouchka* or *Ibéria*, the astounding mechanical construction of these interpretations, the way every note is set securely in place to perform its own small function in the total complex movement. Not a hint of faulty workmanship here, nor an intimation of defective parts. But let not these splendors of construction blind us to other qualities. There is far more to Ansermet's conducting than the precise translation of a blueprint. Ansermet has himself written revealingly on this point: "The executant never finds in his text more than a diagram of the propulsive tensions to be produced; he must always go beyond these mere indications. Fundamentally, *he never plays what is written*—conversely, he should never play that which does not conform to what is written."

Structural clarity, tonal sonority, above all an intellectual toughness of fiber—these qualities inform everything Ansermet touches, and they place him among the most accomplished conductors of our day. One cannot accept all his interpretations; neither can one agree with every statement by Bernard Shaw. But one listens to Ansermet with the avidity with which one reads Shaw—for keenness of mind, sincerity of expression, and an Olympian loftiness of purpose.

☼ Sir Thomas *Beecham*

WITH deliberate, stately tread—straight-backed, arms stiffly to side—he paces his way to the conductor's stand. Here is none of the brisk efficiency that delineates the entrance of an Ormandy or the nervous tension impelling a Toscanini to assault the podium. Beecham's very manner of presenting himself gives a key to his musical personality: his measured steps portend relaxed and genial urbanity. It is not in Beecham's province to cleave the general ear with musical demonism run riot. He enters upon an evening of music-making with gracious informality. Beecham regards his calling with affection, and also with a reasonable sense of proportion. You will not find him staggering like an overburdened Atlas under the weight of interpretative responsibility. A man of towering standards, he yet continues to regard music as a diversion rather than as a religion. He is wonderfully, anachronistically Edwardian. And he is one of the great custodians of musical culture.

For years Beecham was known as a talented amateur, a man who dabbled in music as Disraeli dabbled in literature—brilliant, but not professional. Even today this notion persists, despite assurances from Sir Thomas that the description is so much poppycock. His musical training followed few orthodox trails. At six he was initiated to the piano by a local Lancashire teacher who idolized Mozart, and by the age of fourteen he was proficient enough to accompany the tenor Ben Davies on the occasion of a shipboard concert. He had no commerce with conservatories, his formal schooling having been restricted to Rossall (a Lancashire public school) and two abortive years at Wadham College, Oxford. In his late teens Beecham began to compose songs and little instrumental pieces under the guidance of John Varley Roberts, organist of Magdalen, who also furthered his knowledge of musical theory. Later he studied with Frederic Austin, then professor of composition at the Liverpool School of Music; with Charles Wood, assistant and eventual successor to Charles Villiers Stanford at Cambridge, and with Moritz Moszkowski. Like most conductors he never took a lesson in conducting; having organized a small amateur orchestra when he was barely twenty, he simply began to conduct.

Because of his improvised education and his early indecision about a musical career, there may be areas where Sir Thomas is somewhat less adept than the most professional of professionals. An instrumentalist who spent years in Beecham-directed orchestras once ventured the opinion to me that Sir Thomas has never mastered the alto clef. ("You can almost see Beecham ticking off the notes on his fingers," was the way he put it.) I have heard it asserted that Beecham could set down from memory the entire orchestral score of *Ein Heldenleben*, so retentive and encompassing is his musical intellect, and I have heard it asserted with equal authority that he could no more do this than copy out the Koran from memory. It would be difficult to set with precision the exact limits of Beecham's professional competence. And, really, it is of minor consequence. His deficiencies (if they in fact exist) pertain to the small change of music. What matter if Beecham bluffs his way through certain orchestral intricacies, so long as he makes compelling music? He is a master in the things that count: tempo, balance, tone, and style. As a strategist he has won innumerable campaigns; it would be uncharitable to require that he be a peerless tactician as well.

Those campaigns, the focal points of a rich and varied career, can merely be touched upon in a few pages. Beecham was born on April 29, 1879, in St. Helens, a drab Lancashire town spawned by the Industrial Revolution, where his grandfather had built up an immensely profitable business. That it still prospers can be attested by anyone who has seen the ubiquitous advertisements for Beecham's Pills ("Worth a Guinea a Box") spread throughout Great Britain. His father, Sir Joseph, from whom Sir Thomas inherited his baronetcy, had a lifelong affection for music and was thus kindly disposed when his son demanded piano lessons. Oddly, the Mozartian diet prescribed by his teacher did not appeal to the boy who would subsequently become celebrated for his Mozart readings. Young Beecham much preferred to hammer his way through opera scores.

Throughout his school years it was assumed that Beecham would contribute in some manner to the family's commercial enterprise. As a young man he looked upon music as a hobby rather than a goal, and it was with this attitude that he organized and directed a small orchestra in St. Helens upon his withdrawal from Oxford in 1899. This first venture must have fallen somewhat short of perfection, but it at least convinced him that conducting and not pianism was his proper interpretative métier. In St. Helens that same year he conducted the celebrated Hallé Orchestra when its regular *Dirigent*, Hans Richter, fell ill just before a concert.

Despite these preliminary flirtations, Beecham might well

have settled into a life of commerce had it not been for a serious falling-out with his father which ruptured relations between the two for nine years. As the son was not exactly cast into the street penniless (he could rely on a substantial income provided by his grandfather), he spent three years commuting between London and the Continent, garnering musical impressions and composing vocal works under the ægis of the several teachers already mentioned. One of these compositions, an opera in English, he submitted to Kelson Truman, impresario of a minor traveling opera-company. Truman was flabbergasted at the mere thought of producing an opera by an unknown English composer, but on learning of the young man's other proclivities he countered with the offer of a job as conductor. Beecham toured the provinces for three months, and during his short tenure formed an accurate notion of how opera should *not* be produced. There followed another interlude of cross-channel commuting. In Paris, while studying with Moszkowski, he became aware of eighteenth-century French opera—Grétry, Méhul, and Dalayrac—and hired "a small company of young men" to transcribe scores for him in the Bibliothèque Nationale. His interest in Grétry and Company, let it be emphasized, was the interest primarily of a composer, not a conductor. These were the years when Beecham cherished the conviction that his mission was to write The Great English Opera.

By 1905, six years after his first efforts in St. Helens and three years after the short opera-engagement, Beecham began to slacken in his zeal for composing and to think more seriously of conducting. He threw in his lot with a recently formed chamber ensemble and directed sporadic concerts of unfamiliar music, old and new, to medium-sized audiences. In 1907 this group, known as the New Symphony Orchestra, expanded to full symphonic size. It was not long after the enlargement that Beecham made the personal acquaintance of Frederick Delius, whose *Paris: The Song of a Great City* soon figured on the New Symphony's programs. Delius's reputation owes much to Beecham as propagandist for his music, but there is a less-known debt in the other direction: it was Delius who convinced Beecham finally to forgo composition in favor of his undeniable interpretative gift.

In 1908 Beecham and the New Symphony parted company, the first but not the last time that he would sever an unamicable orchestral relationship with peremptory dispatch. The implication would seem to be that he is a tyrannical and disputatious taskmaster. Actually, he has quite the opposite reputation. "To laugh and smile at a Beecham rehearsal," writes Reginald Kell,* "is part of the show most of the time, for he is no baton-biting, carpet-chewing, stand-slinging tyrant who relies on fear to command respect." Probably it is Beecham's disinclination to brutalize an orchestra which has flecked his career with stormy resignations. Rather than impose his will on a body of sullen players, Beecham prefers to begin afresh and create a new orchestra. That is what happened in 1908. It had been the practice for regulars in the New Symphony to send deputies to rehearsals. Obviously, one cannot perfect an interpretation if the orchestra at rehearsal and the orchestra at concert-time are composed of different men. Beecham laid down a fiat against deputies, ran into opposition, and quit. Soon he had formed a new group of eighty players, the Beecham Orchestra, and with typical success in attracting top-grade talent secured the services of such men as Albert Sammons and Lionel Tertis. The Beecham Orchestra made its first public appearance in London in February 1909 with this program:

* "The Beecham No One Knows," *Saturday Review of Literature*, October 28, 1950.

Carnaval Romain Overture BERLIOZ
In the Fen Country VAUGHAN WILLIAMS
(FIRST PERFORMANCE)
Sea Drift DELIUS
(FIRST LONDON PERFORMANCE)
Te Deum BERLIOZ

London, like the rest of the world, was then dominated by Germanic tradition. Conductors, if not German by birth, were almost always German by training, and programs were weighted with works of Beethoven, Brahms, and Wagner. Beecham endeavored to counteract this emphasis from the very start of his career. In the years prior to 1910 he brought to London such non-Germanic novelties as Lalo's G minor Symphony and D'Indy's *La Forêt enchantée* and (from Bohemia) Dvořák's *Golden Spinning Wheel* and Smetana's *Sarka.* Above all, he gave concert recognition to the rising English school. During these early years he gave six works by Delius (*Paris*, *Sea Drift*, *Brigg Fair*, *Over the Hills and Far Away*, *Appalachia*, and *A Mass of Life*) and at least two by Vaughan Williams (*Norfolk Rhapsody* and *In the Fen Country*). When he did present music of the established masters, he continued to indulge his penchant for novelty. If he chose a Mozart symphony, it would be the "Prague" or the "Linz" or the "Paris" rather than one of the famous last three.

Up to this point the young conductor had hardly become the cynosure of Britain's attention. He was known (if at all) as a second-rate, rather queer conductor, whose home-grown musical culture fell far short of the Continental subtleties offered by Willem Mengelberg, Artur Nikisch, or Felix Weingartner. But with his entrance into the operatic arena Beecham achieved a measure of notoriety. Reconciliation with his father gave him financial backing with which to form his own opera company, and early in 1910 he rented Covent Garden for a short season. *Elektra*, the first of Strauss's operas to be performed in London, set the town agog, and the season was extended to satisfy demand for tickets. Although the other offerings engendered far less enthusiasm, Beecham was emboldened to follow in short order with another operatic venture. He rented His Majesty's Theatre, in the Haymarket, for a summer season of opera in English, and opened with what was later to be a great Beecham specialty, Offenbach's *The Tales of Hoffmann*. London clamored for more *Hoffmann*, though it snubbed the succeeding *Werther* of Massenet, *Feuersnot* of Richard Strauss, and *Seraglio*, *Figaro*, *Così Fan Tutte*, and *Impresario* of Mozart. Only with another light work, *Die Fledermaus*, was Beecham able to garner good attendance. Again he finished with a financial deficit; also with the satisfaction of having brought to life several masterpieces long quiescent in the English capital. As the Beecham fortune could easily withstand these buffets, he embarked immediately on another round of "grand opera" at Covent Garden, following again the policy of presenting unfamiliar works with a leavening of operatic best-sellers. In the former category were D'Albert's *Tiefland*, Thomas's *Hamlet*, and Strauss's *Salome*, and of these only *Salome*—by reason of its reputation for indecency—filled the house.

Thus ended the first year of Beecham's opera-giving, a twelvemonth resplendent with *premières* and revivals such as London had never witnessed. Of the twenty-odd unfamiliar works given that year, only four—two Strauss "shockers" and two light operas—enjoyed substantial support. As the result was a deficit of one hundred thousand pounds sterling, Beecham decided to pull in his reins, merging his forces with the established Covent Garden Grand Opera Trust and taking a back seat in the management of London's operatic affairs for two years. Even with his own company Beecham had not directed all the performances; after the merger he conducted still less, though he managed to continue his record of Strauss *premières* by conducting the first London performance of *Der Rosenkavalier*. These were the years when Diaghilev and his ballet overwhelmed Covent Garden's patrons. Beecham was sometimes at the conductor's desk (it was his own symphony orchestra), where he seems to have made little impression. One well-placed authority, Vaslav Nijinsky, while watching Beecham from the wings, wryly observed: "*Comme l'orchestre dirige bien Monsieur Beecham ce soir.*"

When England found itself unexpectedly at war in August 1914 the first phase of Beecham's career ended. In a dozen years he had organized two symphony orchestras, launched several opera enterprises, imported Russian ballet and opera, introduced new music both native and foreign, and resurrected neglected scores with vigorous determination. He had lavished care and money on works that London should have relished but perversely did not. Occasionally his projects had shown a profit. Always they had injected a stimulus into English musical life. As an impresario and a source of fresh musical currents young Thomas Beecham had made his mark. Not as a conductor. Contemporaries were wont to appreciate Beecham the impresario but to depreciate Beecham the conductor. Thus, Muriel Draper can be found complaining (in *Music at Midnight*) that "Beecham was responsible for some of the less memorable performances," her reference being to his 1914 season of Russian ballet and opera. And Sydney Grew, recollecting the Beecham concerts of this era, concludes that "few impressions remain of the grander and more noble kind." While Grew acknowledged Beecham's insight into the César Franck Symphony, Mozart adagios, and orchestral sparklers on the order of Chabrier's *España*, "where the substance of music is essentially weighty" (Bach, Beethoven, Brahms) he saw no lasting merit, and he could remember "a shatteringly, batteringly noisy and uncontrolled execution of the last movement in Tchaikovsky's Fifth Symphony, which remains with me as my worst experience of coarse orchestral tone."

The most detailed estimate I have found of Beecham's prewar attainment comes from the pen of Boston's astute critic H. T. Parker, who visited London in 1913. In a long article about Beecham and his enterprises, published in the Boston *Evening Transcript* of July 12, "H.T.P." wrote:

> It is not likely that Thomas Beecham will ever prove more than a mediocre conductor. He is old enough now and he has had experience enough to give proof of unusual talents if he possessed them. As he is, there is scarcely a sign of them. In concerts his conducting is exceedingly mannered and exceedingly unproductive of visible results. . . . He beats a beat that seems extremely difficult for an orchestra to follow. Now and again he pounces upon some detail of the music and strongly emphasizes it; then overlooks a dozen others quite as important. He lacks the divine faculty that chooses as by instinct enforced by imagination the pace and the accent that will reveal and animate music. . . . In opera Mr. Beecham is curiously disposed to forget the stage. His mind seems concentrated on the score before him and the orchestra around him. . . . His conducting of *Ariadne auf Naxos* seemed ill-prepared, rough, even obtuse. . . . It was not exactly the part of wisdom to produce operas at the pace of two a week and often in performances so hastily prepared that they did music and drama scant justice. It is good to revive neglected classics, but not in such lumping performances that they reconduct the chosen music into what seems a deserved oblivion.

A more inaccurate prophecy can hardly be imagined. But Parker was no fool (compare his brilliant 1915 estimate of

Toscanini, page 69), and if he describes a Beecham far removed from the Sir Thomas of later years, it can only be concluded that maturity and growing experience have wrought a striking change.

Musical activity in England ceased the moment war broke out in August 1914 (it was to happen again a quarter century later at the start of World War II). "Concert societies all over the country were closing down," Beecham recalls,* "and it soon began to be clear that unless some countermove were made quickly, England would find itself without music of any sort." Armed with energy, talent, and a powerful checkbook, Beecham initiated a series of historic "countermoves." Perhaps on the principle that charity begins at home, he turned his attention first to his native Lancashire. The Hallé Orchestra in Manchester, having just lost the services of its German-born conductor, Michael Balling, was momentarily adrift. Beecham offered to conduct (without salary) whenever he could, to find suitable substitutes when he was away, and to underwrite the orchestra's expenses. With the Hallé Orchestra on an even keel, Beecham directed his ministrations Londonwards, and insured continuance of the London Symphony and Royal Philharmonic Society concerts. He conducted all of the Royal Philharmonic programs and a portion of the London Symphony's (Vassily Safonoff, Emil Mlynarski, and Henri Verbrugghen were his associates). In both cases Beecham made up the deficits.

Opera then claimed his attention. No longer was Covent Garden playing host to the world's celebrated singers, who either had returned to the Continent or had taken refuge in neutral America. But did the absence of a Chaliapin, a Caruso, or a Destinn signify that opera in England must go into eclipse? Thomas Beecham thought not, and in the autumn of 1915 organized his own company, composed mainly of na-

* Sir Thomas Beecham: *A Mingled Chime* (New York: 1943).

tive talent. Again, though he acted as artistic overseer, he did not always conduct, often entrusting performances to Percy Pitt or Eugene Goossens, an unknown young man of twenty-two. So greedy were London audiences for good opera that Beecham's company played for half a year, first in the Shaftesbury Theatre and later in the Aldwych. In the spring of 1916 the company moved to Manchester and repeated its London success. How did this wartime enterprise compare with Beecham's "international seasons" of prewar years? Here is what that perceptive observer Neville Cardus has written:*

> At Covent Garden he seemed frequently frustrated; in the Beecham opera of Quay Street, Manchester, he was in his element, especially when he conducted Verdi's *Otello* with Frank Mullings as Othello, the greatest actor, next to Chaliapin, ever seen in opera in England, and a singer who, by imagination, transformed the defects of his voice into expressive assets. The Beecham opera of 1916, which would fill Manchester's largest theater for three months at a stretch, eight performances weekly, was the best, in range and finish of style, ever known in England. Glyndebourne alone has equaled it, but the scope there was smaller.

The Beecham that we know, musician of elegance and molder of impeccable ensemble, begins to emerge. Cardus terms the wartime production of *Figaro* "the most vivacious and yet the most pathos-shaded that I can recall in a lifetime," and Beecham himself acknowledged that "this production topped a peak so far unscaled in the annals of any native organization . . . certainly nothing has appeared since to excel it." Cardus was admittedly recalling performances far in the past, to which time may have lent enchantment. But here is Francis Toye writing (in the *Bystander*) in 1915 of these

* In his *Autobiography* (London: 1947).

same performances and saying substantially the same thing, albeit in more guarded tone: "Mr. Beecham has more than 'made good.' Despite natural defects of temperament he stands out today as the most important personage in English musical life. He is the only English conductor who has anything 'Dionysiac' about him."

The company continued a steady round of performances until 1920, playing throughout the provinces as well as in London and Manchester. Its wide repertory, with such Beecham favorites as *The Seraglio*, *Die Zauberflöte*, *The Fair Maid of Perth*, and *A Village Romeo and Juliet*, served to maintain the level of English musical taste for several otherwise barren years. Yet it was not for this, nor for his underwriting of England's major orchestras, that Beecham was knighted in 1916, but rather for his services as a cultural emissary to Italy when that country (as yet neutral) was being wooed by the British Government.

Sir Joseph Beecham died in 1916, leaving a good proportion of the family's cash immobilized in the purchase of Covent Garden (not only the two theaters, but also the vegetable market and surrounding real estate). Because of various legal difficulties raised by Sir Joseph's will and by wartime financial legislation the estate could not liquidate this vast investment. In complexity the affair rivaled that unending chancery action in *Bleak House*. A full report can be found in Beecham's autobiography, *A Mingled Chime*. Here it will suffice to say that by 1920 Sir Thomas Beecham found himself without cash or credit and officially declared a bankrupt, despite the fact that he was heir to one of England's greatest fortunes. He was forced to withdraw his support from the various British orchestras with which he had been connected since 1914 and to disband his opera company. For three years he busied himself with commerce and finance, until he had extricated the estate from the courts and gained control of his patrimony.

On April 8, 1923, Sir Thomas once more ascended the podium, conducting the London Symphony Orchestra in a program typically Beechamesque (Mozart, Berlioz, Delius, and Richard Strauss). Londoners soon realized that the three-year hiatus had effected a perceptible change in his interpretative powers. At last he seemed to have attained full command of his medium. "Having for the first time in his life had leisure to look round and to reflect," writes Dame Ethel Smyth,* "Beecham was at last master of his own soul. Up to the present, the multifariousness of his gifts, combined with his inexhaustible energy and the high tension of his spirit, had in a certain sense been his undoing. Owner and organizer of everything he touched, as well as artistic factotum, repetitor, and conductor, he had been trying to put through a task single-handed that was beyond mortal powers." With the hurly-burly of his prewar experience still fresh in mind, Beecham was loath for some time after his return to musical activity to take on the responsibility of fresh enterprises. He assumed direction of the well-established London Symphony, which he conducted more or less regularly, and began to make history as an interpreter rather than as an entrepreneur.

His performance of *Messiah* in December 1926 helped to free this score of the bombastic exaggerations that had so securely attached themselves to it during the nineteenth century. Perhaps even more revelatory was his performance that same year of the Beethoven Second Symphony. "One knew it very well indeed," Gerald Abraham recalls,† "almost too well, even then—though better, indeed, in piano-duet form than

* In *Beecham and Pharaoh* (London: 1935).

† "'Tommy' in England," by Gerald Abraham, *Saturday Review of Literature*, October 28, 1950.

in orchestral flesh-and-blood; yet one found one had never really known it at all. Don't ask what he did with it; though I remember he put down the baton in the slow movement and took it a shade less slowly than one was accustomed to. But the general impression was of something that was neither objective nor objectionable, neither polished conventionality nor a 'personal interpretation.'" Richard Aldrich summed up the changed attitude toward Beecham's conducting when he reported to the *New York Times* in 1927: "London has long since got through laughing at the pill-maker's titled son and no longer stays away from his concerts. . . . The attendance and closeness of attention paid were something in the nature of a tribute to something in the nature of a genius."

Yet when Beecham made his American debut as guest conductor of the New York Philharmonic in January 1928 he was only temperately received. The Tchaikovsky Piano Concerto, which served as a vehicle for Vladimir Horowitz (also making his debut), may not have been Beecham's cup of tea; but otherwise the opening program—Handel excerpts, Delius's *Walk to the Paradise Garden*, Mozart's Symphony No. 34, and the "*Chasse Royale et Orage*" from *Les Troyens*—would seem to have been well calculated to display the new conductor in a favorable light. To W. J. Henderson, however, the titled Britisher "did not seem to set himself shoulder to shoulder with the other generals who have commanded the Philharmonic forces." New York's other critics responded in similar tenor. On a return visit to the Philharmonic in 1932 Beecham got friendlier notices, though it was only in 1936—during another guest conductorship—that American critics accepted him as an artist of the highest stature. The platform eccentricities in which Sir Thomas then indulged may well have stood in his way. His vitality in Carnegie Hall once proved so intense that his suspenders snapped in midconcert; with all the nonchalance he could muster, Beecham held up his trousers with his left hand through the rest of the composition, while continuing to conduct with his right. On another occasion, he became so transported during a passage of quiet reverie that he lost his balance and fell off the podium.

A parallel to Beecham's break with the New Symphony in 1908 occurred twenty-four years later with the London Symphony. This ensemble had begun the practice of forming its business committees from among the players. Beecham took a dim view of this and certain other aspects of the orchestra's operation. His objections went unheeded, and he resigned forthwith. Within two months he had formed the London Philharmonic Orchestra, which with its galaxy of eminent instrumentalists (Reginald Kell and Leon Goossens, to name two) has been described as the finest of Europe's prewar orchestras. Its first concert, on October 7, 1932, initiated a glorious period not only for English audiences, but for record-collectors the world over.

The London Philharmonic was engaged for the concerts of the Royal Philharmonic Society as well as for the Courtauld-Sargent Concerts and Harold Holt's Sunday Afternoon Concerts. Britain's giant gramophone combine, His Master's Voice-Columbia, contracted for its services in the recording studio. Under the name of the Royal Opera Orchestra it played each year during the International Seasons at Covent Garden, where Beecham was Artistic Director from 1933 to 1939. Yet with all this patronage the orchestra operated at a loss. One reason was its distinguished (and hence high-salaried) personnel, but a more basic cause for its recurrent deficit was Beecham's refusal to economize when to do so involved a musical sacrifice. He would think nothing of rehearsing a "simple" Mozart symphony for days before entering the recording studio, nor did he boggle at demanding "retakes," costly as they are.

Several wealthy patrons in collaboration with Sir Thomas

were needed to bridge the gap between the London Philharmonic's expenditure and its income. Toward the mundane aspects of music-making Beecham reportedly professes a complete indifference. Berta Geissmar quotes him as saying, "I never trouble about money. It doesn't interest me." Apparently it did interest the orchestra's other backers, for they tired in time of financing Beecham's extravagances. By early 1939 the famed orchestra was tottering. Enough money came in to see it through the London Music Festival, but with the declaration of war in September it became evident that the orchestra could not continue along the old lines. The players then took over and revivified the orchestra on a co-operative basis. Sir Thomas was invited (!) to conduct, which he did on several occasions (both in concert and in the recording studio) until his departure from English soil in April 1940. He stayed away for over four years, much to the disappointment of those Britishers who looked to him to repeat his heroic efforts of World War I.

After a season in Australia, Beecham came to America, where he was associated with many musical institutions, not all of them venerable. At the Metropolitan Opera House he directed memorable performances of *Faust*, *Carmen*, *Louise*, *Falstaff*, and *Tristan*, and with such well-trained bodies as the New York Philharmonic and Chicago Symphony orchestras he achieved expectably fine results. But Beecham made his profoundest impression with the several "scratch" orchestras which he conducted during these war years in America. In Seattle, Detroit, Rochester, Vancouver, and New York (with the WPA City Symphony) he proved anew his vaunted gift of coaxing first-rate sound from second-rate ensembles.

His return to scarred London in September 1944 was not productive of the happiest consequences. He resumed direction of a London Philharmonic considerably altered from the ensemble he had left four years before. In this interval it had been playing one-night stands to provincial audiences often more enthusiastic than discriminating. Many of its virtuoso members had gravitated to other orchestras or volunteered for war work. No longer was it in the vanguard of Europe's orchestras. This was hardly a state of affairs calculated to upset Beecham. Given a free hand, he was prepared to reconstitute the ensemble as of yore. However, he soon found that his hand was more than a little tied. Dealing now with a cooperative orchestra, he could no longer call every note of the tune. When it came to his replacing personnel or exacting extra rehearsal time, the players—through their executive committee—on occasion said him nay. For a year Beecham tried to adapt himself to the new order, while the orchestra tried to meet him halfway. But recriminations arose, and in 1945 he took leave of the London Philharmonic, simultaneously announcing his intention of forming yet another orchestra. Again he lured some of Britain's most gifted players into his service and quickly molded an ensemble that in tone and fineness of execution bore the Beecham stamp. When the Royal Philharmonic Orchestra crossed the Atlantic in 1950 to tour America, it reinforced an impression previously derived from phonograph records that once more Sir Thomas had created an orchestra rivaling the best.

If Beecham affects British musical life less today than before it is because he and the times are out of step. The Edwardian baronet did not take kindly to an England governed by socialists and reduced to austerity. His view of state-supported music is anything but amicable. For years he badgered the management of Covent Garden, which had become officially subsidized after the war, peppering his strictures with personal diatribes that served his argument ill. Only in 1951 did he consent to conduct again in the venerable opera house on Bow Street which he had once owned and managed. Because of his aversion to the government-sponsored Festival of Britain he refused for many months to conduct in the new Festival Hall. His sympathy for modern British composition ends, chronologically, with Vaughan Williams. He has called our times "the golden age of musicians and the leaden age of music." No wonder, then, that Beecham's leadership has lessened, that many Britishers regard him more as a colorful institution—like the Changing of the Guards—than as the animating force he once was. It was even possible for the 1951 Festival of Britain to open with Beecham *in absentia*.

"Could it be," asks an editorialist in the London *Observer*, "that, in his own country, Beecham's wit, dandyism, and scathing speeches have led people to overlook his standing as one of the great musicians of his age?" Let the British answer for themselves. In America his standing has been secure since his first phonograph records began coming our way. To many he represents an embodiment of the ideal musician, a man who blends lettered culture with invigorating enthusiasms. His rapport with Handel, Mozart, Berlioz, Chabrier, Delius, Strauss, and Sibelius is incontestable. The corollary sometimes added, that he is at a disadvantage with other composers (the "three B's" in particular), may well be more automatic than accurate. The temptation to brand him as a specialized musician arises, I think, because his specialties are so very special. It would seem reasonable that a man who plays Chabrier with rare éclat may be deficient in understanding of Beethoven—save that Beecham does not stand to reason. Everywhere he is contradictory. He finds himself on equally good terms with the rhetorical Berlioz and the subdued Delius. He revels in complex bric-a-brac by Richard Strauss, then addresses himself with undiminished passion to the spare purity of early Mozart. You cannot make predictions about him, not even within his own acknowledged realm. Justly as he is acclaimed for his readings of Mozart, there are occasions when he treats this composer ill. He may conduct the "Prague" Symphony with unbelievable grace and style one night, only to disappoint his listeners a few evenings later with a "Jupiter" unaccountably erratic and lumpy.

Sir Thomas enjoys the amateur's great privilege of nonchalance. Almost alone among contemporary conductors, he avoids the path of demonism; he takes music in his stride and does not press it with febrile intensity. At a supper party one night, just before he was to conduct a performance of *Götterdämmerung*, Lady Cunard voiced the plea that Beecham rely on a score. "You know very well," she challenged, "that you won't remember all the rhythmical changes." To which Beecham replied with sovereign aplomb: "There are no rhythmical changes in *Götterdämmerung*, my dear Emerald. It goes on and on from half-past five till midnight like a damned old cart-horse." But there is danger in arguing this quality of urbane relaxation to the point where the reader will mistake it for carelessness or softness. The adjective "lackadaisical" has never been applied to Beecham. His music-making bubbles with the froth of high spirits. Yet even at his raciest, in a galloping rondo of Mozart or a piece of fluff by Offenbach, he allows music to breathe naturally. With him it will not pant under the crack of a relentless whip.

Totting up the various aspects of Beecham's genius, I would begin by listing this gift of relaxation and proceed to his faculty for finding a tempo at once just and revelatory. Tempo is one of music's imponderables. It is a foolhardy man who expects any widespread agreement on a particular pace for a particular work. Beecham's tempos do not always please, but one learns to respect them even when on first hearing they seem questionable. He is wont, for instance, to take the last movement of *Eine kleine Nachtmusik* at a speed much slower than tradition or the allegro marking would seem to warrant. On first acquaintance this sedate pace may appear indefensible. But Beecham's tempos have a way of justifying themselves. One discovers that this jogtrot finale to Mozart's famous Serenade has its own cogency as a revelation of courtly grace. Again, for the first few seconds the pace of the "Prague" andante may seem laggard, even sluggish, but by the tenth measure the justice of his tempo is established beyond cavil, and as the movement progresses one recognizes how perfectly he maintains its relaxed tread, achieving variety not by the easy devices of accelerandi and stringendi, but rather by imaginative accentuation and luminous orchestral balance.

The reference to orchestral balance introduces another of Beecham's claims to genius, his ability to summon forth equilibrated masses of sound. He has been quoted as insisting that "music should first and last have a beautiful sound"—which to Beecham means not so much voluptuousness as precise "adjustment of the component parts of the machine." In his autobiography one finds, amid a welter of diverting fustian, this *obiter dictum:* "The supremely important factor in any choral or instrumental ensemble is the relationship between the different sections of the forces of play." A commonplace? Perhaps in theory; certainly not in practice. Even with ensembles of minor rank this conductor's gift of adjusting orchestral balance makes for magnificent sound.

To compare the Beecham described by H. T. Parker in 1913 with the Beecham of today is to be confronted with opposites. "The divine faculty that chooses as by instinct enforced by imagination the pace and the accent that will reveal and animate music," noted as lacking in the conductor of 1913, is exactly what today's Beecham possesses *in excelsis*. "It is good to revive neglected classics, but not in such lumping performances that they reconduct the chosen music into what seems a deserved oblivion," wrote Parker in 1913. It would be difficult to maintain today that Beecham's revivals—the Mozart symphonies from K.199 to K.338, Bizet's *Fair Maid of Perth*, Handel's *Il Pastor Fido*—have been conducted to an oblivion either deserved or undeserved. The "hastily prepared" performances of 1913 have given way to the most painstaking care and finish of execution. I have yet to hear a performance more impeccably prepared than Beecham's recorded *Zauberflöte.* It is not with intent to depreciate an excellent critic that I draw these comparisons, but rather to show how remarkably Beecham has mastered his métier and confounded an informed prognosis. H. T. Parker was unquestionably justified in doubting that "Thomas Beecham will ever prove more than a mediocre conductor." More praise, then, to the "pill-maker's son" for proving the Boston critic so very wrong.

Dimitri *Mitropoulos*

Dimitri Mitropoulos belongs to the century of the common man. This conductor's Gargantuan appetite for contemporary music, his choreographic behavior on the podium (so volatile a contrast to the time-beating of former generations), his functional way of life reflect the very form and figure of our age. Reference books insist, however, that he was born in Athens as long ago as 1896. As a young child, he evidenced a religious nature common to his family. Dimitri's paternal grandfather was a priest in the Greek Orthodox Church, two of his uncles were monks, and one of his great-uncles an archbishop. His father was a businessman with spiritual leanings who lost his life in 1921 while ministering as a sort of unofficial priest to disease-ridden refugees from Turkey. As a boy, Mitropoulos paid regular visits to monasteries near Athens. Occasionally he would preach mystical sermons to his playmates. His announced intention was to enter a monastic order.

As it happened, music pre-empted the callings of religion. At the age of twelve Mitropoulos entered the Athens Conservatory to study composition under Armand Marsick, a Belgian musician who was then conductor of the Athens Symphony. For over a decade his life centered on the Conservatory. World War I retarded his early career, for soon after his eighteenth birthday, just when he might normally have journeyed afield for further schooling, Europe's frontiers closed. Not until 1919 could he travel beyond Greece. During that year an opera composed by him was performed at the Athens Conservatory. Eighty-four-year-old Camille Saint-Saëns, on a cultural mission to Greece, happened to attend the opera and subsequently wrote a favorable critique for a Paris newspaper. Praise from this respected pen made Mitropoulos an object of civic concern, with the result that several rich citizens cooperated with the municipality of Athens to finance study abroad for the young composer.

Mitropoulos went first to Brussels, where he worked with the composer Paul Gilson. One presumes this to have been an unfruitful period, for he soon gravitated to Berlin and Ferruccio Busoni. Busoni exerted a lasting influence on Mitropoulos, as he did on almost every young musician with whom he came in contact. In this particular case the Busoni influence set in train a metamorphosis from composer to conductor. Busoni found Mitropoulos's compositions freighted with what he termed "too much passion." The criticism produced a far-ranging effect. Mitropoulos was strongly attracted by Busoni's classical æsthetic, but his inherent romanticism raised a barrier to the practice of this æsthetic theory. The resulting conflict—a strong dislike for his own music and an inability to compose differently—soon turned him from composition to conducting. He attributes whatever stylistic versatility he shows as an interpreter to Busoni's influence, his own natural rapport with passionate, romantic expression having been complemented by the elder musician's convincing advocacy of the classic, intellectual idiom.

Shortly after Mitropoulos's arrival in Berlin, friends secured him a job as assistant conductor at the Staatsoper. There he stood by, score in hand, while singers and orchestra rehearsed under Germany's most accomplished conductors–Leo Blech, Fritz Stiedry, Erich Kleiber, Wilhelm Furtwängler, Bruno Walter, Richard Strauss. "To them," Mitropoulos acknowledges, "I owe my learning of conducting." On occasion he himself would conduct, usually one of the cornerstones of the repertoire, like *Lohengrin* or *Faust.*

Athens did not lose track of the young man's progress during this apprenticeship. When Armand Marsick resigned his post in 1924, Mitropoulos was appointed conductor of the Athens Symphony. By then he had evolved his individual style of conducting. He had dispensed with the baton (unaware, he says, of Stokowski's example) in the attempt to convey interpretative ideas through expressive physical gesture. As this technique is so integral a part of his musical personality, it merits a brief aside.

It can be said of Stokowski and Ormandy that they conduct with their hands. Of Mitropoulos it must be acknowledged that he conducts with his body. When the music soars, he is like a bird in flight; when it droops, he huddles as though broken in spirit. Always the whole man reacts. One might call his podium maneuvers "acrobatic," though Mitropoulos would prefer the adjective "choreographic." To his way of thinking, the baton is a limiting appendage. "It can achieve ensemble," he says, "but it cannot be expressive." Mitropoulos does not mean to suggest that a baton-waving conductor is by definition unable to transmit expression; rather he means that the older school achieves expression in spite of the baton. Over the years he has worked out the means whereby his movements will communicate exactly what he intends, to the point where his desires are apprehended even by an unfamiliar orchestra. Mitropoulos believes that his kind of conducting pays dividends on both sides of the footlights. "It is easier for the audience to understand the meaning of music if the conductor is a bit of an actor. Don't mistake me; I wouldn't recommend that a conductor deliberately make his gestures with the audience in mind."

In Athens, Mitropoulos worked for "almost nothing," but found ample compensation in having a first-class orchestra at his disposal. After gaining experience in Athens, he was invited in 1930 to Berlin as guest conductor of the Philharmonic Orchestra. For his debut he contrived a program of Berlin *premières:* the Symphony in C by Dukas, Prokofiev's Third Piano Concerto, and his own Concerto Grosso. When Egon Petri, engaged as soloist for the Prokofiev work, fell ill at the last minute, Mitropoulos undertook the solo part himself, conducting the orchestra from the keyboard. Subsequently the capitals of Europe made his acquaintance as a conductor-soloist. From 1934 to 1937 he directed an annual three-month season of symphony concerts at Monte Carlo. It was after one of these concerts on the Côte d'Azur that Serge Koussevitzky invited Mitropoulos to Boston. During two guest-conducting engagements in 1936 and 1937 the unknown Greek conductor captivated Boston critics and audiences. Among his Boston listeners were emissaries from Minnesota on the lookout for a man to replace Eugene Ormandy. They engaged Mitropoulos, who began in 1937 his twelve-year tenure as musical director of the Minneapolis Symphony.

Minneapolis audiences warmed to their new conductor. They approved his simple habits (Mitropoulos was content with a single room in a University of Minnesota dormitory); they appreciated his pious sentiments (he made a practice of addressing church groups on Sunday evening); they relished his lack of rapacity (he refused a five-thousand-dollar increase in salary, and often paid for extra rehearsals of difficult works from his own pocket). They even came to accept the regimen of contemporary music he imposed. Under Ormandy the Minneapolis Symphony had excelled in highly scored music of the post-romantic era—Bruckner, Richard Strauss, Rachmaninoff, Kodály. Mitropoulos did not let this repertoire lapse, but he endeavored to admit more challenging fare by Milhaud, Hindemith, Busoni, and the atonalists. In the early forties his name became known beyond Minneapolis as Mitropoulos-conducted recordings gained wide currency. It must be owned, however, that they were not always the most winning ambassadors, for Columbia's engineers had never fully mastered the acoustic vagaries of Northrup Auditorium.

In 1940 Mitropoulos made his New York debut as guest conductor of the Philharmonic. Two years later the Philharmonic-Symphony Society began to betray more than casual interest in his future plans. That season the orchestra's board of directors engaged a parade of guest conductors with the intent of choosing a successor to John Barbirolli. In the end Artur Rodzinski was appointed. There can be little doubt that Mitropoulos's advanced views on program-making had been held against him. Five years later, following Rodzinski's sudden departure, the Philharmonic was troubled anew with the same problem. This time the board viewed Mitropoulos's candidacy more leniently, though as a safeguard he was offered only a divided command with Leopold Stokowski. For the season of 1950–1 the Philharmonic decided to entrust Mitropoulos with full responsibility. As expected, he presented an abundance of difficult contemporary music. The Philharmonic did not founder. Quite the contrary, critics and audiences found the new regime stimulating and eminently worthwhile. Mitropoulos considers his "victory" a portent of America's maturing attitude toward music: "I didn't play down to the board of directors. It was they who changed their minds about contemporary music."

Mitropoulos, who generally includes a major contemporary

work on the program every other week, devotes himself to new music "like a monk to his monastery." "With me," he explains, "playing new music is always an act of love, never just a duty." Among the frequent recipients of this conductor's affection have been the dodecaphonists: Schönberg, Webern, Berg, Křenek. I asked Mitropoulos whether he valued twelve-tone music more highly than other contemporary writing, and he replied that it was not so much a matter of value as of need; he favors the twelve-tone composers because of their neglect by other conductors. Bitterly he exclaimed: "Because most musicians won't pay the price of solitude, twelve-tone music languishes. It is condemned because that is the easy thing to do." When he proceeded to speak of an "inevitable evolution to twelve-tone music," I ventured the opinion that music of the Schönberg persuasion seems too limited to serve all varieties of artistic expression, wonderfully equipped though it is to portray high-strung, bizarre states of feeling. Mitropoulos acknowledged that twelve-tone music has taken a neurotic turn, but sees no reason why it should continue so. He believes it merely the geographical accident of its birth in post-Mahler Vienna that set twelve-tone music careening down morbid paths, and he looks to the day when a dodecaphonic Ravel will appear, composing twelve-tone music with wit and classical understatement.

Once, following a concert in which Mitropoulos had conducted Rachmaninoff's E minor Symphony, the composer went backstage to express his satisfaction with the interpretation. But one question had been puzzling him. How could Mitropoulos find room in his heart for both Rachmaninoff *and* Schönberg? Were not these tastes mutually exclusive? "Rachmaninoff was prejudiced," Mitropoulos comments, "just as some art lovers are prejudiced when they say that a man who appreciates Velásquez cannot possibly see beauty in Picasso." Mitropoulos finds no conflict in widely disparate styles. He prides himself on his ability to vault with ease from Rachmaninoff to Schönberg; he would deny possessing a loyalty toward any particular school. "It is the duty of a good performer," he states, "not to be a character actor."

Many listeners, notwithstanding, would account Mitropoulos more of a character actor than he admits. In handling the intricate rhythms and unconventional balances of contemporary music he is amazingly adept. He summons ordered sound from a seeming morass of dissonance and responds with obvious relish to fresh and challenging forms of expression. His rapport with more traditional writing is not always so demonstrable. Although he will give himself wholly to Schönberg's *Five Orchestra Pieces,* he may hold Schumann's "Rhenish" Symphony at arm's length, rendering it correctly but without the ring of conviction. Not always is this so (the Rachmaninoff symphony mentioned above can be noted as one shining exception), but it happens often enough so that we may justifiably wonder whether Mitropoulos is indeed the "repertory actor" that he fancies himself.

On the occasions when Mitropoulos dispatches a standard work with no more than dry efficiency it is reasonable to suspect a want of encompassing interest. Yet psychic affinity (or the lack of it) may not tell the whole story. It is conceivable that this conductor's technique of expressive gesture, so well adapted to music of our century, stands in the way of the repertoire extending from Bach to Brahms. Especially in Mozart does one miss the cohesive tick-tock of firm, baton-inflected beats. Account must be taken, too, of the unprepossessing tone Mitropoulos commands from the orchestra, a tone sometimes harsh and ragged, often bleak and colorless. The unprejudiced ear must avow that in the blending of sound Mitropoulos is the competent pharmacist rather than the inspired alchemist.

His sense of cultural mission and his imposing musical integrity help to right the balance. In the belief that a conductor's mission is to ensure the continuity of musical culture, he incessantly proselytizes for the new and unconventional. Mitropoulos would consider himself derelict were he to attend entirely, or even principally, to established masterpieces. He rebels at the conception that symphonic repertoire should constitute a musical museum; he prefers grappling with second-rate Křenek to perfecting first-rate Schubert. It is his concern to keep audiences up to date and on their intellectual mettle. Were all conductors of like disposition, we might have just cause to complain of short supply in the basic victuals of music, but there being no dearth of musicians to play accepted classics Mitropoulos deserves our thanks for heading frequently in uncharted directions.

His musical integrity, his sense of responsibility, is not limited to program-making. It motivates his insistence on conducting both in concert and in rehearsal from memory. When he performed Alban Berg's *Wozzeck* in 1951, its labyrinthine patterns were so imprinted in his mind that even during rehearsals Mitropoulos dispensed with the printed score. "Go back to bar 237," he would request, and he would then begin to direct this tortuously difficult music as if the score were open before him. If the reader will examine an orchestral score of *Wozzeck*, with its twenty-odd staves each representing an autonomous line, the enormousness of this feat can better be appreciated. What is germane to the argument is that memorizing has always been difficult for Mitropoulos. But early in his career he concluded that a conductor should no more rely on a score than an actor should appear on stage holding a prompt book. For over twenty years he has got by heart every work he plays.

Beyond the conviction that a conductor should know his score as an actor knows his lines lies another compelling motive for memorization. "Conductors," Mitropoulos avows, "are the most cowardly of musicians. They take no risks. They have not to watch intonation like a string player, nor live in constant fear of blowing a 'clinker' on the clarinet or horn. When they make a mistake the public hardly ever knows it." The conductor's ease of burden obsesses Mitropoulos. He imposes memorization upon himself as an act of penance: "I must jump this hurdle; otherwise I could never justify myself."

☼ Charles *Munch*

CHARLES MUNCH first came to America's attention as conductor in some prewar concerto recordings of French origin. Record-collectors began to see his name in the late thirties, when Munch led the Paris Conservatoire Orchestra in recordings of such works as the Ravel Concerto for Left Hand and the Saint-Saëns Concerto No. 4, both with Alfred Cortot. By these tokens he was adjudged a conductor of quality, though hardly a musical force to be reckoned with. But those who had heard Munch conduct in Paris knew otherwise. As early as 1935 Virgil Thomson had predicted, with amazing prescience, that Munch would one day succeed to the conductorship of the Boston Symphony. When he made his New York debut in January 1947, as guest conductor of the Philharmonic, it was easy to see why he had been named as the man foreordained to inherit Koussevitzky's podium, for in personal bearing and musical inclinations he seemed ideally fitted to Boston requirements. Fate worked out according to Mr. Thomson's prescription when in the autumn of 1949

Munch succeeded Serge Koussevitzky (who retired after twenty-five years as conductor). The French musician aligned himself squarely with Boston tradition in espousing contemporary works of substance and quality, and though he could not quite command his predecessor's plangent string tone, he allowed no significant deterioration in aural quality. By the end of his first season, there was no doubt that Munch was performing the job to Boston's taste.

We tend to look upon Munch as a musician oriented exclusively toward French traditions. Actually, he spent the majority of his formative years under German influence. He was born in Strasbourg on September 26, 1891, when that city was part of the Kaiser's German Empire and spelled its name Strassburg. (The conductor's own name has undergone two orthographic mutations: he was born Münch; when he became a Parisian the name was changed to Muench; now that he is a Bostonian he prefers the spelling Munch.) His father, Ernst, taught at the Strasbourg Conservatory and directed the choir at L'Eglise-St. Guillaume. Young Charles soon became attentive to music in the dedicated atmosphere of his home. After a few years at the local gymnasium he transferred to the Strasbourg Conservatory, where his principal teacher was Hans Pfitzner, composer of several post-romantic operas and a musician of *echt Deutsch* inclinations. Munch chose the violin as the instrument with which he would make a living, and in 1912 went to Paris to work with the most eminent of French string teachers, Lucien Capet, founder of the Capet Quartet and editor of many excellent editions of violin music. One by-product of this change of locale was Munch's Paris debut—as a violin recitalist; another, and more important, was his introduction to French musical culture.

In the summer of 1914 he returned to spend the vacation months in Strasbourg. When war broke out in August, Munch—a healthy twenty-three years of age—was drafted into the

German Army and obliged to wear its spiked helmet for four years. In the course of service he was gassed at Peronne and wounded at Verdun. He came home to find the tricolor flying over Strasbourg and himself a citizen of the French Republic. For a while he stayed on native grounds as concertmaster of the Strasbourg orchestra and teacher at the conservatory. But though his passport had become French, his musical allegiance still went to Germany. In the early 1920's he recrossed the Rhine and spent the better part of a decade playing in the violin sections of German symphony orchestras. For many years he was concertmaster of the Leipzig Gewandhaus Orchestra under the regimes of Wilhelm Furtwängler and Bruno Walter. From them he can be said to have received his first lessons in conducting, indirect though the tutelage may have been. Munch might have remained in Leipzig indefinitely had not the orchestra insisted on his taking out German citizenship papers. Not relishing the notion of becoming re-Germanized to this extent, he quit his job, and in 1931 set out for Paris, where his career was to take a radical turn.

Munch did not direct an orchestra until he was forty-one years old, later in life even than that other tardy starter, Ernest Ansermet. When he did begin to conduct, the opportunity was owing principally to the bank account of his bride, heiress to the Nestlé chocolate fortune, who hired the hall and the orchestra for Munch's Paris debut in 1932. For most of us, I think, a career served up on a silver platter is always rather suspect; but the examples of Sir Thomas Beecham, Serge Koussevitzky, and Charles Munch are sufficient to establish that merit and money need not necessarily go in inverse proportion. Actually, neither Beecham nor Koussevitzky nor Munch could have climbed eminence on a financial ladder alone, though in each case money provided the first opportunities for talent to assert itself. During the thirties Munch made the rounds of Paris orchestras, injecting a new, romantic flavor into a milieu that had been dominated by able but rather desiccated conductors. One gathers from the remarks of French critics that Munch was regarded in prewar Paris as a sort of Alsatian Stokowski, a musician of glamor and magnetism, much given to stunning effects. His popularity increased rapidly, particularly among feminine auditors, who earned the nickname of "*les muenchettes*" by reason of their partisan devotion to the handsomely mournful conductor. Engagements in Central Europe and England followed, and in 1938—a scant six years after he started to conduct—Munch secured the most coveted podium in France when he was appointed conductor of the Orchestre de la Société des Concerts du Conservatoire de Paris.

For eight years Munch guided the destiny of the Conservatoire Orchestra, a period when he developed from a competent aspirant to the finished workman that he was on his first visit to the United States. Much of his tenure with the Conservatoire Orchestra coincided with the Nazi occupation. Through those difficult years, Munch continued to conduct in Paris, and is said to have turned over all his fees to the resistance movement. Never was there any suspicion of collaboration in his case; like most French musicians, Munch continued to provide his countrymen with music while avoiding intimate contact with the Germans. In a sense, the occupation of Paris redounded to his benefit. With the capital cut off from normal relations with the rest of the world, Parisians were dependent upon resident musicians for cultural sustenance. As a consequence, Munch undoubtedly mastered a more extensive repertoire between 1940 and 1944 than he would have mastered in normal times, when guest conductors from abroad were wont to preside over a large proportion of Paris concerts. The catalogue of records made during the occupation years gives an index to the important role he played in French musical affairs at that time. Soon after the liberation of France, Munch conducted in London a series of concerts which brought him to the attention of the English Decca record firm, just then beginning to expand its catalogue of serious music. Almost simultaneously with the conductor's debut in America came the release of his first Decca records, made with Paris Conservatoire Orchestra, among them his notable interpretations of *Ibéria*, the *Daphnis et Chloë* suites, and Roussel's *Festin de l'araignée*. As was the case with Ernest Ansermet, the "ffrr" trademark helped measurably to disseminate his interpretations and make known his name in the United States.

Munch resigned full-time direction of the Conservatoire Orchestra in 1946. Until he was named music director of the Boston Symphony three years later, he led an itinerant life that took him on guest-conducting visits to a dozen European countries, the Near East, South America, and seven cities in the United States. Upon assuming his Boston post he curtailed much of this globe-trotting, though he still managed to conduct many concerts in France each summer until 1951; but with the sudden death of Serge Koussevitzky on June 4 of that year, the direction of the Berkshire Music Festival devolved solely upon Munch, and he was forced to forgo most of his remaining engagements in Europe. If present indications are any guide, Munch's ties with the Continent will grow increasingly tenuous.

This conductor's career divides into opposing halves. Prior to 1931 he was subject almost wholly to German domination; following that date his theater of activity and musical outlook centered entirely in France. It would seem that this artificial division should have served to intensify the ethnic and cultural duality of his Alsatian lineage, but with Munch *la patrie* has quite overpowered *die Heimat*. Musically, he is thoroughly French, with a transcending sympathy for the Gallic idiom. It is a sympathy, however, that does not always follow prescribed French tradition. Munch favors a conception more romantic than most French conductors would endorse, indulging in *rubato* and warm, expressive nuance where others keep to strict metrics and cool objectivity. Fortunately, there is more than one way of scaling Mount Parnassus, and as the way of Munch makes persuasive sense it would be foolish to deny its validity. In such a work as Ravel's *Rapsodie espagnole* he is surpassed by none. While conducting this music he seems almost to be composing it, so freely and insinuatingly do the phrases form under his baton. He plays the *Symphonie fantastique* in like manner, taking fearless liberties with the composer's markings, demanding a crescendo here and an allargando there, suddenly subduing one section of the orchestra and intensifying another, but all to the end of a total effect at once improvisatory and exciting, though not to the taste of those who view Berlioz as a misunderstood classicist. His reading of Debussy's *Ibéria* departs, too, in some details from the letter of the score, though here again he convinces by his strong personal identification with the music. This *Ibéria* is more Iberian than French renditions traditionally allow, with flamboyant dance-rhythms and contortions of emphasis more flamenco than Parisian, but resulting in an interpretation of vivid effectiveness.

With music *outre-Rhin* Munch is respectable if not always revealing. He plays Beethoven and Brahms properly, observes all the customary niceties, blunders into no solecisms. But in this area he displays little interpretative originality. He recreates Berlioz; he merely translates Brahms. In non-French repertoire I have been most impressed with Munch's conducting of Bach, as evidenced by his all-Bach programs at the 1951 Berkshire Festival. In several of the "Brandenburgs," the two concertos for three claviers, and the *Magnificat*, Munch conducted Bach as few today can, maintaining the Latin and Teutonic elements of Bach's writing in splendid equipoise.

Perhaps these Berkshire concerts presage a widening of his interpretative competence. As a conductor, it should be remembered, he is a relative neophyte. His actual working experience on the podium is less than that of any of his contemporaries, and his potentiality for further development is probably that much greater.

✲ Eugene *Ormandy*

EUGENE ORMANDY began life as a violinist. This statement is to be taken literally. His father, a Budapest dentist, had resolved many years before Ormandy's birth that his son was to be a great violinist. To facilitate this consummation he named the baby Jenö (of which Eugene is the English equivalent) after the then-reigning Hungarian violinist, Jenö Hubay. He was born November 18, 1899, and by the age of four he was making headway with a pint-sized violin. Taken to a violin recital, he is said to have shrieked to the startled performer: "You played F-sharp instead of F-natural"—a show of musical erudition to be deplored at whatever age. At five he was sent to the Royal Academy of Music and four years later progressed to the master classes of Hubay. Ormandy recalls that he was loath to practice the eight hours a day prescribed by his teacher, though frequent beatings by his father encouraged an industrious attitude.

He left the Royal Academy with a professor's diploma in 1917 and set about building a career, a bad leg having exempted him from military service. At his Berlin debut (with the Blüthner Orchestra conducted by Paul Scheinpflug) he played no less than three concertos: the Brahms, the Mendelssohn, and the Vieuxtemps in D minor. Thereafter a concert bureau booked him for recitals throughout Central Europe, and for a time he joined a small instrumental group that traveled from hospital to hospital playing for wounded soldiers. In 1919, when Hubay was appointed director of the Budapest Academy, Ormandy became head of the violin department. His colleagues, many of them more than twice his age, resented being outranked by so young a man. Their unceasing intrigue obliged him to resign within two years.

With inflation making existence in Central Europe increasingly precarious, it was only natural that America should beckon as the most likely place for a fresh start. Shortly before leaving for America, Ormandy gave a recital in Austria for a single United States dollar bill—and considered himself well paid. Two Hungarian acquaintances, more naive than malevolent, lured Ormandy into an ill-conceived journey overseas. One of these gentlemen was a doctor who had never traveled much farther west than Vienna; the other had once toured the United States as a "champagne salesman" (a sobriquet which Ormandy later discovered to mean bootlegger). Between them they devised a contract whereby their protege was to make a cross-country tour of the United States, playing a modest three hundred concerts in one year—for which he was to receive thirty thousand dollars.

On paper the scheme looked promising. Only after their arrival in 1921 did Ormandy and his backers realize the folly of their undertaking. The violinist was duly auditioned by various concert managers in New York. Ormandy found them ready to enter his name on their rosters—provided he would defray the cost of his initial recitals. The minimum estimate came to three thousand dollars. As the Hungarian triumvirate possessed nothing approaching this sum, the ambitious contract was declared null and void, and Ormandy set out to find a job. The Keith Circuit offered him $250 a week to play in vaudeville shows. In the proposed act he was to perform light music while acrobats accomplished their gyrations. Was this the best that lay in store after a decade's study with the great Hubay? Ormandy thought not, and turned the job down. Later, with the fabled last nickel in his pocket, he met the conductor of the Capitol Theater (New York) orchestra, his compatriot Erno Rapee, who offered him a job in the violin section. He joined the orchestra in December 1921. Within five days he had been appointed concertmaster, and within two years had become the associate conductor.

Circumstances threw Ormandy into the role of conductor, but ability kept him there. He remained as conductor at the Capitol Theater until 1929, thriving on the good pay and using his spare time to profit. Lessons in conducting were not part of his regimen. (Indeed, Ormandy seriously doubts that conducting can be taught; he agrees with Mahler's *obiter dictum* that "conductors are born, not made.") But experience had taught him that a trained musician with the inherent capabilities of a conductor could benefit vastly from attendance at rehearsals. During his decade in New York City Ormandy seldom missed a rehearsal of the Philharmonic when that orchestra was enjoying its great years under Toscanini. Among the Italian conductor's many admirers none was more devoted than young Ormandy, who would attend regularly, score in hand, in the rear of an empty Carnegie Hall while Toscanini drilled his orchestra. Even now, Ormandy still marvels at this conductor's imagination, his rare taste, his ability to discover the subtleties that elude everyone else. He refers to Toscanini as his "one and only musical influence."

While New York endured the vicissitudes of Jimmy Walker, speakeasies, and the Vitaphone, the penniless violinist Jenö Blau matured into the promising conductor Eugene Ormandy. Gradually his reputation spread beyond the world of show business. The *Sun*'s venerable critic, W. J. Henderson, descended into the nether regions of the Capitol and emerged with an approving report; radio stations began to bid for Ormandy's services; a record company set him to recording light classics. Emboldened by this accumulating evidence of his worth, Ormandy abandoned his lucrative job at the Capitol and consigned his future to Providence and the managerial sagacity of Arthur Judson.

Under Judson's management Ormandy secured engagements with the New York Philharmonic in Lewisohn Stadium during the summer of 1929 and with the Philadelphia Orchestra in Robin Hood Dell a year thereafter. It was against Judson's advice, however, that he took advantage of the fortuitous opportunity that came his way in 1931. Toscanini had agreed to conduct a few of the Philadelphia Orchestra concerts that year while Stokowski was to reciprocate with the New York Philharmonic. Sudden illness prevented Toscanini at the last minute from performing his half of the exchange. Several conductors who were called upon to substitute in Philadelphia declined the artistic suicide likely to attend replacing Toscanini and succeeding Stokowski. But Ormandy, when approached to fill the vacancy, accepted—despite his manager's counsel to the contrary; and though he did not precisely fill Toscanini's shoes, the Philadelphia audiences received him amicably. The story of the substitution, reported by the United Press, was read in Minneapolis, where the conductor of the Symphony—Henri Verbrugghen—had that very day been stricken with a serious illness. There was a hurried phone call to Philadelphia. Was it possible for Mr. Ormandy to fill in at Minneapolis until Verbrugghen's successor could be chosen? It was possible. And the successor turned out to be Ormandy.

During the next six years the achievements of the Minneapolis Symphony were heralded far beyond Minnesota. One underlying cause was the orchestra's contract with the musicians' union, a contract stipulating that the orchestra men could be employed without extra compensation for purposes of recording. The significance of this provision in fine print was brought to the attention of RCA Victor. That company, hard pressed by a deflated record-market, quickly took advantage of this economical source of recorded repertoire. From Minneapolis came recordings of popular encore-pieces (dances from *The Bartered Bride*, Strauss waltzes) and standard symphonies (Schumann Fourth, Rachmaninoff Second), plus such uncommon fare as Kodály's *Háry János* and Bruckner's Seventh Symphony. Although a contractual quirk had suggested these recordings, it was the quality of musicianship they purveyed that earned them worldwide distribution and praise. For Eugene Ormandy had thoroughly revitalized the Minneapolis Symphony, to the point where it could compete, on records, with orchestras of long-established reputation.

With the Minneapolis recordings serving as advance ambassadors, Ormandy began to enlarge the area of his activity. He returned to Philadelphia yearly as a guest conductor, further cementing the connection he had formed when substituting for Toscanini in 1931. During his vacations in Hungary, he would occasionally appear as guest conductor of the Budapest Philharmonic. Once, when an important ecclesiastical festival took place in Budapest, Ormandy was selected to conduct the Philharmonic at a special performance with Joseph Szigeti as soloist—a rare honor in a country often censured for neglect of its native sons. After the concert, Ormandy and his father attended a party in honor of the two guest musicians. En route the elder man maintained a dour silence. His son wondered what was amiss. Had his father disliked the concert? No, it appeared that the performance had been first-rate. "Perhaps you didn't care for the program?" the conductor queried. But that too merited approval. What, then, was the matter? Finally, with tears in his eyes, Ormandy's father blurted out: "I couldn't help thinking all through the concert that if I had only beaten you a little harder perhaps Ormandy would have been playing the violin and Szigeti conducting." A father's desire is not easily stilled.

When Leopold Stokowski decided to attenuate his conducting activity in 1936, Ormandy was appointed co-conductor of the Philadelphia Orchestra. Two years later he became its musical director; he has held this position ever since. Ormandy inherited not only one of the world's great orchestras, but also one of the most perilous assignments that can befall a conductor. To rescue an orchestra from mediocrity, as Ormandy did in Minneapolis, though it requires a musician of parts does not entail much risk; comparison is all in the newcomer's favor. But to succeed a luminary like Stokowski, whose personal magnetism and virtuosity had made the Philadelphia Orchestra a touchstone for tonal grandeur, was a task calculated to trip the surest-footed of aspirants. One is reminded of how the New York Philharmonic fell to pieces for several years after Toscanini left the helm (indeed, it has never quite regained its former eminence). The finest tribute one can pay to Ormandy is to say that he let the Philadelphia Orchestra suffer no deterioration. Under his care the virtuosity and luster of this ensemble have been maintained as in Stokowski's heyday.

Indeed, it was for orchestral conservation rather than for musical interpretation that Ormandy gathered praise during the first decade of his Philadelphia incumbency. He could be depended upon to tender a solid, workmanlike performance, but his interpretations did not exhibit that insight and audacity which announces genius. He was essentially a prosaic conductor, the thorough, dependable man of reason, playing Horatio to the volatile Hamlets in New York, Boston, and Europe. About the time of his fiftieth birthday, however, he began to assume stature as an interpreter with ideas of his own. His rigidity slackened and his readings partook of a personal rhetoric previously absent. To the surprise of many, the matter-of-fact Philadelphia drillmaster showed every sign of becoming an artist of consequence. He had begun at last to plow furrows of his own instead of following discreetly in the ruts left by more independent musicians.

Ormandy is an eclectic conductor who confesses to no blind spots, who acknowledges no particular affinities, who feels himself equally *en rapport* with Haydn and Rachmaninoff. What personal predilections he allows himself are confined to the area of contemporary music. He ranks Béla Bartók as the greatest of modern composers, with Prokofiev, Hindemith, and the pre-1930 Stravinsky following close behind. Among American composers he is partial to William Schuman, Paul Creston, and Samuel Barber. His enthusiasm for contemporary music is reflected in his programs, though he does not proselytize on the scale of Mitropoulos or propagandize like his predecessor, Stokowski. The staid audiences in Philadelphia's Academy of Music desire programs that accord with Webster's definition of music as "a pleasing combination of tones," and he will not alienate his listeners by an overdose of contemporary asperities. Ormandy and his orchestra are at their best in performing complex, richly orchestrated scores. When Berlioz, Rachmaninoff, Strauss, or Ravel appear on the program, the odds are strong for a rousing evening of music. But it would not do to put Ormandy in a bottle marked, "Open only for tonal display." He ranges with assurance from Purcell to Prokofiev, and extracts from everything he undertakes a competent and appetizing performance.

☼ Arturo *Toscanini*

DO we remember that Arturo Toscanini first stepped onto a podium in the year 1886, when Richard Strauss was a fledgling composer of nothing more consequential than the *Burleske* for piano and orchestra, when Elgar's reputation was still confined to his native Worcestershire and Debussy was busy sending *envois* to the Académie des Beaux-Arts, when Tchaikovsky had yet to compose his Fifth and Sixth symphonies and Dvořák his Fourth and Fifth? We remember nothing of the kind. Toscanini refuses to seem thus ancient. We find it somehow beyond belief that the beginning of his career should antedate Debussy's. He is too sprightly, too modern. For all his years, no one has ever pinned the adjective "venerable" on Toscanini. No one would dare!

He was born in Parma on March 25, 1867, of poor *petit bourgeois* parents. His mother and father detected in him nothing noteworthy, though they acknowledged the keenness of his musical ear. But a Signora Vernoni, his second-grade teacher, amazed at the ease with which Arturo memorized words and music, counseled his parents to enroll him in the local conservatory. He began at the age of nine with the study of solfeggio; two years later he entered the cello class of Severino Leandro Carini and the composition class of Giusto Dacci. He spent extracurricular time in the library studying scores and transcribing music for a tiny orchestra that he directed himself. His talent and zeal soon earned a scholarship, and to eke out the family's resources further he played the cello at Parma's Teatro Reale for one lira and fifty centesimi (then about thirty cents) an evening. His schoolfellows acknowledged Toscanini's gifts by nicknaming him "Genius"; already he was one apart, a student "very reserved, not very fond of amusements," to quote the conservatory's proctor. On July 14, 1885, the eighteen-year-old musician was graduated with a rating of 160 points out of a possible 160 in cello, 50 out of a possible 50 in piano, and 50 out of a possible 50 in composition.

Soon thereafter came the famous trip to South America. Thanks to a revealing essay by Alfredo Segre * and an equally helpful book by Andrea Della Corte,† this episode as well as many other details of the musician's early years have been rescued from the realm of legend. Claudio Rossi, an impresario of traveling opera-companies, had organized a group to appear in Brazil for the season of 1886. Toscanini was hired as cellist and second chorusmaster. After several weeks in São Paulo, the company proceeded to Rio de Janeiro. There some of the papers criticized the troupe's Brazilian conductor, Leopoldo Miguez, for a shoddy performance of *Faust*. Miguez countered with the assertion that his efforts were being sabotaged by the Italian instrumentalists and singers, and that because of these impossible conditions he would have to resign. A performance of *Aïda* impended. Carlo Superti, the assistant

* "Toscanini—The First Forty Years," *Musical Quarterly*, April 1947.
† *Toscanini* (Lausanne: 1948).

conductor, was to take the place of Miguez. But Superti, on the night of the performance, was received with jeers and catcalls; a partisan audience had decided to uphold the honor of Brazilian musicianship. When Superti fled from the untenable podium, his baton passed to Aristide Venturi, chorusmaster. Venturi, too, receiving nothing for his pains but a stream of hisses, quickly retired.

At this juncture, according to the traditional story, young Toscanini rose from the obscurity of the cello section, walked to the conductor's desk, shut the score, and treated his stupefied hearers to an incandescent reading of *Aïda.* The rags-to-riches element in this account has an undeniable appeal, but a knowledge of the background makes the incident somewhat less spectacular. Toscanini had rehearsed the chorus on many occasions, and everyone in the troupe knew of his astonishing memory and his authority with the baton. It was known, too, that he had thoroughly studied the score of *Aïda.* With the assistant conductor and the chorusmaster disfranchised, the succession clearly passed to the assistant chorusmaster, Toscanini. It was not quite as though a nobody had leaped into the breach to improvise as best he could.

Why the unruly audience suddenly quieted when Toscanini took over has never really been explained. It is possible that his dominating magnetism was even then operative, possible also that his superior musicianship manifested itself from the first tremulous notes high in the violins. It is most probable, however, that the audience had had its fill of uproar. Two gladiators thrown to the lions had appeased the crowd. Now they were eager to get their money's worth, and the prospect of seeing a nineteen-year-old conduct was not without its charms. Whatever the reasons, everything went smoothly. The applause was cordial and the newspapers were laudatory. Thenceforth, Toscanini conducted regularly for the remainder of the season in Brazil. A local critic averred that he gave "complete proof of his ability, coolness, enthusiasm, and energy."

Toscanini returned to Italy to find himself a musician without particular honor in his own country. Only one small paper, the home-town Parma *Riforma*, had published a notice of his exploits in Rio de Janeiro. No impresario having met him at the boat with tempting offers, he returned to his study of the cello and began to coach singers for a livelihood. Apparently there was nothing of the "pusher" in his make-up; one might have expected an energetic person, flushed with recent triumphs, to regale every opera house in Italy with tales of his abilities. Fortunately for the history of conducting, other members of the Brazil troupe were less inhibited about advertising Toscanini's gifts. One of them, a tenor named Nicola Figner, had been engaged to sing in Alfredo Catalani's *Edmea*, which was shortly to receive its *première* in the Teatro Carignano of Turin. The rehearsals under the conductor Franco Faccio were proceeding poorly. Figner saw an opportunity for his young friend, and proposed that Toscanini come to Milan to meet Catalani. Toscanini impressed the composer by his sympathetic sight-reading of *Edmea* at the piano. Faccio made way for the nineteen-year-old conductor, who received a friendly pat on the back from the press. The *Gazetta Musicale* of Milan spoke of "the irreproachable chorus, the exceptionally attentive and well-prepared orchestra." "The debut of Toscanini," this journal added, "has been a triumph. It is a splendid dawn that has broken on the artistic horizon. . . . He conducts by heart, with the confidence and energy of an experienced maestro. . . . A thoughtful, studious, intelligent young man." The *Piedmont Gazette* remarked on Toscanini's calm, coldblooded approach and his "infallible memory," but found "the chiaroscuro effects a little unbalanced and uncertain."

His career as a conductor burgeoned. It would be pointless

to follow him as he journeyed through Italy, filling engagements in provincial opera houses. Suffice it to record that though the press handed out a fair share of compliments there were also objections, mostly centered on Toscanini's disregard of "tradition." Amintore Galli, critic of *Teatro Illustrato*, gave voice to such reservations when he wrote: "Toscanini should not give us a mere rendition of our masterpieces: he should try to master the most spiritual part of art and to translate it with the intelligence and love of a true musician. To achieve all this it is not enough to know the score by heart and conduct without using it, but it is necessary to study the spirit of a composer and the tradition of the various interpretations." Alfredo Segre, writing in 1947, attempted to put these remarks of Galli in an unfavorable light. He said:

> As far as Toscanini was concerned, these traditions had to be ignored, and he didn't wait until he became famous to fight them. . . . From the beginning of his career, Toscanini fought mercilessly against all odds: incompetent musicians, the despotism of singers, the nepotism of publishers, the ignorance and corruption of impresarios, the bad habits and insolence of audiences. . . . He fired stars, and instrumentalists with an ill-gained tenure in orchestras; he questioned the competence of famous publishers who wanted to intervene with their advice during rehearsals; he refused to conduct whenever he thought the preparation had been insufficient. It is hardly surprising, therefore, that acrimonious remarks were thrown at him. No, he didn't support such a tradition.

Well, there are two sides to most questions, and Signor Galli is no longer alive to advocate his. That there was some justice to his strictures I do not doubt. Assuredly, Toscanini's impatience with operatic barnacles was well founded; even so, Galli's criticisms seem apposite to a neophyte conductor.

Especially to *this* conductor. Might not the admonition to "study the spirit of a composer" be applicable, in certain instances, to the Toscanini of six decades later?

Soon Toscanini's repertoire widened. As the nineteenth century approached its last decade, all Europe—even Italy, where there had been strong initial resistance—knuckled under to the Wagnerian domination. Toscanini was first called upon to conduct Wagner (*The Flying Dutchman*) in 1892 at the Palermo Opera. Two years later he directed performances of *Tannhäuser* at Genoa. This was tried and proved ground; but not so *Götterdämmerung*, which received its Italian *première* under Toscanini in 1895. Two other first performances entrusted to the young conductor should be mentioned. At Milan's Teatro Dal Verme, Toscanini presided over the brilliant birth of *Pagliacci* (May 21, 1892) and at Turin's Teatro Regio he conducted the far less successful *première* of Puccini's *La Bohème* (February 2, 1896).

Studying the press reports from Toscanini's first decade as conductor, one can derive a hazy but generally consistent picture of the young musician. He appears as a straightforward interpreter not given to contrived, applause-stimulating effects. His memory and grasp of orchestral technique already astonish his contemporaries. His artistic relationships are stringent: he will brook no carelessness of execution and he allows no singer to exercise an unmusical whim; from impresarios he exacts sufficient rehearsal time, adamantly refusing to conduct if it is not granted; he does not truckle to the will of an audience, refuses to permit encores when he deems them inappropriate. His regard for the musical text is unusual.

The year that marked Toscanini's tenth anniversary as a conductor saw his first sally into the realm of symphonic music. On March 20, 1896, in Turin, he conducted a program consisting of the Schubert C major Symphony, the *Tragic* Overture of Brahms, the *Nutcracker Suite* (then but four years old), and the "Entrance of the Gods into Valhalla" from *Das Rheingold.* Italy had come late to an appreciation of symphonic music. Readers of Berlioz's *Evenings in the Orchestra* may remember the unmerciful drubbing that that hyperbolic commentator gave the mid-nineteenth-century Italian orchestra. "In all the theaters," he wrote, "there is in front of the stage a black hollow filled with wretches blowing and scraping, as indifferent to what is being shouted on the stage as to what is being buzzed in the boxes and parterre, and possessed of but one thought, that of earning their supper. The assemblage of these poor creatures constitutes what is called an orchestra." Substantial improvements had been effected in the intervening half-century, especially as regards standards of execution, but from an interpretative standpoint Italy still lagged far behind the rest of Europe. The Italian critic Della Corte once asked Toscanini to describe the nature of the interpretations he had heard in his early youth. Toscanini gave as their principal characteristics "rigidity of movement" and "heaviness of sound." The letter of the law was severely observed; one had to beat time "without flexibility, without elasticity, without inflection." Hearing the great symphonic classics interpreted without passion or profundity, young Toscanini must have been moved to rebellion just as had young Richard Wagner under parallel circumstances sixty years before.

Like Wagner, Toscanini was destined to rekindle many musical embers. But he did not change the history of symphonic interpretation overnight. The refinements of Toscanini's maturity—the happy mean that keeps rhythm precise yet supple, and sonority clear yet full-bodied, the intuition that goes beyond the raw dictates of a score without transgressing a composer's intentions—were still embryonic during his early years. That he already had a superior grasp of symphonic literature is evident from the number of engagements that followed the Turin concert of March 1896. More than this one would hesitate to say, for knowledge of symphonic music was so slight in Italy at the time as to make newspaper criticism an unreliable index of Toscanini's abilities.

From Turin he went to Milan for four concerts at La Scala, this being his first appearance in that venerable and imposing theater. His programs included Beethoven's Second Symphony and Haydn's "Clock," the complete "Norn Scene" from *Götterdämmerung*, Grieg's *Holberg Suite*, and the *Danse Macabre* (Saint-Saëns was present and complimented Toscanini on his properly restrained tempo). A much more ambitious symphonic project was entrusted to him two years later, in 1898, when Turin became the scene of an international exposition. One of the attractions was a series of concerts (forty-three in all) under the direction of Toscanini. (The music shed was built in easy hearing of tramways, a scenic railway, and a toboggan chute!) One can gather from the 133 compositions listed a fair idea of the Maestro's musical predilections in his thirty-first year. Wagner and Beethoven predominated, followed by Brahms (the First and Fourth Symphonies) and Weber. Schumann's Fourth and Schubert's "Unfinished" were heard, but of Mozart only the "Jupiter" and the *Magic Flute* Overture—a choice typical of the *fin-de-siècle* impatience with the "simple tunesmith." Contemporaries figured prominently in the Turin programs. Dvořák was represented by his Symphonic Variations, Overture to *Othello*, and "New World" Symphony (then an infant of four years), while other modern symphonies came from Saint-Saëns, Charles Villiers Stanford, and Martucci. Humperdinck and D'Indy were performed, but not Richard Strauss or Debussy. Perhaps Toscanini considered the latter composers too difficult for orchestra and public alike; rehearsal time was limited, and the exposition audiences might not stomach such advanced music.

In connection with Verdi's *Pezzi Sacri*, the composer's swan song, which received its *première* at these concerts, there is an illuminating story. Toscanini had been troubled over a tempo indication, and in search of advice he visited the eighty-five-year-old composer in Genoa. When the question of the perplexing tempo was broached, Verdi asked the young conductor to sit down and play the passage on the piano. Toscanini let his convictions get the better of his discretion and performed the passage with all the rhythmic freedom he felt necessary. "*Bravo!*" cried Verdi, "that's just the way it should go." Toscanini then dared to inquire why the ritardando that he had played had not been indicated in the score. "For fear that the passage might be played *too* slowly," replied Verdi. How disturbingly this testified to the inadequacy of musical notation! The lesson was not lost on Toscanini. Contrary to popular impression, he has never been a slave of the printed score. Like every interpreter of stature, he brings to the sketchy and often ambiguous pages of notes his own æsthetic intuitions. To do otherwise (as the experience with Verdi showed) is to play falsely with a composer's thought.

The years of wandering from opera house to opera house ended in 1898, when La Scala added Toscanini to its roster of regularly employed conductors. He opened the season the day after Christmas with *Die Meistersinger*. Nearly thirty days of rehearsals preceded this performance—wearying sessions, during which the conductor made demands on singers, chorus, orchestra, and stage managers unparalleled in La Scala's history. Never had a Scala conductor been so concerned with ensemble as this tyrant, whose insistence on proper lighting and acting was as intense as his passion for correct intonation and phrasing.

Despite his tightening of discipline, not all listeners were favorably disposed to the new conductor. Of Toscanini's *Falstaff* the critic of the *Gazetta Musicale* uttered sentiments that have echoed for half a century. "The *Falstaff* of today," he wrote, "no longer resembles the sympathetic, fascinating thing it was when Verdi himself was in charge." This "metallic execution" was likened to an "inexorable pendulum." "Accuracy should not be transformed into rigidity," etc. Fifty-two years later, in 1950, when Toscanini was practically *hors critique*, an American writer ventured a similar opinion concerning the conductor's broadcast performance: "It doesn't become me to pretend that I know more about *Falstaff* than Toscanini does, but I found the pursuit of musical truth in this instance a little grim and beside the point." * Again and again the *Gazetta Musicale* deplored his "inexorable beat," while admitting to the power and general intelligence of his interpretations. It seems probable that at this stage of his career Toscanini had reacted too far against the abuses of "tradition." His aversion to the excesses of singers and to those interpretative "niceties" which invariably went counter to the dictates of the score engendered an understandably Procrustean attitude toward music. He was certainly not the only young conductor in history to have thrown out the baby with the bath water in advocating rhythmic firmness and dry sonority.

Of Toscanini's five seasons at La Scala between 1898 and 1903 there is occasion here to mention only a few highlights. His 1899–1900 season encompassed the Italian *première* of *Siegfried* and a tour through northern Italy with the Scala orchestra. The following year witnessed the first performance of Leoncavallo's *Zaza* and a production of *Tristan* which is said to have attracted music-lovers from all over Europe. His fourth season opened with *Die Walküre* and included a restudied and rehabilitated *Il Trovatore*, an opera that had lost its soul over the years through careless, routinized interpreta-

* Irving Kolodin in the *Saturday Review of Literature*, April 15, 1950.

tion. The season of 1902–3 brought to a head a smoldering discontent. From the start of his career Toscanini had fought against the prevalent Italian practice of according encores in the opera house whenever the audience demanded them. He would give in to applause only when the break was not injurious to musical and dramatic continuity. Considering Toscanini's basic opposition to encores, it is surprising to learn what he did allow in the early years of his career. For instance, he could be persuaded to repeat part of the overture to *William Tell*, and he permitted baritones to encore "*Quand' ero paggio*" in Verdi's fluid *Falstaff*. But the stronger his position grew, the less was he inclined to truckle to a claque. In the spring of 1903 a *contretemps* over the propriety of an encore in *Un Ballo in Maschera* led to a rupture of Toscanini's relations with La Scala. For the next three seasons the conductor resumed an itinerant life, giving Milan's opera house a wide berth—and, incidentally, adding some important new works to his symphonic repertoire, among them Elgar's "Enigma" Variations, Debussy's *Nuages*, and Smetana's *Moldau*.

By his absence Toscanini won his point. When posters were affixed to the walls of La Scala announcing the season of 1906–7, a new regulation struck the eyes of passing Milanese: "Reasons of public and artistic discipline have prompted the management to forbid encores. . . . The public is requested to abide by these arrangements." Also, the posters were once more graced with the name of Toscanini. Audiences swallowed the new imposition with ill grace, but sour feelings were assuaged with musical sweetmeats. That season and its successor glittered with productions of Gluck's *Orfeo*, Strauss's *Salome*, and Charpentier's *Louise*. The limpid masterpiece that is *Pelléas*, however, failed to impress Milan's public. At the end of the first performance, according to a newspaper account, Toscanini "expressed his own satisfaction by appearing before the footlights himself and applauding . . . that small group of enthusiasts who, in a theater already half empty, called him to the 'honors of the proscenium.' "

Early in 1908 a rumor circulated through Italian musical circles that Toscanini and La Scala's director, Giulio Gatti-Casazza, were negotiating with the rich Metropolitan Opera House in New York. When the news became official in February, the two men found themselves rebuked in the press for preferring "American millions" to the enhancement of Milan's operatic splendor. Money *did* count in determining the conductor's decision, though not principally in respect to his own financial profit. "American millions" translated into superior artistic resources were the prime influence governing his withdrawal from the less favorably endowed Scala. During the weeks preceding Toscanini's Metropolitan debut, New York newspapers were salted with information and anecdotage about the new and much-discussed Italian conductor. Assurances were given, with liberal quotation from European pundits, that Toscanini's performances in Milan had set a standard for the rest of the Continent, that New York could count itself fortunate in having secured so eminent a musician. Astounding stories were told of his memory; the incident of his South American debut in 1889 was lavishly embroidered. At his first rehearsal Toscanini sweated the orchestra remorselessly for four hours, which was expected, and talked to the players in English, which was a surprise. Finally, came the day of unveiling (November 16, 1908), when Gatti's first season opened with a performance of *Aïda.* The *Tribune*'s critic, Henry E. Krehbiel, rhapsodized: "In the best sense he is an artist, an interpreter, a re-creator. Signor Toscanini brought to the understanding and the emotions of the audience all of Verdi's score, body and soul, as it lives in him, mixing with it an abundance of sympathetic affection." If other commentators—W. J. Henderson in the *Sun*, for one—mustered less enthusiasm, none doubted the new conductor's authority and individuality.

Full approval was reserved, however, until Toscanini's performance of *Götterdämmerung* later in the season. It seemed heretical to entrust this score to an Italian; wherefor three thousand ticket-holders arrived prepared to pronounce a damning "I thought as much." But ingrained Teutonic prejudice foundered in the wake of Toscanini's revelations. "How he rises to its climaxes," gasped one critic, "lingers on its luscious passages, and revels in its melodious intricacies! None of the subtle features of this score escapes him, nor does he miss those subtle modifications of tempo and dynamics which give life to the score, as the *rubato* does to the Chopin mazurka." And if W. J. Henderson chided Toscanini for the Apollonian effeminacy of this interpretation (the bluff strides of Hercules were more to his liking), even he could not ignore the conductor's glowing perception of "all the sensuous quality of Wagner's melody."

For seven seasons Toscanini dominated the operatic life of New York, years when the Metropolitan Opera House reached its apogee of artistic splendor. The results were bought dearly—Toscanini exacted long and abundant rehearsals, canceled performances if the proper artists were not at hand, frayed tempers by his irascible zeal—but they showered on appreciative ears. Just how appreciative can be detected from the eulogy of the Boston critic H. T. Parker written a few months after Toscanini's last Metropolitan appearance, in 1915:

> Whatever piece he undertook in his seven years at the Metropolitan—German music-drama, Italian opera buffa, the romantic Verdi, the theatrical Puccini, the adroit Massenet, in the whole range of music of the theater from Gluck to Dukas—he penetrated substance, style, and spirit

> and transmitted them eloquently to his audience. He was thrilling to hear in his mastery of rhythm; magnificent in the advance and the breaking of musico-dramatic climax; wondrous in the adjustment of detail to the whole tonal mass in the orchestra and the instant that it enforced or illuminated on the stage. . . . The nervous force within him he infused into music and play, singers, band, and audience until, when he was at his highest and fullest, and in the music that stirred him, it made the atmosphere of the opera house electric.

Toscanini's conducting of *Otello*, *Die Meistersinger*, *Orfeo*, *Tristan*, and *Boris* established standards that have been approached rarely in New York's subsequent history. To detail the landmarks of those years would stale the argument by needless repetition. It is enough to catch the glint in Parker's evocative phrases.

In the summer of 1915 it was announced to a regretful New York that Toscanini would concern himself no longer with the musical world centering on Broadway and Thirty-Ninth Street. Officially, he remained on the eastern side of the Atlantic "solely because of his interest in the war." In actual fact, the roots of his decision were imbedded in artistic principle. During his last season, the powers ruling the Metropolitan had decreed that expenses were to be pared and the institution established on a self-sustaining basis. This retrenchment jeopardized the standards to which Toscanini had grown accustomed. Rather than compromise, he declined to lend his services further.

Toscanini's tenure at the Metropolitan had not put a complete quietus on his other activities. In 1910 he had led a season of Italian opera at the Paris Opéra, and in 1912, at the Teatro Colón, Buenos Aires, he had conducted twenty-two different operas. Returning to Europe in the spring of 1915 (he had canceled at the last moment a passage on the *Lusitania*'s final crossing), Toscanini entered on the five least active years of his career. He directed scattered concerts, led military bands in the rear lines, participated in La Scala's 1918 "Victory Season." In the elections of 1919 he stood as candidate for parliament on the Fascist Party ticket, but, like Mussolini himself, failed to attract sufficient votes. To bring down any eyebrows raised by mention of this episode, it should be noted that the 1919 Mussolini was ostensibly a socialist reformer whose dictatorial ambitions were as yet concealed.

This fallow period came to an end in the summer of 1920, when Toscanini set about forming an all-Italian orchestra for a long American tour. Arriving in New York on December 13, 1920, the musicians went immediately to the Victor studio at Camden. Toscanini's initial bout with the recording turntable is said to have caused him great anguish. The conditions of acoustical recording—cramped studios, the necessity for rearranging orchestral forces to suit unwieldy recording horns, the restricting brevity of a four-minute disc—set in train an impatience with mechanical reproduction which has ever since plagued this conductor. The tour opened on December 28 at the Metropolitan Opera House. Seven years earlier New York had sampled his symphonic vein in a concert (only once repeated) with the regular opera house orchestra. The eloquence of that Sunday evening in 1913, especially of the interpretation of Beethoven's Ninth Symphony, had quickened three thousand expectant pulses. "It was recognized as a remarkable performance," wrote Richard Aldrich in the next morning's *New York Times*, "and one of its obvious results was to prompt the wish that a way might be found for Mr. Toscanini to conduct more symphonic concerts for the New York public."

But when the way was found via an Italian orchestra, the enthusiasm of Mr. Aldrich—always an ardent Toscanini well-wisher—hardly coruscated. "The quality of the orchestra," he wrote, "did not add much to the distinction of the occasion. It is a large body, but it was not notable for fullness, richness, nor body of tone." This tonal deficiency operated with particular ill effect, the *New York Times* critic observed, in Debussy's *Ibéria* and Respighi's *Fountains of Rome*. They were played "with an exquisite and flexible manipulation of their ingenious and complete instrumental effects, but it seemed as if the chief aim and object of these instrumental effects—color, atmosphere, movement, the suggestion of exterior effects and visual images . . . somehow escaped and eluded players and conductor." General critical agreement focused on the pure virtuosity of the ensemble—the astonishing *fortes*, razorlike string attacks, delicate balance, and lucid articulation—but the net result was adjudged dry and contrasty. Surveying these contemporary estimates from a vantage point three decades away, one wonders whether the imported orchestra may not have been unjustly anathematized. Doubtless even the cream of Italy's performers could not duplicate the sound of America's long-established polyglot ensembles. But the characteristics of the playing as described in 1920 are so akin to what is heard from the Maestro now as to suggest that Toscanini's influence, and not the quality of the orchestra, was largely responsible for the "shortcomings." Aldrich and his confreres, comparing the Toscanini approach with the accustomed ways of Muck or Stokowski, found it strikingly different, and hence difficult to accept. It is a common critical failing.

Following his American tour came the climaxing years of Toscanini's efforts in the opera house. The stage of La Scala had been dark since 1917 except for the short "Victory Season" of 1918. From the day it had opened, in 1778, the house had led a precarious existence. Two successive wealthy patrons—members of the Italian nobility—had met the annual deficits from 1898 to 1917, but the war and a subsequent slump in Italy's economy had made it impossible for a single benefactor to assume this responsibility further. Instead, a group of prominent Milanese banded together after World War I to form the corporation "Ente Autonomo della Scala" with the aim of reopening the house under the most favorable circumstances. The stage was re-equipped, the lighting modernized, and the artistic direction entrusted to Toscanini. La Scala became "his" theater, and the eight-year reign that began on December 26, 1921, with a performance of *Falstaff*, will shine forever in Italy's annals of opera. The history of La Scala in the twenties merits a chapter to itself, a chapter, however, that could properly come only from the pen of an eyewitness. Those of us who were not present must catch what we can from the secondhand evidence of recordings. I say "secondhand" because Toscanini never committed any of his Scala performances to wax. But there are glimmers in the old complete-opera recordings made at La Scala under other conductors to suggest the effect of Toscanini's vitalizing influence.

By 1929, Toscanini had withstood the intrigues and debilitations of the opera house for forty-three years. It was time for him to cry "Hold, enough!" In terms of physical effort alone, the task of ruling La Scala held diminishing appeal as the years wore on. (It was not unusual for Toscanini, already in his sixties, to conduct fifty times during a season.) More important than the physical strain was his growing impatience with opera, or rather with the compromises inevitable in the opera house. The work of an opera conductor, like that of a newspaper editor, is compacted of compromise: there is no getting around an inexorable curtain-time or press-deadline. Thenceforth Toscanini would conduct opera only when the spirit moved him and/or when he was given the optimum resources of musical talent. Before concluding his Scala tenure, the conductor took the company on tour so that foreign ears might hear the estate to which Italian opera had been raised.

When Toscanini left La Scala, he had already been installed as conductor-in-chief of the New York Philharmonic-Symphony. His first appearances with that orchestra dated from January 1926, when he came as a guest conductor for a total of eleven concerts, and introduced the New York players to such famous Toscanini interpretations as the Haydn "Clock" Symphony, the Brahms *Variations on a Theme by Haydn*, Debussy's *La Mer*, and Respighi's *Pines of Rome*. So impressive were these few concerts in 1926 that Toscanini was asked immediately to return the following year. Although a nervous malaise forced him to cancel all but three of his 1927 concerts, that trio—all-Beethoven, as befitted the centenary year—securely established Toscanini in the estimate of New Yorkers. On the morning following his interpretation of the Ninth Symphony (Elisabeth Rethberg and Louise Homer were among the soloists), the New York press delivered a flood of critical panegyric, and on March 30, 1928, at the end of Toscanini's third guest-season, Clarence Mackay announced that the Italian conductor was to be chief steersman at the Philharmonic's helm.

Toscanini's decade with the New York Philharmonic is considered by many the high-water point in his varied career. Rash though it is to make so confining a declaration about an artistic life compounded of triumphs, it is nevertheless clear that in these ten years the conductor's full musical maturity met in happy confluence with an orchestra of enviable properties. Individual memories and the witness of a few breathtaking recordings attest the richness of these performances. During his tenure with the Philharmonic there were cycles of Brahms and Beethoven symphonies, the *Missa Solemnis* and *Ein deutsches Requiem*, delvings into Berlioz, and resuscitations of Verdi. Though minor carpings were flung at the scarcity of soloists and the plethora of modern Italian composers on Toscanini's programs, the tone of New York criticism was adulatory to excess. The critic of the *New York Times* echoed firmly entrenched admiration when he wrote in 1928 that "the Toscanini performance of the Elgar variations is not only an exciting feat of virtuosity, it is in itself a creation."

Distressing news from Wall Street notwithstanding, the Philharmonic-Symphony Society sent Toscanini and the orchestra on a junket through Europe in the spring of 1930. The tour opened at the Paris Opéra on May 3 amid a chorus of praise and a famous dissenting solo. The chorus consisted of Paris concert-goers and ecstatic critics, who made the unprecedented admission that a foreigner could conduct French music with the comprehension of a native. The sole dissent came from Maurice Ravel, whose *Boléro*, then eighteen months old and at the summit of its popularity, concluded Toscanini's first Paris concert. When Ravel conducted the *Boléro* he favored a measured tread and a conception more elegiac than frenetic. Toscanini preferred the music at a perceptibly faster tempo, and so played it in Paris. What transpired between composer and conductor at the concert's end is variously reported, but the general description shows a displeased Ravel and an impenitent Toscanini. From Paris the American orchestra went to Zürich and thence to several Italian cities. Turning north, they gave two concerts in Vienna, proceeded to Berlin by way of Budapest, Prague, Leipzig, and Dresden, and after four performances in London sailed for home, having accumulated rapturous compliments and a deficit reported at $250,000.

Toscanini's Italian concerts with the Philharmonic turned out to be his last public appearances on native soil for sixteen years. His famous clash with the Fascist authorities occurred in Bologna early in 1931. The conductor had agreed to direct a commemorative concert devoted to the music of his onetime mentor Giuseppe Martucci. City officials demanded that the program begin with *Giovinezza,* the Fascist anthem. Toscanini declared publicly that he would not introduce such musical trash on his program. When he arrived at Bologna's Teatro Communale on the evening of the concert, a band of ruffians lay in ambush, ready to beat him up. Thanks to the prescience of a chauffeur, Toscanini suffered only a few bruises and was soon far away from the auditorium. Italy, which would not again hear its greatest living musician for fifteen years, suffered from the encounter far more heavily.

Paris having accorded its accolade, it followed that that other bastion of musical chauvinism, Bayreuth, must also fall. "Toscanini conducts it [*Tristan*] in a manner entirely different from ours," Mahler once said, "but magnificently in his way." "His way"—the way of precision, tonal clarity, and freedom from the cant of tradition—ran into some squalls within the sacrosanct walls of Bayreuth. The Festspielhaus orchestra lacked the virtuosity and cohesion of the trained ensembles to which Toscanini had become accustomed. More than once he threw down his baton and fled from the rehearsal, despairing of ever coaxing the musicians to make music properly. But a few minutes later he would be back, and—to judge from the recorded 1930 Bayreuth performance of *Tannhäuser*—the final results were extraordinary. Again the evidence is secondhand, because Karl Elmendorff, and not Toscanini, conducted the orchestra for this recording; but as all singers and musicians were rigorously prepared by Toscanini, these discs bear at least partial witness to his accomplishment. In 1930 Toscanini directed the Bayreuth productions of *Tannhäuser* and *Tristan*, and the following year addressed himself to *Parsifal.* The walls of the Festspielhaus vibrated to a thitherto unheard lyrical sweep. But this irradiation, this intense distillation of Wagner's meaning, this impatience with Germanic muddiness masquerading as "tradition," cost him dearly in point of nervous expenditure. Tempers flared regularly. The fiery Italian had little respect for those who steered the artistic destinies of Bayreuth. In departing from Bayreuth in 1931, he is reported to have declared: "I leave Bayreuth disappointed and embittered. I came here with the expectation of discovering a grail, and I found a banal theater." In 1932 the Bayreuth stage was dark, and when it came to life again during the summer of 1933 the swastika flew over Germany. Toscanini's refusal as a matter of principle to conduct in the Third Reich is justly celebrated. It in no wise detracts from this honorable stand to observe that he was also unfavorably disposed to Bayreuth on purely musical grounds.

The political and artistic climate of Austria proved more salubrious. Beginning in 1933, Toscanini made yearly appearances in Vienna, conducting the Philharmonic, and from 1934 through 1937 he directed concerts and opera each summer at the Salzburg Festival. When Hitler's invading army precluded further activity in Austria, Toscanini went instead to Lucerne to participate in a festival hastily created to compete with the Nazified endeavors at Salzburg. And he gave a further demonstration of his anti-Nazi sympathies by flying to Tel-Aviv to conduct a newly formed orchestra of Jewish refugees.

When the Philharmonic-Symphony Society announced Toscanini's resignation in 1936, a great dolor enshrouded American musical circles. In reporting Toscanini's final concert with the Philharmonic, New York newspapers did everything but print their margins in black. Events proved this lamentation to have been premature. Eighteen months later Toscanini returned to New York as conductor of a new orchestra. Since the days of P. T. Barnum and Jenny Lind no musician had been lured to these shores more temptingly. The Radio Corporation of America not only offered Toscanini a custom-made orchestra (the NBC Symphony) and the freedom to do with it exactly as he pleased; RCA also provided an audience of millions and a contract of twenty concerts per season at five thousand dollars per concert. How could he decline?

The radio career of Toscanini, which began on Christmas night, 1937, is too well known to require extensive detailing here. For the first few years his broadcasts suffered from the acoustical defects of NBC's Studio 8-H. An acute lack of reverberation stole the ring and bloom from the conductor's crescendos and transformed them into shattering blares. (The recording of Haydn's Symphony No. 88, a product of Toscanini's first NBC season, remains as a sad legacy of these engineering deficiencies.) Extensive remodeling of the studio ensued, and to good effect, though even at the end of its short life Studio 8-H could not bestow the tonal patina of a Carnegie Hall or an Academy of Music. Finally, in the summer of 1950, NBC's concert hall was ripped apart and turned into a television studio, after which the Toscanini broadcasts emanated from Carnegie Hall—a desirable shift of locale, if rather tardily accomplished.

Toscanini's programs with the NBC Symphony have been built largely of the music that has engaged his attention for half a century—the nine Beethoven and four Brahms symphonies, the virtuosic variations of Brahms and Elgar, Debussy's *La Mer* and *Ibéria*, orchestral excerpts from Wagner's operas, Verdi's *Manzoni* Requiem, overtures by Rossini. But there were and continue to be happy departures. After years of neglect the conductor's interest in Tchaikovsky revived—rather more fortunately with the *Manfred* Symphony than with the First Piano Concerto. The war encouraged him to explore territory that he had previously neglected. He reconnoitered the domain of contemporary American composition, with absorbing if not always successful results. Less absorbing were the *longueurs* of a Sunday afternoon when Toscanini had the doubtful honor of presenting to American listeners the Seventh ("Leningrad") Symphony of Shostakovich, not to mention other equally tedious occasions when he dabbled severely with the marches of John Philip Sousa. Such reservations notwithstanding, no one could point an accusing finger at this old man to berate a sluggish or atrophied mind.

Nor could anyone level the charge of flagging energy at a conductor who in his seventy-seventh year began preparing full-length operas for broadcast. To the vast majority of American listeners, Toscanini's prowess as a director of opera was known only by hearsay. On December 10, 1944, with a broadcast of *Fidelio*, the reputation became reality. Subsequent seasons have brought *La Bohème* (on the fiftieth anniversary of its *première*), *La Traviata*, *Otello*, *Aïda*, and *Falstaff*. On occasion the singers have been unequal to the conductor; at times the forward surge of these concert performances has stood in the way of dramatic verity. But despite their minor faults, the opera broadcasts have been major musical experiences. To a new generation of listeners they have demonstrated what was evident in Italy half a century ago: that the precision, faithfulness, and good taste of a Toscanini performance throw brilliant and unsuspected illumination on the commonest of opera warhorses.

Toscanini has been a figure of public concern for well over six decades. A span of such magnitude must inevitably nurture the growth of legends, half-truths, and misconceptions. It is the lot of any public man to be misunderstood. Hegel, in a fit of exacerbation, once avowed that "of all my numerous disciples, only one has ever understood me, and even he understood me falsely." Were Toscanini to peruse a cross-section of the literature purporting to explain his art there is little doubt that he would fall prey to equally uncharitable thoughts. (Fortunately for the state of his spleen, he is said never to read what is written about him.) But some blame for the misunderstandings must be borne by Toscanini himself, for seldom has a person of his eminence been so little articulate, so little inclined to share his mind with an inquiring public. *Some* of the blame. Most of it must be assigned to our insatiable appetite for the easy generalization.

In the mid-thirties, when Toscanini idolatry reigned triumphant, misinformation followed copiously in the train of dull-witted panegyric. In particular, encomiasts gabbled over the conductor's sedulous regard for the printed score. "Toscanini," they breathlessly explained, "plays every note in the score exactly as the composer wrote it." As if it were a virtue to give a bald, verbatim transcription of the printed note! Provided he has the technical wherewithal, any student can place a piece of music before him and mechanically translate what he sees. For the regrettable aural result, listen to any sure-fingered but unimaginative child pianist as she (it is usually she) drums her stolid way through a Mozart sonata. It is imagination, filling in the vital elements that a score cannot precisely express, rather than literalness, which gives stature to a musical interpreter. The printed language of sound is woefully inexact and leaves unanswered a multitude of questions. How is one to shape a phrase? Where should it "give" and where should it strengthen to a peak? The score says nothing or, at best, offers but the sketchiest notion. How should one determine the correct tempo? The score will usually start off with a general description (such as allegro assai) and sometimes with a metronome indication, but it is not always clear just what the composer meant by those nebulous words "very quick," and metronome indications are notoriously inexact. Was it not Brahms who said that every composer who set down metronome marks lived to regret it? And these hints, inexact as they are, govern only the general tempo-boundaries of a musical entity. The instructions for ebb and flow within the over-all framework are even more enigmatic. The word *rallentando* under a phrase signifies a slowing of tempo. But how slow, and where does the slackening begin and where stop? Again, the score is silent. On the matter of coloration the printed page is mute; neither does it speak helpfully about balance or about the quality and extent of variations in volume. The imagination of an interpreter must eke out the insufficiencies of musical notation. Every musician takes liberties in translating a printed score. Toscanini is no exception: he is only more subtle than most.

Samuel Antek, who has played under Toscanini since the NBC Orchestra was organized, speaks illuminatingly on this subject.* "It will probably surprise many readers," he writes, "that Toscanini is the 'freest' of all conductors; but that 'freedom' is taken so subtly, with such discretion and good taste, that one is hardly aware of its occurrence. This expressive ebb and flow *within* the phrase without disturbing its 'line' is one of the unique aspects of his music-making." The operative words here are "discretion" and "good taste." Any musician feels impelled to interpret the printed score freely rather than literally, for in freedom resides the principal means wherein music comes to life; the extent and quality of the freedom are what really matter. There are conductors of worldwide reputation who will reorchestrate Tchaikovsky's "*Pathétique*" Symphony or insert blatant ritardandos in Beethoven's "*Eroica*" or accentuate a melody in the Brahms Third to ludicrous extremes. For these practitioners, "freedom" descends to "license"; their deviations from the letter of the text traduce rather than liberate the composer's thought. It is because Toscanini stands at the opposite extreme from those who

* "Playing with The Maestro," by Samuel Antek, *Saturday Review of Literature*, March 25, 1950.

"interpret" by misrepresenting that he has earned a dubious reputation for mechanical literalness. To be sure, there are instances where Toscanini fails to present a composer's work in the most favorable light. But his lapses are predominantly because of congenital blind spots, a temperamental antinomy, or an æsthetic viewpoint based on postulates that seem to many of his listeners inappropriate; they are almost never due to willful neglect of clearly expressed wishes.

Second only to the myth of Toscanini's literalness is the fiction of his inflexibility. A massive and inexorable rigidity is ascribed to Toscanini in the most trustworthy quarters. One of England's keenest critics, Neville Cardus, would have it that "Toscanini, after scrupulous rehearsals, is not likely to alter the charted course, change gear, or change a semiquaver, at any one of twenty subsequent performances." Unfailingly, commentators will insist that this conductor's tempos are as reliable as the finest Swiss chronometer, that he is nothing less than a human metronome whose spring never slackens. Fortunately for the vitality of Toscanini's performances, it is not so. For those who subscribe to the chronometer simile, no more instructive eight minutes can be spent than in comparing two Toscanini recordings of the *Midsummer Night's Dream* Scherzo. Exhibit A, recorded with the New York Philharmonic in 1926 for Brunswick, seems to proceed at a sprightly enough pace until one hears Exhibit B, recorded with the same orchestra four years later for Victor. The latter interpretation is so much faster and more nimbly articulated as to make the first version, on replaying, seem quite stodgy and heavy-footed. Here, in the space of four years, the human chronometer can be caught ticking at demonstrably different speeds. And there are fluctuations within a period far shorter than this. At a first rehearsal Toscanini will choose one tempo, presumably firm and unshakable. At the next rehearsal he will decide on another. And at the concert the following day he will conduct at a tempo different from that of either rehearsal. This flexibility is standard operating procedure for Toscanini—and happily so. For how could his performances be so animated if everything were anticipated, if each facet of his interpretations were chiseled at the same unvarying angle year in and year out?

His tempos change, and so do his general musical conceptions. Returning to his orchestra one autumn to rehearse the Beethoven Fifth, Toscanini said to his men: "Forget everything I ever told you about this work. It was stupid, uncomprehending. . . . *Now* I realize for the first time how it ought to be played." And this in his eighties! A mark of intellectual vigor is the ability to change one's mind. If Landowska has basically revised her approach to Bach's *Well-Tempered Clavier* three times, is it so surprising that Toscanini has evolved several differing interpretations of the Beethoven Fifth? The real cause for surprise is that these two vital performers are still characterized as artistic die-hards, wedded to dogma, impervious to change.

What of Toscanini's much-mooted "disregard of contemporary music"? Before weighing the indictment it would be well to consider what is contemporary in the case of a man born in 1867. Is the term to cover Strauss and Debussy, both of whom needed the good offices of proselytizing conductors at the very time that Toscanini was building his own reputation? Or is it meant to connote Shostakovich and Benjamin Britten, who were infants when Toscanini was verging on middle age? If one accepts the former definition, there is no cause to prate about Toscanini's lack of interest in the moderns: he performed Strauss, Debussy, Dukas, and Elgar at a time when their works were far from acceptance as "classics," and he has continued for half a century to give their music the most persuasive consideration. Even for such relative youngsters as Ravel, Kodály, and Respighi he has been more than solicitous. If later he fell behind the vanguard, that is cause for disappointment, but not for censure. The conductor brought unreceptive ears to a 1925 contemporary-music festival at Venice, where the fare concentrated on Stravinsky, Schönberg, and Milhaud. "Much of this does not seem to me to be music," was his observation at the time to Paul Stefan. And at another concert of contemporary music Toscanini left no doubt as to his feelings: "Open the windows; we need fresh air." When Dimitri Mitropoulos conducted Alban Berg's Violin Concerto for a 1945 NBC Symphony broadcast, Toscanini attended rehearsals as well as the actual broadcast performance. He studied the score assiduously. Finally, he admitted to Mitropoulos: "I try very hard, but I still think you are crazy—and Berg also."

For a man with views thus decided, Toscanini has showed himself remarkably yielding. On the eve of his seventieth birthday he played the First Symphony of Shostakovich—a composer forty years his junior. Even later, in his mid-seventies, he directed his attention to the American muse. I believe it is customary to deprecate the results of this gesture. Fashion decrees that Toscanini is quite incapable of warbling our native wood-notes wild. Nevertheless, I must insist that I have yet to hear the *Rhapsody in Blue* or *An American in Paris* delivered with the fervor, zest, and profound appreciation that were evident in the interpretations of this benighted foreigner. So rewarding, indeed, have been his sporadic performances of contemporary music as to make one wish that Toscanini really fulfilled Bernard Shaw's dictum that the true progressive turns more radical the older he grows. It has not been so with Toscanini. His forays into the modern idiom remain isolated deflections from the current of his life work. For such divagations as he has vouchsafed we are grateful, though our gratitude is tinged with the regret that his illuminating genius has not more often been put at the disposal of a Barber or a

Copland, to say nothing of a Stravinsky, a Hindemith, or a Milhaud.

As more and more of his recordings have been issued, the myth of Toscanini's infallibility has withered. The pitiless testimony of repeated listening has demonstrated that even this paragon can nod. Some writers, reveling perhaps in the luxury of finding fault in so hallowed a quarter, have pursued his weaknesses too far. Virgil Thomson is wont to picture Toscanini as a musician bereft of culture, lacking in the humane marriage of learning and inspiration. In this critic's portrait he emerges as little more than the canny maestro of the Italian opera house, able to whip an orchestra into a state of excitement, capable of wooing an audience with the relentless clickety-click of a fast beat but, for all that, "spiritually unenlightening, except when he plays Italian music." Other writers, less sweeping in their reservations, allow him pre-eminence in most quarters—Beethoven, Verdi, and Wagner—while putting a few composers (Mozart, for instance), beyond his ken. This is a stand more readily defensible, but hardly impregnable. For Toscanini is likely to confound one by a taut, squarely driven performance of the "*Eroica*" followed by a wonderfully plastic and evocative interpretation of the Mozart G minor. And by no means is he ignorant and unlettered. If he favors a certain musical style, it is certainly not because he is unaware of the alternatives. He often consults manuscript originals, compares editions, and studies letters and biographies to resolve seemingly minor interpretative difficulties. He reads widely, and—like any intelligent man—becomes impatient with unenlightening books. He will pick up a volume in search of a factual detail and, finding instead only fatuous commonplaces, will throw it aside with a disdainful: "Written by a musicologist!"

Despite the perils of pigeonholing Toscanini's personality, one general observation may be ventured without too great danger of its confutation by this unpredictable genius. However charming and good-humored he may be in everyday life, his musical temperament does not run to geniality. Something of Savonarola informs his nature. Intensity is wont to run at too extreme a pitch, with high seriousness lacking the warming grace of relaxed urbanity. This unyielding disposition often prejudices his readings of Mozart, which strive so hard to make a point, are argued with such determined vitality, as to giddy the mannered music. To say that Toscanini's spirits can prove too strong and rigorous for Mozart does not imply that this composer fares any better at the hands of slipshod, mincing interpreters, but there is a happy mean between taut *dämonisch* and peruked flummery, and if comparisons were not said to be odious I would observe that Sir Thomas Beecham usually achieves such a balance far more successfully than Toscanini. I do not wish to press this criticism too far. Toscanini's Mozart, for all its lack of gentle animation, will yet reveal unique marvels of inflection and steadiness of outline. But it does not bask in the sunset glow of maturity. To hear Richard Strauss conduct *Don Quixote* in his seventy-eighth year (on a treasurable set of German records) is to hear the tonal equivalent of Wordsworth's "old age serene and bright," a way of making music with all the good humor and relaxed grace of a life fallen into the sere and yellow leaf. Toscanini ordains it otherwise. With strengthening determination he refuses to mellow into old age.

I cannot leave off without a word on Toscanini's rehearsals. It is customary to describe these sessions with the awed appreciation that might attend a description of Etna in eruption. Toscanini hurling his watch over the heads of the orchestra men, Toscanini vituperating an offending player, Toscanini breaking off a rehearsal in blind fury—the picture has been sketched enough. I find it neither pretty nor especially commendable. My sentiments lie with those of an English instrumentalist once courted by Toscanini, who recommends that "that man be soundly spanked when he starts to behave so badly." Those whose weekly job it is to play under Toscanini do not hold with this doughty viewpoint. They accept the conductor's storms as ineluctable freaks of nature. While he accosts them in raging choler, they murmur to themselves Toscanini's credo, "Democracy in life, aristocracy in art," and turn the other cheek for music's sake. Doubtless we should follow their example and raise our eyes from the tirades to the higher musical matters that coexist with them.

Some "bootlegged" recordings of Toscanini rehearsals convey the volatile atmosphere of these sessions. In a foggy, croaking voice he "sings" the way the phrase should go—and manages to transmit not only its shape but its hue as well. The rehearsal record of "Siegfried's Rhine Journey" gives an uncanny demonstration of this instantaneous communication of tonal color. On the record of Mozart's "Haffner" Symphony in rehearsal, the last movement begins neatly with eight nimble measures by strings alone. Then on the downbeat of the ninth measure the entire orchestra enters with a resounding fortissimo crack. Yet the crack will not do. It is not loud, not brittle, enough; it lacks passion. "Are you asleep?" Toscanini shouts. Then, stamping his feet and uttering a curdling bark, he demonstrates the power and energy that he expects to go into the orchestral *tutti*. Even over the loudspeaker it frightens. Inspired with "the power of a divine terror" (in Stefan Zweig's acute phrase), the men pick up their instruments once more. This time the playing snaps like a spring. The conductor is satisfied; the rehearsal continues.

His constant concern is to release from his players untapped reservoirs of musical passion. There is none of the dry pedant about him. Rehearsing Berlioz's *Roméo et Juliette*, he adjures the orchestra: "*Disperato!* You are all *disperati!*" To him music always calls up a "program" of his own devising. Thus, in this same score, a cello phrase in the adagio signifies to him "*Juliette, je t'aime.*" At a later point, in the Reconciliation scene between the warring families, he is so moved by their gradual turning from anger to pity that he "sees heaven opening." I am sure he would object to Stravinsky's conception of music as the organization of time by human invention. To deny music expression would be, for Toscanini, to deny it its highest function.

Excepting only contemporary music, Toscanini's tastes are imperturbably catholic. This impartiality may sometimes spell trouble in navigating the shoals of stylistic differentiation, but it insures the most concentrated care for the music at hand. In giving his utmost to every note and in laying down the highest standards of technical discipline, Toscanini has profoundly influenced modern conceptions of conducting. He is idolized and emulated wherever music is made. At his best, he has never been equaled. Allow him his failings—there is still no one like him in music. Future generations, through the heritage of phonograph records, will marvel at the extraordinary level to which he has raised the musical experience. Those of us fortunate enough to have known the sway of his personal magnetism are luckier. To have lived in the Toscanini era has been an inspiration and a privilege.

☼ Bruno *Walter*

IN the course of a review written during Bruno Walter's first season with the New York Philharmonic (1932), Lawrence Gilman observed: "Mr. Walter is especially to be valued as an interpreter because he represents with a singular completeness and authenticity what one might call, for want of a more sharply indicative term, the great central tradition of German musical culture." Even at that time, German influence was fast on the wane; but Gilman, writing in the days of the respectable Weimar Republic, could not have foreseen the depths to which that influence was destined to sink. Today Bruno Walter not only represents the German tradition in America with "completeness and authenticity"—he represents it almost singlehanded. Other conductors presently before our public—Fritz Stiedry and George Szell to name two—have also been exposed to Germanic cultural radiation, but none so much as Walter. He is the sole conductor now active in the United States who can claim succession to the royal line of Bülow, Nikisch, and Mahler.

At the turn of the century, by contrast, it was as customary to import conductors from Germany as chefs from France or governesses from England. In New York the symphonic scene was dominated by Leopold Damrosch and Anton Seidl; in Boston the orchestra was under the leadership of Wilhelm Gericke, having previously passed through the hands of Henschel, Nikisch, and Paur; and at the head of Philadelphia's newly formed orchestra was Lübeck-born Fritz Scheel. This Germanic monopoly obtained for many years under the succeeding influence of Karl Muck, Gustav Mahler, Max Fiedler, Frederick Stock, Felix Weingartner, and Josef Stransky—all, if not actually born within German boundaries, being by training and inclination stout protectors of Teutonic musical culture. The year 1910 can be said to have marked the floodtide of this influence. By the end of World War I, German domination had already begun to slacken, and Hitler's anticultural folly, followed by World War II, reduced it almost to nonexistence. At midcentury New York's two major orchestras were conducted by an Italian and a Greek; in Philadelphia a Hungarian was in charge (trained in Budapest, not Vienna like Nikisch or Leipzig like Seidl); Boston's affairs were directed by an Alsatian (who had inherited the orchestra from a Russian); Chicago's by a Czech; San Francisco's by a Parisian.

The decline and fall of Germanic influence is probably the most significant single phenomenon of twentieth-century musical history. Germany's retrogression as a political force offers a partial explanation, as witness the careers of Muck, Furtwängler, and Gieseking, but more pertinent is that nation's retrogression as a fount of musical creation. The Germanic creative tradition, which continued without a break from Bach to Richard Strauss and Mahler, began to flicker perceptibly at the very time when Germanic interpreters began to lose their dominance. The two facts are not unrelated. A

Germany devoid of genuine creative vitality could still produce interpretative musicians of merit, but its musicians could hardly command the international respect accorded to them in the nineteenth century, when they swam in the mainstream of music.

Bruno Walter, who began his conducting career in Cologne in 1893, belongs to that departed era. During his formative student and apprentice years, Wagner and Liszt were but lately deceased, Brahms and Bruckner basked in well-earned approbation, Clara Schumann still preached the gospel according to Saint Robert, Richard Strauss and Gustav Mahler had yet to create the works of their maturity, and not too far distant in the past lay memories of Beethoven and Schubert as recollected by Moscheles and Schober. Is it any wonder that Walter conducts the music of this culture with reverence, with love, and with the authority born of close communion with the wellspring of artistic creation? Other conductors may throw fresh light on the masterpieces of Germanic musical culture, or realize their intentions with greater éclat, or tend to an approach more individual and therefore more provocative, but no one in America today brings to this music quite the intimate associations of Bruno Walter.

This custodianship of a great tradition is the source of both Walter's strength and his weakness, for if it enables him to interpret the Central European repertoire with rare comprehension, it lends also a rather elegiac complexion to his music-making. To hear him conduct a series of all-Brahms programs, as he did in New York during the 1950–1 season, with his fine command of mellow orchestral tone, his harmonious kinship with Brahms's *Weltanschauung*, and his searching knowledge of the scores, is an inspiring experience—but a little deadening too, at least to this listener, who has the utmost respect for Bruno Walter's interpretations, but who finds the cumulative atmosphere of his concerts just a little stuffy.

Of course, in his long career Walter has often strayed from the confines of German music. Vienna acclaimed his performances of Italian opera, of middle-period Verdi in particular, and justly so, as we learned when he conducted *La Forza del Destino* at the Metropolitan. His infrequent brushes with French music have revealed a *Symphonie fantastique* of fine persuasion on the one hand, a *La Mer* weighty and overstated on the other. The record shows a few contemporary works entered under Walter's name—the Second Piano Concerto by Křenek, symphonies by Daniel Gregory Mason, John Alden Carpenter, and Samuel Barber, the Vaughan Williams *Fantasia on a Theme by Thomas Tallis*, *La Péri* by Dukas, Prokofiev's *L'Enfant-prodigue*—but save for the first- and last-named these keep on the safe side of modernity. If exceptions can be made to prove a rule (and I have never understood just how), these few detours should underline the constancy with which Walter has stuck to the main highway running from Hamburg to Vienna by way of Düsseldorf, Leipzig, and Prague.

The detours have become more and more infrequent as Walter has grown older. Inclination restricts him now to a territory bounded geographically by the Rhine and the Oder, temporally by the demarcating year of 1911 (when Mahler died). Assuredly, these boundaries admit of much *Lebensraum*, and at many points within them Walter is a peer of the realm. His conducting of Schumann and Mahler is unsurpassed. I have heard him do complete justice to Schubert's C major Symphony, Dvořák's Fourth, Brahms's Third, and the *Symphonia Domestica* of Richard Strauss in performances sometimes equaled, but never bettered, by others. He is not quite a match for Beecham in Haydn and Mozart or for Toscanini in Beethoven and Wagner—an evaluation that still need not detract from the warmth and fervor that he can inject into his readings of these composers.

Walter has the enviable ability to command rich autumnal sound from whatever orchestra he leads. No sooner does he commence his annual engagement as guest conductor of the New York Philharmonic than this polyglot ensemble is turned into a band of easy-going Viennese—in startling contrast to the rest of the season when, under Mitropoulos, these same men play with sharp and metallic efficiency. Walter brought about a similar transformation when he conducted the NBC Symphony in the spring of 1951, completing a season during which the orchestra had been directed by Ansermet, Guido Cantelli, and Fritz Reiner, as well as by Toscanini. Under the latter conductors, the players had become inured to a continuing demand for cool, transparent sound, but Walter required no more than a quick run-through of the overture to *Le Nozze di Figaro* to endow this tense, precision-tested orchestra with Viennese nonchalance and warm opacity. The means by which he achieved this metastasis were not perceptible to the naked eye. At rehearsal time there was no special instruction, no colloquy on tone. I could assign the cause only to what Frederick Goldbeck terms "action of presence," by which the conductor need have merely a strong mental image of how a piece of music should sound for the instrumentalists to respond by reproducing his thoughts. According to this theory, if Bruno Walter hears Viennese tone in his imagination, the orchestra men will hear it too, and will play accordingly. "It is up to psychologists to explain such facts," writes Mr. Goldbeck.* "They are common experience inside and outside music. How many times have we not, in animated conversation, heard beforehand the very words that were going to be spoken? 'That is just what I was going to say!' Musical performance has greater focusing power than most subjects of dialogue. Eighty musicians concentrate upon Beethoven and the conductor's guidance. Is it such wonder that

* Frederick Goldbeck: *The Perfect Conductor* (New York: 1951).

they are 'just going to say' what the conductor thinks about it, when his technique consists in perfect concentration (corresponding to theirs) on every detail of the score?" Doubtless this oversimplifies the imponderables of conducting, but it helps to explain how Bruno Walter can for a single concert Germanize Toscanini's own mercurial orchestra.

I mention first Walter's ability to shape an orchestra in his own image that I may balance with an adequate counterweight what Walter lacks in technical address. He does not always make an orchestra toe the line: attacks may be ragged and instrumental execution slipshod. Walter is capable of commanding a technically impeccable execution—firmly beat, carefully enunciated; rather too often, though, there are minor blemishes, not significant in themselves but tending in sum to blur an image otherwise sharply focused. I can recall two performances of the Verdi *Requiem* a few weeks apart, the first by Toscanini, the second by Walter, which put this failing in strong relief. Walter conducted the *Requiem* with obvious sympathy, but the conspicuous lack of razor-sharp precision in the execution robbed his reading of the dynamic surge that had made Toscanini's earlier performance so convincing. Walter is no tyrannical drillmaster; he does not goad an orchestra with abuse or sarcasm. Dissatisfied with the way a passage is played, he will turn to the second violins and query cajolingly: "You could give a little more expression?" This makes for amicable relations and puts the players in that state of relaxation from which Viennese nonchalance exhales, but it can leave a loose and indeterminate end-effect.

I will pass over the tragic political vicissitudes of Bruno Walter's career, referring readers to the conductor's detailed autobiography * for a moving account of how the artistic conscience can maintain its constancy, and deal here only with a few highlights of his musical development. He was born in

* Bruno Walter: *Theme and Variations* (New York: 1946).

Berlin, September 15, 1876, into a lower middle-class Jewish family. (Walter is a *nom de baton;* his name was originally Bruno Schlesinger.) At the age of nine he entered the Stern Conservatory, Berlin, and for four years directed his talent to the piano. He made his debut as a pianist in 1889, aged thirteen, playing the Moscheles E-flat Concerto with the Berlin Philharmonic. Soon after he attended a concert conducted by Hans von Bülow and resolved to follow in Bülow's footsteps as a pianist turned conductor. Accordingly his curriculum at the Stern Conservatory changed, the emphasis thenceforth being on composition, score-reading, and conducting technique. Through the good offices of this school Walter obtained his first job, as coach at the Cologne Opera.

He began work at Cologne when he had just turned seventeen, and after six months of routine rehearsal duty was entrusted with the conducting of Lortzing's *Der Waffenschmied.* As few other conducting assignments followed—despite general commendation of the young man's talent—he applied for, and got, a contract with the Hamburg Stadttheater. For the next seven years, from 1894 to 1901, he made the circuit of German opera houses which took him to Hamburg, Breslau, Pressburg, Riga, and Berlin. These were years during which he was usually in a subordinate position, often working with mediocre artists and playing to undiscriminating audiences, but years also when he mastered the operatic repertoire from Mozart to Wagner and learned that to bring off a performance without mishap and to re-create a work of art are two quite different achievements. At the age of twenty-five, already established as an opera conductor, he moved on to the Vienna Opera, where he fell under the two dominant influences of his life: the musical personality of Gustav Mahler (then General Manager of the opera house) and the insouciant charm of Austrian society. He remained in Vienna for eleven years, most of them filled with success, though at first his conducting met with outspoken criticism. The bulk of his activity centered on the opera house, but occasionally he conducted symphony concerts, among which took place the first performances of Mahler's Ninth Symphony and *Das Lied von der Erde*. Walter's reputation filtered beyond the Germanic orbit. Beecham invited him to conduct at Covent Garden, an engagement soon followed by concert appearances in Rome and Moscow.

In 1911, after a decade in Vienna, Walter took out Austrian citizenship. It seemed as if he had taken firm root in Viennese soil. However, a change of directorship at the Vienna Opera ushered in a new regime and an artistic policy with which he could not agree. Fortuitously, he was approached just at this time by the Munich Court Opera with an offer to succeed Felix Mottl as General Musical Director of Bavaria and artistic head of the Opera. Walter assumed this position on January 1, 1913, after protracted negotiation with Vienna to abrogate his contract. He was then thirty-six years old, and for the first time in full control of a major opera house. Actually three opera houses were under his artistic direction: the Residenz Theater, where Mozart had once conducted, the large Court Theater, and the "Wagnerian" Prinzregenten Theater. During his ten years in Munich, Bruno Walter conducted time and again the main operatic staples (with special emphasis on Mozart and Wagner) and explored the ample territory of post-Romantic German opera (Strauss, Wolf, Pfitzner, Schreker, Korngold, Braunfels). Occasionally he would entrain for Vienna to conduct one of that city's three orchestras, and shortly after World War I he began a series of annual guest-appearances with the Berlin Philharmonic.

Walter resigned from the Bavarian post in 1922, frustrated by the impossiblity of maintaining artistic standards in the face of a damaging inflation. For three years he led an itinerant life. At the invitation of Walter Damrosch, he conducted the New York Symphony for a few weeks beginning on February 15, 1923. During Walter's first season in America the press was seldom given to praise of his work. Some critics complained that his orchestral discipline was lax, others that his interpretations were stodgy. However, these were not the opinions of Damrosch, who asked Walter to return for two successive years, nor of the several American orchestras that made bids for his services.

It was inevitable that the intense musical renascence in Berlin would sooner or later ensnare this eminent native son. In 1925, Walter gave up his independent career to assume the directorship of Berlin's Municipal Opera. For four years he guided the destinies of the Charlottenburg opera house and helped to make the Berlin of this era the center of world musical attention. His concert activity abated somewhat, but did not end. Vienna and Leipzig welcomed him often, as did Paris and London. New ports of call were Leningrad and Milan, where respectively he made the acquaintance of Shostakovich and Toscanini. He was to be heard regularly at the newly founded Salzburg Festival. When Walter withdrew from the Berlin Municipal Opera in 1929, he succeeded Wilhelm Furtwängler as director of the Leipzig Gewandhaus Orchestra. Other centers also heard him conduct during those years. The New York Philharmonic-Symphony, midway in the Toscanini era, engaged him for seven weeks in 1931 and repeated the invitation for two successive seasons. This time Walter's efforts fell on far friendlier ears. There were still unfavorable criticisms, but offered now within a context that accorded Walter a position among the world's great conductors.

The date March 16, 1933, should enjoy a prominent place in any chronology of infamous events, for it was on that day that the Nazi police canceled a Leipzig Gewandhaus concert on the grounds that a Jew, Bruno Walter, was to conduct.

A few days later Walter and his family were obliged to flee. Austria again became his home, where for the next five years he played the leading role in a cultural efflorescence emanating from Vienna and Salzburg. In the Viennese swan song of the thirties one observed none of the daring brilliance and modernism of Berlin in the twenties. Vienna had become an anachronism, a museum of past glories, but the collective instrument was wondrously perfected. Some recorded mementos of this era—Act I of *Die Walküre*, Mahler's *Das Lied von der Erde*—bear witness to Walter's encompassing artistry and to Vienna's opulent musical resources.

Hitler's annexation of Austria closed another frontier. Overnight Walter became a man without a country and without a valid passport, a situation to which France responded by conferring honorary citizenship on him. For a year he carried on his work—in Switzerland, Holland, Scandinavia, England, and particularly in the country that had adopted him—until the outbreak of war and an engagement with the NBC Symphony hastened his removal to America. In the years since, Walter has become a United States citizen (the Vichy government abrogated his French passport) and has exerted a strong and beneficent influence on our musical development. His continuing association with the New York Philharmonic-Symphony ripened to the point where he was asked to take over its direction following Rodzinski's sudden departure in 1947, though he agreed to act only as a "musical adviser" until a younger director could be chosen. For over a year he set the Philharmonic's artistic policy, and he was still returning as a regular visitor in the year that marked the seventy-fifth anniversary of his birth. He has been a welcome visitor, too, in the Metropolitan Opera House.

The change of environment from Central Europe to the Western hemisphere might have seemed risky for a musician of Bruno Walter's powerfully Germanic orientation. In actual fact, it invigorated him as an artist. In Vienna this conductor had succumbed too readily to connotations of *Weltschmerz* and *Gemütlichkeit.* Although suffused with a sunset radiance and inflected with easy tenderness, his interpretations had often lacked fiber. All their glow could not disguise a sagging structure. In his latter years in America, Walter's interpretative sinews have toughened. The mellow, weighty tone is still present, but it is allied now to a more vital beat and to a more rigidly controlled conception of pace and form. A comparison of his prewar recording of the Schubert C major Symphony with the one he made in America in 1947 gives an excellent ear-witness accounting of this welcome increase in expressive strength.

As a conductor Bruno Walter has not been a seminal force. He has not revolutionized the standard of orchestral execution like Toscanini, or revitalized discarded masterpieces like Beecham, or trumpeted the march of progress like Ansermet or Mitropoulos. He belongs to a distant past when Germany ruled the great domain of music. He is the custodian, not the originator, of tradition. Whether that tradition will recapture its erstwhile eminence is problematical, but as long as Bruno Walter continues to argue its virtues, a precious link with departed glories survives.

Singers

☼ Pierre *Bernac*

OF late years Nature's way with vocalists has been niggling. Dividing her largess with painstaking care, she offers a singer voice or brains—never both at full strength, and often neither. If we are to believe yesterday's mentors, it was not always so. Of Jean de Reszke it is said that intellectual probity kept easy pace with vocal talent; Wilhelmine Schröder-Devrient moved Wagner to apostrophize both an intensity of singing and an enlightenment of interpretation; Lilli Lehmann astounded with extraordinary sagacity of mind no less than with staccato roulades to D in alt. I am content to grant these powers to singers long since dead. Perhaps their like will be seen again. Today, unhappily, Nature's favors are sorely split. Optimum vocal brilliance there is, and optimum musical intelligence; but, to the best of this listener's knowledge, they will be sought in vain from the same artist.

Pierre Bernac, French baritone, belongs to the company that has been meted intelligence. Taking a Gigli or a Flagstad as touchstone, Bernac's voice *qua* voice clearly belongs to a lesser category. Its volume is small, its range limited, its quality of no startling appeal. This singer can lay claim neither to the Italian's warm, satinlike voluptuousness of utterance nor to the Norwegian's strong and solid shafts of ringing sound. On intellectual counts, however, the Frenchman takes clear precedence. His repertoire (from Rameau to Poulenc by way of Schubert, Schumann, Debussy, and Ravel) encompasses more varied and adventuresome music; his knowledge of style ranges farther; his interpretations exhibit a greater awareness of literary and æsthetic fundamentals. What matters in a Bernac recital is plainly gray matter.

Vocal deficiencies and cerebral assets of this order have given rise to a standard response applied almost automatically to singers of Bernac's persuasion. Someone is sure to remark: "I can't *stand* the sound of his voice, but how intelligently he sings!" Let me dissociate myself at once from this inevitable observation. If a singer's vocal resources remind one of nothing so much as the love-yelps of a tomcat, then surely all the intelligence in the world goes for naught. What matters it that a phrase be modeled to perfection if the aural experience causes the listener to wince? This custom of respecting intelligence while execrating a voice pays no compliment to any singer. It is, indeed, the most devastating damnation with the faintest praise.

Brainpower must make itself felt in beauty of sound. In Bernac's case that is what occurs. His is the example *par excellence* of a singer whose mind has triumphed over matter. One can on the morrow of a recital and in the light of cold analysis compile an elaborate list of his vocal shortcomings. Yet on the previous evening how insignificant they appeared! At the moment of hearing, Bernac's vocal equipment seems compounded of many virtues it does not really possess. I take this to be the mark of the truly intelligent artist, that he so knows how to capitalize on vocal resources as to bring full musical satisfaction. The vocalist of high IQ whose voice is a trial to auditors can hardly be said to sing intelligently.

Enough said about these alleged vocal inadequacies. What of that other point of contention, Bernac's stage deportment? Showmanship pertains to the recital hall no less than to the opera house, but it must be of a different, more subtle order. Carry the broad movements of face and body from operatic to concert stage and the result is embarrassing and sometimes ludicrous. Our mind's eye can easily picture the diva of lurching hips, clasped hands, and tearful mien. So awful does this visage loom that many concert singers run pell-mell to the other extreme. Especially does this apply to the men. Planting their feet stubbornly in one spot, with an immobile mask serving for facial expression, they remind one of a raw recruit snapping to attention under the baleful eye of his first sergeant. How stale this sort of thing can be! But puritanism is infectious; we begin to take it as norm and paragon. Bernac's first appearance in this country (November 1948) brought forth the criticism that his platform manner was too expressive, too calculated, too precious. Concert-goers expecting bluff fixity were nonplused to find a singer lithe and supple who dared move on the stage. His body and face, no less than his voice, interpreted the song, yet so skillfully and tastefully that no suggestion of the cumbrous or excessive obtruded. Here we enter into the subjective. There are those (and not limited only to this country) who are put off by Bernac's manner. To appreciate his art they must close their eyes, divorcing actor from singer. For my part, I shall always choose temperament and showmanship. One should add, as postscript, that Bernac on the stage and Bernac across the dinner table are two contrasting personalities. In private life he presents the very antithesis of flamboyance. The drunken gusto of "*Chanson à boire*" (Ravel), the dreamy nostalgia of "*L'Hôtel*" (Poulenc), the broad clowning of "*Voyage à Paris*" (Poulenc)—they are all acts. As with any act, you either like it or you do not.

Songs were Bernac's first love, and to them he has remained faithful. As a boy he composed them, frequented recitals where he could hear them, sang them himself. Unlike most embryo singers, he never fell in love with opera, never pictured himself forging Siegfried's sword, upbraiding Gilda's seducer, or twirling Escamillo's cape. Toward the end of World War I, aged eighteen (he was born in Paris on January 12, 1899), Bernac first appeared in public singing a few songs at a charity concert. The response emboldened him to take singing lessons. Various teachers came and went—none of them, one gathers, very impressive. Little import attached to these lessons, for their purpose at that time was purely avocational. Bernac entered his father's prosperous brokerage business. But recurrent bad health and a revulsion from figures put a quick end to his apprenticeship. Music, especially the music of his contemporaries, came more and more to occupy Bernac's time and thoughts. His appearances as an amateur singer multiplied.

During the winter of 1922 Bernac sang in a concert devoted to the music of Roland-Manuel. At its conclusion he received the classic backstage visit: André Caplet, friend of Debussy and an estimable composer in his own right, came to urge Bernac to make music his profession. As happens so often, the musician was willing but the parents were weak. Prudence having dictated his father's every move in the stock market, prudence was to inform his son's career in the speculative sphere of music. To hedge on attendant risks, Bernac was prevailed upon to take part-time work in a jewelry shop.

While this arrangement lasted Bernac studied under many teachers—some good, some bad. No single teacher can be said to have molded his technique of voice production, which is a synthesis purely his own drawn from several sources. Interpretative traditions stemmed mainly from his two counselors, André Caplet and the conductor Walter Straram, who took over supervision of Bernac's studies after Caplet's death in 1925. For the occasion of his professional debut in 1928 the singer changed his name from Bertin to Bernac, another Pierre Bertin, an actor at the Comédie Française, having established prior claim. Bernac soon gained a reputation among the cognoscenti as an interpreter of twentieth-century song. Those were exciting days for a partisan of contemporary music. Ravel's genius was in full flower, while every year brought forth a freshet from the *enfants terribles*, Honegger, Milhaud, and Poulenc.

Yet it became increasingly evident to the young singer that music did not begin with Debussy and end with Françaix. German lieder beckoned, and to explore this genre Bernac took as guide Reinhold von Wahrlich, a German authority on the lied, then resident in Paris. Of all influences on Bernac, that of Wahrlich seems to have been the strongest. Certainly it is an influence least expected of a singer from the most musically chauvinistic of nations. At Bernac's 1948 New York debut a large audience came prepared for masterful interpretation of the French repertoire. Yet nothing was more enthusiastically applauded than a group of Schubert lieder from which little had been expected. I, for one, had never heard the terror of "*Der Doppelgänger*" more thrillingly conveyed, the charm of "*Lachen und Weinen*" more adroitly communicated. At a later recital Bernac astounded us anew with an interpretation of Schumann's *Dichterliebe* remarkable for musical poetry and textual insight.

The summer of 1934 Bernac spent in Salzburg at work with Wahrlich. One evening following a recital there by the pianist George Copeland he was invited to a garden party at the home of a wealthy American. The hostess approached him with a request. Would M. Bernac favor the company with a few songs? There followed a search for an accompanist. Among the guests was Francis Poulenc, who volunteered to accompany. Thus, in the small hours of a warm Salzburg night a famous association began. A year later the two began giving joint recitals in public.

This is not the place to enter into an appreciation of Francis Poulenc. His position as the pre-eminent song-composer of our day is almost unanimously conceded by informed opinion, and I shall not repeat encomiums made elsewhere. It is enough to suggest that Bernac has been fortunate in riding to success on the crest of these contemporary masterpieces, that Poulenc has been equally favored in finding so ideal an interpreter. Bernac's intense feeling for musical atmosphere, his infectious rhythmic brio, his mordant wit—these qualities, valuable in whatever he performs, are especially apposite to Poulenc. There is more to the songs of this composer than meets the untutored eye. In his interpretations Bernac discloses secrets that the printed score does not always reveal. The tradition he is establishing enjoys the double virtue of authenticity and artistic insight; not always are "official interpreters" thus happily endowed.

September 1939 found France at war and Bernac in the army, driving a truck at what was euphemistically called "the front." His military career lasted a scant three months, for the French government, following Germany's example of proselytizing neutral countries with musical talent, pressed the team of Bernac-Poulenc into service. Preparations for a South American tour were halted by the debacle of June 1940. Bernac drove his brother's family to safety in the south of France and then returned to Paris, where he remained throughout the German occupation, singing occasionally and teaching.

Riches, the prophet said, are not given to men of understanding. Neither are they the lot of French concert singers. The Bertin fortune having fallen from its high estate, Bernac has had of late to eke out concert earnings with the more stable rewards of the teacher. It is a source of continued dismay to him that talented pupils are usually paupers, dull ones invariably rich. Talent apparently has not gone begging at his doorstep, however, as witness Bernac's accomplished pupil, Gerard Souzay. Teaching occupies Bernac from April to August. He prepares his forthcoming recital programs in the autumn, then spends the winter touring with Poulenc on an itinerary that always includes the major cities of Europe and often the United States.

Perhaps the most striking aspect of Bernac's singing is his acute regard for text. I am reminded of his interpretation of "*Ein Jüngling liebt ein Mädchen*" from *Dichterliebe*, in which Schumann has set a sad verse to a light and tripping melody. Most singers, falling into the bubbling spirit of the music, jettison verbal meaning for melodic grace. Not so Bernac. Without destroying the rhythmic vitality of Schumann's writing, Bernac leaves the listener in no doubt that Heine's poem ends with the words "breaks the heart in two." So with the Apollinaire texts of Poulenc or the Verlaine texts of Debussy, it would seem that the word is all-important in forming Bernac's conception of a song. Yet when this singer approaches a new work he disregards the text until every nuance of the music has been absorbed. Approaching a song words first is the easiest way, Bernac feels, to violate a composer's intention.

His interpretations often change with experience and further thought, but so gradually that the evolution is imperceptible. Listening to an old recording, however, Bernac is usually startled to discover a considerable metamorphosis in his conception of a song. Here, by the way, is cause for a rankling dissatisfaction with phonograph records. "They capture," he complains, "but one moment of an interpretation." He dislikes, too, singing for an "unreceptive" microphone instead of an audience. Nevertheless, Bernac is represented by an enviable number of fine recordings. His first records were made in Paris during the late thirties for French HMV; after the war he recorded extensively in the London studios of English HMV; now his allegiance has shifted to New York and American Columbia. In most of these recordings Poulenc accompanies, and in many he is the composer.

Today Bernac turns more and more to classical music, to songs "with a good tune." For the proverbial desert island he would unhesitatingly choose Schubert. Having solidly demonstrated his rapport with the difficult modern idiom, he now admits to a sneaking regard for Puccini. Twenty years ago Bernac avidly seized upon each new work as it came from the presses. Now he is more disposed to study Schubert and Wolf and Bach. But let a young song-composer of promise, like Samuel Barber, appear and he will find in Bernac his most enthusiastic and persuasive apostle.

Ernest Ansermet

Sir Thomas Beecham

Dimitri Mitropoulos

Charles Munch

Eugene Ormandy

Bruno Walter

Arturo Toscanini

Pierre Bernac

Lotte Lehmann

Kirsten Flagstad

Joseph Szigeti

Pablo Casals

Budapest String Quartet

JOSEPH ROISMAN, JAC GORODETZKY, MISCHA SCHNEIDER, BORIS KROYT

Reginald Kell

Andrés Segovia

Robert Casadesus

Walter Gieseking

Myra Hess

Vladimir Horowitz

Artur Rubinstein

Wanda Landowska

☼ Kirsten *Flagstad*

IN the world of opera times are seldom what they were. At the zenith of Jean de Reszke's career habitués of Covent Garden would speak wistfully of the days of Mario. But in Mario's day they spoke with equal nostalgia of Rubini, just as later on they were to find Caruso a poor substitute for the departed De Reszke and, later, Gigli a pale shadow of the departed Caruso. Opera needs a Gresham to formularize its own law of diminishing value. When this savant addresses himself to the task, he will find that though opera is held always to be in decline there are some periods when its state appears particularly egregious. Such was the case at the Metropolitan Opera during the 1930's. Loud were the complaints of patrons that the venerable company had fallen on evil times. There was nothing to equal the old days: the staging was pedestrian, the orchestra ragged, the singing mediocre. In the wake of these complaints attendance dipped alarmingly (the Great Depression was a contributing factor), and within two years the Metropolitan's backlog of one million dollars had disappeared. By dint of much hat-passing the company somehow managed to limp along, with threatened bankruptcy and suspension of activity serving to counterbalance, at least partially, a state of general apathy. But on the lips of many opera-goers the question posed itself whether the Metropolitan, in its sorry pass, really merited saving. Then Kirsten Flagstad came to rekindle enthusiasm and revive attendance. Almost overnight the Metropolitan assumed once again its wonted patina of glamor. Following the evening of February 2, 1935, it seemed as if the Metropolitan might be worth saving after all.

The Norwegian singer had been engaged to replace Frida Leider, a German soprano of unequal voice but commanding intensity, who had decided against returning to the Metropolitan in view of the dollar's decreased value in foreign exchange. Flagstad was virtually unknown abroad and was untouted even by the Metropolitan before her debut. Yet that debut (as Sieglinde in *Die Walküre*) and a performance of *Tristan* four days later brought skeptical New Yorkers to their feet. The morning after this first *Tristan* readers of the *Herald Tribune* found Lawrence Gilman writing of the new Isolde:

> . . . an embodiment so sensitively musical, so fine-grained in its imaginative and intellectual texture, so lofty in its pathos and simplicity, of so memorable a loveliness, that experienced opera-goers sought among their memories of legendary days to find its like.

Musicians were astounded by Flagstad's "inhuman" vocal accuracy, her rigorous fidelity to musical text. They heard, almost for the first time since Lilli Lehmann, due regard given to Wagner's chromatic intervals—for example, the descent from G-sharp to F double sharp in the phrase, "*das schenkte mir die milde Magd*," which every other contemporary Isolde could sing only diatonically (G-sharp to F-sharp). They heard, too, the top B-flats given with a ringing strength of tone unparalleled in recent Metropolitan history.

During her first season Flagstad gave twenty-three performances with the company, all of them sold out after the February 6 *Tristan*, initiating not only a revival of Wagner but a revival of the Metropolitan as well. The next season began, appropriately enough, with a performance of *Die Walküre* featuring Flagstad as Brünnhilde. "No other opening since 1929," reported the *New York Times*, "had been characterized by so much excitement, enthusiasm, and good cheer," and the glad tidings continued up to her controversial wartime retirement in the spring of 1941. Despite a schedule calculated to exhaust any singer, Flagstad brilliantly sustained the auguries of her first season. The Metropolitan has seen many aspirants make an overwhelming debut, only to decline precipitously in public esteem on subsequent appearances. If anything, Flagstad added to her reputation. Here, as an instance, is what W. J. Henderson wrote in the New York *Sun* of February 23, 1937, after hearing Flagstad as the *Siegfried* Brünnhilde:

> . . . one of the most flawless pieces of pure vocal technique ever heard on the stage of the Metropolitan. Every note was produced with exquisite floating tone, with a solid foundation, with perfect breath control, and with a consummate ease of attack and a sustained legato of celestial texture. No other singer except Melba ever equaled it in liberation of voice, in the utter freedom from all constraint of production and articulation. The one phrase, "O Siegfried, Leuchtender Spross," with the ravishingly airy head tone on the upper C, was something for the student of vocal technique to keep in his mind forever.

Consider the source of this encomium. It was no rapturous young dilettante who indulged in such superlatives, but a hard-to-please octogenarian who had been hearing Brünnhildes as a professional music critic since 1887.

It is allowable to question Flagstad's pre-eminence as a rounded musical artist; to question her pre-eminence as a vocalist would be to controvert established and demonstrable fact. By the time she first appeared in America this singer had mastered her voice as Casals had mastered the cello or Horowitz the piano; that is to say, with a consummate technique transcending all difficulties, one that would do her bidding "automatically," as naturally and easily as breathing. Those of us who have heard Flagstad in the opera house, with that never-flagging strength of tone, that unfailing accuracy of intonation, and those solid shafts of sound evenly produced over two octaves, will cherish always an image of well-nigh perfect vocalism. She has left few truly representative phonograph records, for at the peak of her career she often labored under the disadvantages of unresonant studios and inadequate orchestral support, but those that do her full justice (and I take them to be principally the recordings made in the Academy of Music with the Philadelphia Orchestra) are bounteous legacies indeed. To hear her negotiate the cruel ascending passage to B natural in Leonore's "*Abscheulicher*" aria will alone suffice to explain to future generations why the post-1935 era at the Metropolitan was as indelibly marked with Flagstad's name as the post-1903 era was marked with Caruso's.

The week after her Metropolitan debut *Time* characterized Kirsten Flagstad as "neither fat nor forty"—a description, as regards her age, that was to hold good for only five more months. This "young woman of grace" (*Time*'s phrase again) had been singing on the opera stage for twenty-two years before she ever set foot in New York. Flagstad was born on July 12, 1895, into a poor Norwegian family for whom the pursuit of music provided a marginal existence. Her father played violin in an Oslo theater orchestra; her mother gave piano lessons and coached singers. Young Kirsten received early instruction on the piano and in music theory, but it was soon evident that her talents and inclinations ran to singing. For many years she worked without professional instruction; it is said that at eleven, having acquired a score of *Lohengrin*, she committed the part of Elsa to memory. Perhaps it was this evidence of zeal that recommended her to Ellen Schytte-Jacobsen, an Oslo teacher who was mainly responsible for Flagstad's early vocal instruction. She made her opera debut at the age of eighteen, December 12, 1913, singing the minor role of Nuri in an Oslo performance of D'Albert's *Tiefland*. Some local patrons were sufficiently interested in her career to finance further study, first with Albert Westwang in Oslo and later with Gillis Bratt in Stockholm. Until 1933 Flagstad labored as a valuable member of several Scandinavian opera and operetta troupes. If her activities were limited geographically to Norway and Sweden, in scope they ranged from American musical comedy and Viennese operetta to grand opera, oratorio, and solo recital. Possessing a voice predominantly light and lyrical, Flagstad gained her early reputation not as Isolde or Brünnhilde, but as Mimi, Marguérite, and Aïda. Otto Kahn, a patron of the Metropolitan Opera, happened to hear her as Tosca when he passed through Oslo in 1929. He suggested that the Metropolitan investigate further. From Eric Simon, the company's European agent, a routine letter went out requesting of Flagstad her press notices, the extent of her repertoire, and other details. She did not bother to reply for several months, and the Metropolitan pursued her no further.

The late twenties, when Flagstad sang her first Elsa (in Norwegian), mark the beginning of her Wagnerian orientation. By then her voice had begun to expand. It was larger still in 1932, when she was engaged to sing Isolde in a production of *Tristan* given in Oslo with a predominantly German cast. With this performance, after nearly two decades on the opera stage, she captured non-Scandinavian attention. Oscar Thompson, surveying Europe for *Musical America*, wrote an appreciative account of her Isolde, and an emissary from Bayreuth engaged her to sing two minor parts (Ortlinde and the Third Norn) in the Bayreuth Festival of 1933. She returned to Bayreuth again in 1934, having advanced to Sieglinde and Gutrune. That summer, in St. Moritz, Gatti-Casazza and Artur Bodanzky—who were seeking a soprano to replace Frida Leider—heard Flagstad in a private audition and recruited her for the forthcoming Metropolitan season.

Six years after her New York debut, at the pinnacle of artistic and financial success, Flagstad disappeared from this continent as dramatically as she had arrived. On April 19, 1941, she stepped aboard a Pan American plane for the first lap of an excursion that would take her, by way of Portugal and Germany, to Nazi-occupied Norway. There she was to remain for the next six years. By so doing she broke the uninterrupted chain of adulation that had been hers since 1935. Charges of Nazi proclivities were leveled against her, and there were repeated rumors of Flagstad performances in wartime Germany. The Norwegian Ambassador to the United States asserted that Flagstad's return to Oslo went counter to the expressed wishes of her government-in-exile. Certainly it disappointed the great majority of her American admirers, who looked to an artist of Flagstad's stature to range herself at least in spirit with the forces fighting totalitarianism.

It is clear that she exercised poor judgment; equally clear—it seems to me—that the charge of collaboration has yet to be substantiated. During the immediate postwar years "the Flagstad case" rocked in a stormy sea of passion and innuendo. She was alternately extolled and reviled according to individual persuasion. Actually, neither side had a very strong case. According to the dossier compiled by John Bartlow Martin in an excellent piece of reporting,* Flagstad's wartime behavior was scrupulously correct, if hardly praise-

* "The Kirsten Flagstad Story," *Cosmopolitan*, December 1950.

worthy. She returned ostensibly to be with her husband, Henry Johansen, a lumber magnate friendly to the Quisling government, whose considerable prewar fortune was increasing rapidly as a result of commercial collaboration between his several enterprises and the occupying Nazi forces. During the long years of her Norwegian retirement Flagstad led a strangely secluded life. On a typical day, according to Martin's informant, she would spend her time knitting, playing solitaire, or singing (on her return in 1947 it was quite obvious that she had kept her voice in top condition). She never once sang publicly in Norway, Germany, or any occupied country. Of her wartime performances two were in neutral Sweden, the others in neutral Switzerland. Her sole intercourse with the Nazis seems to have been in obtaining transit visas.

On May 13, 1945, five days after the German surrender, Norwegian authorities arrested Flagstad's husband, who died in jail thirteen months later under suspicion of treason and collaboration. For one year and a half after Johansen's arrest the Norwegian government refused to issue his wife a passport. Although she was under no suspicion of collaboration herself, authorities required Flagstad's presence in Norway to disentangle her financial affairs from Johansen's–a forcible detention that she found extremely irksome.

Why Kirsten Flagstad voluntarily interrupted her career in 1941 to return to occupied Norway against the advice of her well-wishers and her friends was a question long unanswered. Her side of the matter was finally brought to light late in 1952 with the publication of her memoirs, *The Flagstad Manuscript*. It appears from this that she returned to Norway partly because of homesickness, partly because her husband had repeatedly asked her to return. Flagstad seems not to have been told of Henry Johansen's collaborationist leanings until she arrived in Europe. And she appears to have been blind to the impropriety of deliberately taking up residence in Nazi-occupied Norway when thousands of her own countrymen (to mention no others) were prepared to die for its liberation. Politically, she would seem to have been naïve to a fault.

Her first postwar concert took place at Cannes on January 18, 1947; it was followed by concerts in Paris and London. One Englishman averred that the reappearance of Flagstad was "like the taste of butter after ten years of margarine." Another, the critic Desmond Shawe-Taylor, addressed himself to a consideration of her postwar vocal prowess: "Here was the old ease and buoyancy, the golden notes effortlessly reappearing like the head of a strong swimmer after each orchestral wave, the solid, equable two-octave compass, the sense of security, the ability to maintain the same quality from pianissimo to fortissimo." Then came a concert tour in America marked by sold-out houses, adoring audiences, active picketing, and critical hosannas. For three seasons, while Edward Johnson still held sway, she was barred from the Metropolitan Opera, but with the advent of Rudolf Bing as general manager the old house opened its doors once again to the woman who was by general consent the world's greatest opera singer. By 1950, when New York again heard her incomparable portrayal of Isolde, the political climate had changed. The pickets were no more to be seen. Yet inside the house a hysterically partisan audience committed the *gaffe* of applauding Flagstad to the dying strains of the Prelude. Before the war, admiration for Flagstad was not expressed by interrupting a performance of *Tristan* in one of its most magical moments.

Writing of Flagstad in 1938, Oscar Thompson had found occasion to compare the Isolde of that year with the Isolde he had heard "on a late summer evening in 1932 at the National Theater in Oslo. . . . The voice has unquestionably grown in volume and in dramatic power. It sounds much larger in the Metropolitan than it sounded in the smaller theater in her native Norway. It has heroic accents now that were much less characteristic of it then." Like most big-voiced dramatic sopranos, Flagstad as she matured experienced a settling of the voice that took away some of the upper notes. (Even by 1941 she was shying clear of high C's.) "The elasticity of youth," Thompson put it, "gave way to the solidity of middle age." When she returned after the war this settling of the voice was even more evident. The top notes could still be summoned, but not with the brilliant, carefree strength of yore. Flagstad, sensing this, wisely realized the need to husband her resources. At the age of fifty-five she announced her retirement from Wagnerian opera, her last appearance as Isolde taking place in England in July 1950. Thenceforth she would restrict herself to recitals and to less-taxing operatic roles. London heard her in Purcell's *Dido and Æneas* and New York in Gluck's *Alcestis*. In the latter opera Flagstad bade farewell to America, for in 1952 she decided to confine her further activity to England and the Continent. Flagstad's Metropolitan leavetaking was as spectacular as had been her debut seventeen years before. The classic purity of Gluck's music and the plastic grace of the action admirably suited Flagstad's voice and temperament, and together they combined to create an interpretation of high poetic distinction. The nobility, the humanity, and the still unparallaled vocal virtuosity of this Alcestis will not soon be forgotten by those who heard it.

Whatever the slight postwar decline in Flagstad's vocal estate, it was more than offset by a marked heightening of communication. In the prewar years no one coupled the adjective "intense" to this singer's name. Although she had always possessed a dignified and effective stage-presence, admirably gaited to the unfolding of Wagnerian music-drama, there was latent in her approach a cool reserve that raised an invisible barrier to vivid communicative power. To her, Wagner's texts served more as a medium for great vocalizing than for meaningful discourse. "Apparently," observed Ernest

Newman, "there are certain things which her voice cannot do. It cannot express vehement passion, or fury, or scorn." His reference was to Flagstad in her early forties. In her early fifties, after six years of retirement and introspection, it was observed that she sang as if words and music connoted a good deal more. There was a delirium to her Isolde, a compassion to her Brünnhilde keyed far higher than one would have thought possible before the war. What a pity, then, that this increase in understanding was accompanied by an increase in girth. Just when the stage character made more sense to the ear, it began to make less sense to the eye.

At best Flagstad has never approached the dizzy level of Lehmann as a singing actress. Nor has she as a recitalist been able to distill the essence of a song with the subtlety and imagination of Bernac. Opinion divides on her achievement in the concert hall. To some her straightforward manner is a rare asset: Virgil Thomson contends that "by eschewing exploitation of her personality, she warms all hearts to that personality." Each one to his taste. While I am not insensible to Flagstad's power as a recitalist (her singing of Grieg's *Haugtussa* song-cycle is an impressive accomplishment), I would say of her, as Ernest Newman did of Melba: "Uninterestingly perfect and perfectly uninteresting." A recital by Flagstad is as finely polished as a marble façade—and, to me, as cold. But no singer can possess every virtue. Flagstad showed, in an age much given to vulgar bawling, the very form and figure of perfect vocalism. She has commanded vocal equipment unmatched in our day and has directed it solely to the advantage of sober musicianship. That is quite enough for any mortal.

☼ Lotte *Lehmann*

JUST before the intermission of a Town Hall recital in February 1951, Lotte Lehmann interrupted the applause to make a short and unannounced valedictory speech. "I don't like to celebrate my own funeral," she said, "but this tonight is my farewell recital in New York." From the audience came cries of "No! No!" Lehmann shook her head, as though scolding Octavian for his impetuosity. "Please don't argue with me," she pleaded. "After forty-one years of hard work, inner tension, and nervous strain, I think I deserve to take it easy and to relax. You know," she continued, "that the Marschallin in *Rosenkavalier* has always been one of my favorite parts. This Marschallin is a very wise woman. She looks into the mirror, and she says, 'It is time.' So I, as a singer, look into the mirror, and I say, 'It is time.' " Happily, "taking it easy" did not signify complete retirement. She would continue to give recitals within motoring distance of her Santa Barbara home, to make recordings in near-by Los Angeles, and to teach selected students.

In recent years this unique artist has been taken too much for granted. Her yearly New York recitals (always copiously attended) seldom attracted the interest of our more eminent musical pundits. Indeed, to have read the usual perfunctory notice of a Lehmann recital one would have thought her but another figure in the parade of aspirants who serve as nightly grist for the apprentice critic's mill. Her new records have rated only passing mention, as if nothing more were to be said than "the mixture as before." In sum, though her reputation bulks as formidably as that of any other living singer, it lies today dormant and static. This chapter will have served its purpose if it explains the basis of that reputation and if it transmits even partially the radiation of a great and moving artist.

Lotte Lehmann was born in 1888 (not 1885 as listed in most reference books) in the little town of Perleberg, Germany, midway between Berlin and Hamburg. How the fortunes of war have treated Perleberg I do not know. Considering the damage wrought by two world wars, the inflation of the twenties, the holocaust of Hitlerism, and the present Russian occupation, it must be sorely changed. If at the turn of the century you had predicted any of this to Lotte's father, he would probably have thought you insane. What could have seemed more stable, more peaceful, than this sleepy town and the German Empire of which it was a part? It was a place where one worked diligently and where in due course one retired on a small pension. In this secure environment Lotte Lehmann passed her early years. Soon after her confirmation the family moved from its spacious country house to an apartment in a lower-middle-class quarter of Berlin. Lotte was sent to high school, in preparation for a career as a teacher, but a kindly neighbor, charmed by her untrained voice, secured an audition for her at the Hochschule für Musik, where she was accepted as a student. Her father doubted the practical value of studying music. It was only after Professor Schulze, head of the voice department, assured Herr Lehmann that his daughter might easily secure a State job (with a pension) as a music teacher that the cautious father gave consent to a musical education.

Lotte Lehmann embarked on her career with no higher goal than a teaching post and occasional appearances in oratorio. In her second year at the Hochschule, however, her ambition had so increased that she was dissatisfied with the course of her progress—for Professor Schulze, true to his word, had kept his pupil on the straight path of pedagogy and oratorio. Feeling that a change was indicated, Lehmann transferred, as a scholarship student, to Etelka Gerster's private school. This shift of allegiance almost proved disastrous. However successful Gerster's method may have been with other pupils, it came close to ruining Lehmann's voice. The main stumbling-block was "*Dove sono*" from *Le Nozze di Figaro*, which for some technical or psychological reason Lehmann could not master. Faced with such an impasse, most teachers would have put the *bête noire* temporarily aside. But the Prussian determination ruling the Gerster School knew no such moderation. Drudging at the aria week after week, the singer found her voice becoming more and more constricted, her confidence less and less evident. Indeed, Lehmann never fully conquered her early fear of "*Dove sono*," and because of its terrors rarely attempted the role of the Countess in her subsequent career.

Within a year Mme Gerster had thrown her new pupil out of school. The letter that Lehmann received on this occasion from Gerster's assistant, Eva Rheinhold, makes droll reading today:

DEAR FRÄULEIN LEHMANN:

I shall speak to your father today on behalf of Frau Gerster, but I should like to write you a few lines. I am sorry that your singing instruction at the Gerster School has come to an end in this way, but alas! I have seen this coming for months. I can only say that none of my pupils has ever been such a disappointment as you have, and this has given me many a dark hour. I believe that, if you want to and have to achieve something in the future, you should take up a practical career. . . . Frau Gerster requests me to tell you that your progress is not even that of a mediocre pupil, and that even as a paying pupil you would have been expelled. . . .

With all good wishes for your future, Fräulein Lehmann, and kindest regards

I am, Yours sincerely,

EVA RHEINHOLD

That suggestion for "a practical career" sounded an ominous note. Herr Lehmann entered his daughter's name for the next course at a commercial school. He was certain he could get her a job as a secretary with the bank where he was employed. But Lotte rebelled. She would not relinquish her aspirations that easily. In a long letter to Mathilde Mallinger, the original Eva in *Die Meistersinger*, and then a successful singing teacher, she poured out her troubles. The desired audition was arranged, and with the desired result. Mallinger confirmed what Lehmann secretly felt, that her latent talent had merely fallen into uncongenial hands. Aided by financial help from Baron Konrad zu Pulitz, Herr Lehmann's superior in Perleberg, she began lessons with Mathilde Mallinger. She had found the right teacher. A year later she set out to obtain an appointment with a provincial opera house, not an inordinately difficult task in the opera-ridden Germany of that day.

Before too long the Hamburg Stadttheater offered a contract. The year was 1910. Lehmann made her debut as the Third Boy in *Die Zauberflöte*. There followed appearances as a Page in *Tannhäuser* and *Lohengrin*, an Apprentice in *Die*

Meistersinger, a Bridesmaid in *Der Freischütz*. Eventually, a more important part came her way–Freya in *Das Rheingold*–to which the press did not take too kindly. The critic for the *Hamburger Fremdenblatt* wrote: "Fräulein Lehmann sang and played the part of Freya with touching ungainliness." Another critic commented on her physical beauty, adding that this did not compensate for "her lack of vocal and histrionic talent." Poor notices deterred neither the singer nor her employers. Continued study helped to alleviate the vocal imperfections noticed by the Hamburg critics; practical experience on the stage enlarged her capabilities as an actress.

Thanks to the intercession of the conductor Otto Klemperer, Lehmann was given a truly big part in a subsequent season at Hamburg: Elsa in *Lohengrin*. This time both audience and press responded enthusiastically. She had emerged from the ranks, and by 1914 was already a minor luminary. That summer she sang Sophie in *Der Rosenkavalier* under Beecham in London, as well as Agathe (with Richard Tauber singing Max) in *Der Freischütz* at the Zoppoter Waldoper. In 1915 the Vienna Court Opera engaged her for a guest season. When her contract was extended on a permanent basis one year later, the Lehmann family moved south. Until the *Anschluss* of Germany and Austria in 1938, Vienna remained the singer's home and the focal point of her activity.

Americans are likely to think of Lehmann as a staid liedersinger. If they associate her with opera, it is as the Marschallin in *Der Rosenkavalier* or Sieglinde in *Die Walküre*. But Vienna knew her as Mimi, Tosca, and even Turandot, as Manon Lescaut, Marguérite, and Mignon, as Beethoven's Leonore and Tchaikovsky's Tatjana. From the time when she created the role of the Composer in Richard Strauss's *Ariadne auf Naxos* (1916), she was *unsere geliebte Lehmann* to the Viennese public. Vienna's artistic climate engendered a remarkable transformation. Lehmann arrived in that metropolis with tonal opulence her main asset. A few years in the Vienna opera house served to release all of her talent. Within a decade she had become a musician of subtlety and temperament, an actress imbued with charm and persuasion. Sir Thomas Beecham relates that when she sang Sophie at Drury Lane in 1914 he had the impression of a fairly competent repertory singer who could be trusted to hit the right notes and make the appropriate movements on stage. Of incandescence or originality there was apparently no hint. So great was the ensuing metamorphosis that when Lehmann returned to London in 1923 to sing the Marschallin under Bruno Walter, Beecham failed to recognize her. He had in the intervening nine years forgotten even her name, and was incredulous when reminded that this adept and imaginative singing actress was the nondescript Sophie of 1914.

As Lehmann matured she became a member of the select company of opera singers for whom excuses on the score of histrionics are never necessary. With Lehmann on stage one transcended that ridiculous world of opera where singers tread the boards gingerly to avoid disastrous falls, where mood and action founder abruptly so that an aria may be delivered from the most comfortable and sonorous position. Shaw once questioned whether "it were possible for anyone to become an actress in such an atmosphere of incongruity and nonsense as that which an operatic artist is condemned to breathe." Lehmann's example provides one gloriously affirmative answer.

Her characterization of Elsa can be instanced as an illustration of this singer's ability to vitalize a hackneyed role. She brought Elsa to life, gave cogency and conviction to her conduct. You were persuaded to sympathize with the odd girl, to appreciate her grief, to sense the surging passion that lay beneath her distracted behavior. Lehmann's Elsa, alas, now belongs to the past, but listening to her recording of "Elsa's Dream" and in particular to the phrase, "*In lichter Waffen*

Scheine ein Ritter nahte da," one can recapture in part the impact of its power and beauty. The girlish ecstasy, the naïve trust, the subdued passion embodied in that one phrase speak more for this characterization than paragraphs of prose.

When Lehmann retired from the stage in 1946 she left a void in a certain area of operatic interpretation that has yet to be filled. Fortunately, her recordings are extensive. With Lauritz Melchior as Siegmund and Bruno Walter conducting, she recorded *in toto* Act I of *Die Walküre*, plus the Sieglinde scenes of Act II—a precious and, one would like to think, imperishable document. From the moment of her entrance and her incandescent phrasing of "*Ein fremder Mann,*" it is an interpretation compact of temperament and intensity. The scornful tone of her references to Hunding's clan, the sensual rapture with which she pours out her love to Siegmund, the frenzied terror in the second act when she barks out the phrase "*Sippen und hunde ruft er zusammen*" so as to prickle the scalp—these are still the touchstones of opera at its grandest.

For opera at its subtlest, most charming, and most lettered there is Lehmann's *chef d'œuvre*, the Marschallin in *Rosenkavalier*. It is a matter for infinite regret that her interpretation of the Marschallin was never captured in a complete recording. The records made in Vienna in 1933 offer only fragments of the score, and from a technical standpoint clearly betray their age. But we must take our blessings as they come and be thankful that posterity can sample many of the great moments of this role (to say nothing of Richard Mayr's zestful Baron Ochs and Elisabeth Schumann's virginal Sophie). In *Rosenkavalier* Lehmann had a libretto worthy of her dramatic gifts, and of it she made glorious capital. The mind's eye swims with memories of this brilliant performance. There is the moment when the Marschallin is about to tell Octavian about a former amorous indiscretion and then decides it is wiser to keep silent; what a wealth of artistry there was in that one word "*Einmal*" ("Once")—followed by a half-playful, half-exasperated shake of the head. Or the passage just before the entrance of Ochs, when she recalls having received his letter and then admits, with the most disarming charm, "*und ich hab' keine Ahnung was drin gestanden ist*" ("and I haven't the *faintest* idea what was in it"). One remembers the consummate stage craftsmanship of the entire scene with Ochs, in which, despite all the antics, she maintained the atmosphere of a relaxed, urbane conversation. The hollow sound of her dismissal of the hairdresser, "Today you have made an old woman of me," still rings in the ear, and will the vision ever fade of that moment in the famous monologue when she imitates a member of a street crowd pointing her finger at "the old Princess Resi"? Who that saw it will forget the panniered sweep of Lehmann's entrance in Act III, when, borne in by a great surge of Straussian melody, she suddenly surveys the motley scene with aristocratic *hauteur*? Or the flaring of her anger when Ochs presumes too far? Or her attitude toward Sophie, at once kindly, mocking, and condescending? Or the philosophical resignation of her final "*Ja, ja*"? Perhaps it would not be too much to suggest that Lehmann conveyed more drama, more temperament, more innuendo in those two final words than an ordinary singer does in a whole evening of opera.

Only the highlights of the years following Lehmann's first Vienna success can be indicated. In 1922 she toured South America, singing opera under Weingartner and giving some of her first lieder recitals. The following year she sang the Marschallin in Covent Garden. In 1927 came her first *Fidelio*, performed in Vienna and Salzburg under the baton of Franz Schalk. She visited this country for the first time in 1930, giving a few performances with the Chicago Civic Opera, but did not sing in New York until a Town Hall recital early in 1933. Her Metropolitan Opera debut as Sieglinde in 1934 met with unreserved critical acclaim and prompted speculation as to why the Metropolitan had waited so long to engage her.

The Salzburg Festival of 1937, when the triumvirate of Lehmann, Toscanini, and Walter collaborated in now legendary performances of *Fidelio* and *Meistersinger*, marked the culmination of Lehmann's European career. Dark days impended. The *Anschluss* early in 1938 meant that Vienna no longer was to be her home, for this "Aryan" artist had from the very start voiced her antipathy to Hitlerism. In the autumn of that year she settled in the United States and took out first citizenship-papers. Soon after, her husband, Otto Krause, died following a protracted illness. The strain of those years is evident in an album of records ("Song Recital No. 2") that Lehmann made for RCA Victor at the time.

By the early forties Lehmann began to execute what in military parlance would be called an orderly retreat. Her opera appearances slackened off. She sang in *Der Rosenkavalier* a few times each year, and occasionally in *Die Walküre*. The year 1945 saw her last Marschallin at the Metropolitan, 1946 her final Sieglinde. In truth those final opera performances were in the nature of remembrances of things past, for by this time Lehmann had recast her musical personality to the new requirements of lieder.

Lehmann's first sorties into the domain of the lied, during the early 1920's, were far from ideal. In her lieder records of the late twenties and early thirties one hears a voice of glorious sensuous beauty inflating lieder to operatic proportions. By degrees, she recalls, "there dawned upon me a new and overpowering realization: that as a lieder singer I was at the very dawn of an awakening. This was the first step: the awareness of my ignorance." Between that realization and her later mastery intervened long and difficult years of study. During the First World War she worked under Ferdinand Foll, a friend of Hugo Wolf, who is said to have been a remarkably sensitive accompanist in an era when ponderous playing predominated. Later she studied with Leo Rosenek. But most of her tutelage had to come from the school of experience and introspection. By the late thirties the doors of lieder had opened, though they did not always afford a full and unimpeded view. Even then, as Vincent Sheean once pointed out, "she depended upon the little book of words, the fancy handkerchief, the train, and all the other accoutrements of the diva giving a concert." She was at her best singing lieder in which operatic tricks could be exploited: Schumann's "*Die Kartenlegerin*," for instance, with its opportunities for farcical mugging, or Brahms's "*Therese*," with its Marschallin-like soliloquy.

In an article in *Theatre Arts Monthly* of April 1937 Lehmann wrote: "In studying a song I never begin with the music, but first consider the text, to which the accompaniment is, in the beginning, of secondary importance." But eight years later she was to offer this advice to young singers: "I should like to protect you from this stage which I had to go through: of feeling first the *word* and then the *word* and only finally the *melody*. . . . Learn to feel *as a whole* that which is a whole in complete harmony: poem and music. Neither can be more important than the other." Lehmann's early emphasis on text, together with an unfortunate habit of breathing too often, resulted in frequent breaks of phrasing. Devotees of the lied quite rightly insisted that, for all her vocal luster, Lehmann revealed many grave deficiencies. But during the decade prior to her Town Hall farewell Lehmann's lieder style was shorn of operatic affectations and subjective solecisms. Fortunately, in the quality of her vocal equipment time had marred only the inessential. Needless to say, her voice no longer possessed the brilliance and opulence of youth, but its individual sheen and timbre remained unaltered. She did not hesitate to transpose a song to a more comfortable key, and she preferred to concentrate her attention on works of moderate range, but the power, the dramatic sparkle still lay in reserve.

Lehmann has often been censured for interpreting songs written for male voice; and on the basis of pure logic it would indeed seem inappropriate for a soprano to sing *Die Schöne Müllerin*, that doleful saga of a youth who loved in vain the miller's beautiful daughter. But had we insisted on logic we should have been without Lehmann's "*Tränenregen*" and her enchantingly prosaic delivery of the final line, "*es kommt ein Regen, ade, ich geh' nach Haus.*" Logic would also have deprived us of the tense, spectral quality of her "*Ich hab' im Traum geweinet*" (from Schumann's *Dichterliebe*) and the soft, caressing manner of her "*Und willst du Liebsten sterben sehen*" (Wolf). Faced with these privations, one can only rejoice that Lehmann elected to disregard logic and the animadversions of purists. She has given certain insights into song literature which cannot be found in the performances of any contemporary male singer; these easily outweigh the technicality of her trespassing. Besides, is the art of lieder so dependent on outward circumstances? Lehmann herself gives the answer when she writes: "It would be a very sad indication of incapacity if one could not awaken in the listener sufficient imagination to carry him with one into the realms of creative fantasy."

There must be an end to encomiums. Let me admit that Lehmann is not of unadulterated virtue all compact. Her lapses from grace—the way she gasps for breath in the midst of a phrase; the arch, coy manner in which she will play down to the desires of her doting audience—I readily acknowledge. Hardly the most adventuresome of singers, she excels chiefly in nineteenth-century Germanic repertory. When a complaint is lodged against her program-building, my ears are not closed, for I have squirmed in my seat while she sang one saccharine

Brahms lied after another, at what seemed infinite length. But somehow these reservations seem beside the point. As the reader undoubtedly will have guessed, an infatuation in this instance muddles clearheaded judgment. About Lehmann I feel as did C. E. Montague when he observed of Sarah Bernhardt: "Her faults are rank; they cry to Heaven—when she is not there. Then you see her once more, and you feel as if you were looking again at Florence from Fiesole, or at a pheasant's neck, or Leonardo's Mona Lisa, or ripe corn with poppies in it."

Violinist

Cellist

String Quartet

☼ Joseph *Szigeti*

Joseph Szigeti first came to public notice as a prodigy. His family called him Joska, and so he was billed. His first phonograph records, released in 1909, bear that name. But by the time this player was twenty, Joska had been renounced in favor of Joseph. Along with the baby name went the salon sentimentalities, the gaudy technical flourishes, the meretricious concertos, the brainless crudities that are the average prodigy's stock in trade. In their place came a sense of style refined by reading and sensitive observation, an avoidance of facile shortcuts to vulgar esteem, an inquiring mind that would interest itself in unaccompanied Bach and accompanied Prokofiev.

Through sheer quality of intellect Joseph Szigeti stands apart from the common herd of virtuoso fiddlers. To single him out does not invidiously slight all remaining members of the tribe. Put it rather that even among those few who share his artistic constancy Szigeti holds a commanding position, holds it by virtue of many-faceted accomplishment and steadfast pioneering. For a quarter century he has been the darling of that body, limited in number if vociferous in enthusiasm, which shall be called—for want of a better name—"the intellectual audience." Never has this faction ceased to proclaim his praise or to appear at his concerts. Indeed, viewed in the light of artistic prestige, Szigeti has tasted success in America from the day in 1925 when he made his debut here. On a commercial level his real conquest can be said to date only from 1940 or thereabouts. During the twenties and thirties this player's patrician way of making music was caviar to the general. His name occasioned no queues at the box office. I can remember that Orchestra Hall was blotched with wide islands of vacant seats when Szigeti stopped off in Chicago during the mid-thirties to perform Prokofiev's Concerto in D. A far more gratifying prospect was to be seen in Carnegie Hall many years later, when the violinist marked the twenty-fifth anniversary of his first American concert. On that occasion close to three thousand devotees absorbed a program of proportions immense even for Szigeti: Corelli's "*La Folia*," Bartók's *Portrait No. 1*, plus the concertos of Brahms *and* Beethoven. To say that his present popularity stems from a vast enlargement of "the intellectual audience" detracts nothing from Szigeti's personal achievement. For no one has contributed more to that growth than the violinist himself.

An auspicious influence, an artist of wide-ranging enthusiasms, a musical personality of rare discrimination—yes, and an acquired taste to boot. I am aware that some intrepid *bon vivants* have enjoyed dry martinis from the very first sip, and the knowledge induces me to concede that other advanced souls may have nailed their flag to Szigeti's mast from the first strike of his bow. Most of us, plodding worn paths, are wont to approach him more obliquely. Confronted with his individual style, the neophyte listener tends to be fascinated and perplexed in equal measure. At my first encounter with Szigeti what really caught my fancy was the delight of watching the violinist's bald head bob up and down to Prokofiev's jaunty rhetoric. But along with this engaging display came sounds hard to assimilate, unusual sounds from the violin—sometimes thin and piercing, sometimes gnarled and harsh, often sweet, never treacly. A tone reserved for Prokofiev? No, for it was met again in Bach and Beethoven and Brahms. As acquaintance ripened, my perplexity abated. With all the well-wishers of this artist, I came in time to appreciate Szigeti's unique tone as cause not for discomfiture but for rejoicing, a taste well worth the acquiring. With his tone Szigeti endeavors to put music in proper perspective; he is not concerned with creating the aural equivalent of pile carpeting or Turkish coffee.

Another side of the Szigetian personality contrives to discourage immediate rapture. He does not adorn his programs with sleazy goods or costume jewelry. Search them in vain for concertos by Tchaikovsky, Wieniawski, Glazunov, or Khatchaturian, for *Hora Staccato*, *Rondo Capriccioso*, or *Flight of the Bumblebee*. You will find him concerned instead with the unaccompanied literature of Bach, concertos by Mozart and Alban Berg, sonatas by Beethoven and Ravel and Prokofiev. He prefers Stravinsky to Sarasate, Bartók to Bruch. All this—like his tone—is endearing in the long run. But a repertoire wrought of such substance, giving violinistic trickery wide berth, does not sweep the groundlings off their feet. Szigeti makes his conquests the hard way. He offers fastidious playing, imaginative programs, the culture of a well-stocked mind, knowing that quality will ultimately reap its own reward.

It was not always so. For years Szigeti followed the course of a flashy virtuoso. In his career he has come full circle. Perhaps that is why he holds to the cause of pure music with such tenacity. The most devout are those who have been converted from infidelity.

He was born in Budapest on September 5, 1892. He came of a family that was no stranger to the violin. His father earned a living as first violinist in a Budapest café orchestra. An uncle, pupil of Hubay and the family's pride, had secured a berth in the violin section of the Edouard Colonne Orchestra (Paris). Another uncle gave Szigeti his first violin lessons. This initiation took place in Maramaros-Sziget, a village near the Hungarian-Rumanian border, to which the infant Joska had been sent upon his mother's death. We must assume that the boy showed remarkable aptitude; when he was eight he was fetched by his father to Budapest, there to receive more professional instruction. After several months in a second-rate academy he auditioned for Jenö Hubay and was admitted to the teacher's class.

Few are the truly original interpreters who profess to have learned other than the mechanics of their art from teachers. Landowska and Professor Michalowski, Cortot and Professor Diémer, Lehmann and Frau Etelka Gerster provide random examples in which the pupil acknowledges small debt to the master. Joseph Szigeti belongs to this company of individualists ("ingrates" the teachers might call them). From Hubay he learned the trade of fiddler, nothing more. So bereft of substance was his musical schooling in Budapest that Szigeti retains today hardly any memories of it. The grooming toward virtuosity for virtuosity's sake created a mental vacuum. "There were no improvised sonata sessions with our 'opposite numbers' from the piano classes," Szigeti recalls. Indeed, the atmosphere of Hubay's class made chamber music seem almost reprehensible. So one-tracked were the school's objectives (partly engendered by the vaulting ambitions of parents) that Szigeti deemed it quite beneath his notice to attend more than just a few classes in quartet-playing given by the cellist David Popper, and even those were with an "ulterior motive"—the desire to get onto the concert stage in a public performance of a Haydn quartet.

In 1905, aged thirteen, Joska Szigeti was judged proficient enough for an "official" debut in Berlin. A list of the music with which he was then familiar bears detailing. The concertos of Wieniawski, Ernst, Mendelssohn, and Viotti formed the bulwark of his repertoire. An obeisance to the classics was made with two compositions by Bach, the Chaconne and the Prelude from the E major Partita, both chosen because of their technical difficulty, their opportunities for display. Tartini's "*Devil's Trill*" Sonata, Paganini's "*Witches' Dance*," and assorted encore pieces served to demonstrate agility. Never had young Szigeti so much as opened the pages of a sonata by Beethoven or Mozart; never had he encountered a Bach concerto. With the Beethoven Concerto he had only a nodding acquaintance. Joseph Joachim, before whom Szigeti played soon after his Berlin recital, offered to repair these omissions. He suggested that the boy study repertoire with him; he even volunteered to arrange for a patron to assume the expenses. But Szigeti's father declined this apparently sumptuous offer. A canny man, whose ambitions for his son were limitless, he knew that not one of the aging Joachim's pupils had ever made a notable solo career. Joachim created concertmasters easily, but Joska—so his father thought—deserved another fate.

The Berlin recital generated sufficient commendation to encourage Szigeti's father to break contact with Budapest. Boy violinists had caught the public fancy. Fourteen-year-old Mischa Elman was just then reaping the first harvest of a phenomenal box-office success. What was meet for Mischa was meet for Joska. Reasoning thus, the elder Szigeti abandoned his job in Budapest and set himself the task of managing his son's climb to renown. But events did not follow quite as he had hoped. Perhaps the prodigy market had been cornered by Mischa Elman. Perhaps the diffident Joska cut too pale a figure on the concert platform. Whatever the reason, the boy did not captivate Europe in the Elman manner. His métier lay in directions other than precocious virtuosity. As a prodigy he was an "also ran," his success being sufficient to pay the bills but not to earn a fortune.

After a season in Berlin, father and son settled in London to try their luck in what was then the world's wealthiest country. Attired in velvet, the perfect Little Lord Fauntleroy, Joska Szigeti made an appealing impression at fashionable musicales. In the homes of moneyed benefactors and in provincial concert halls he could hold his own. But in London's Bechstein Hall his puerile and saccharine playing met with an indifferent reception. The phonograph records that Szigeti made for HMV at this time—Hubay's *Zephyr*, Rubinstein's *Romanze*, an abridged version of the variations from Beethoven's "Kreutzer" Sonata—show by their very titles why London critics were not conquered by this latest prodigy from the Continent. Those were years of indolence and torpor. "My natural laziness," Szigeti confesses, "kept from me all disturbing thoughts of self-development, of self-criticism." Nobody wagged an admonishing finger at this disinclination to mature. As a boy violinist he was salable, but who could predict his prospects once he slipped into prosaic adulthood?

Faced with the disparity between these dim beginnings and the man today, one is tempted to look for the "electrifying influence," the "cataclysmic event" that suddenly shunted the direction of Szigeti's life toward a more purposeful goal. But the course of human events does not proceed in so angular and clear-cut a fashion. Quite obviously a few weeks with Ferruccio Busoni did not metamorphose Szigeti from a spineless virtuoso into an eclectic musician. Other congruent experiences—Ysaÿe and Pugno playing the César Franck Sonata, Kreisler playing two Mozart concertos—had effect. Nevertheless, his association with the great pianist Busoni caused a fundamental shift in Szigeti's relationship to music. Before Busoni music had been principally a livelihood; afterward it became a fulfillment.

The two met by chance. It was the custom then for reigning divas to bolster their programs with some violin and piano music. In 1909 Szigeti had been hired as an "assisting artist" to tour England with Nellie Melba. For a few weeks Busoni joined the retinue. Standing in the wings while the famous pianist played Bach, the young violinist grew aware of an absorption and an intellectual command hitherto unsuspected. Under the influence of Busoni, the man and the musician, Szigeti emerged from his chrysalis.

Just as he reached the threshold of real success, critics now taking notice of him as a musician and not as "another Hungarian violinist prodigy," a double catastrophe intervened. Europe fell prey to World War I and Joseph Szigeti to tuberculosis of the lung. Three years in Davos, scene of Thomas Mann's *The Magic Mountain*, restored the violinist to health. He had the good fortune to come under the care of a lung specialist who was also an amateur of music. To pay for room, board, and medical treatment Szigeti had only to play duets regularly with his doctor! With a fresh batch of scores arriving every other week from a circulating music library in Zurich, the duo managed to secure a solid lien on a large body of musical literature.

At the time Szigeti must have felt that fate had treated him badly. His last prewar tour, extending from Portugal to Finland, had presaged that prosperity and acclaim so diligently pursued by Joska and his ambitious father. With the advantage of hindsight, however, one perceives that these years of enforced retirement played a decisive part in shaping the musician we know today. They effected a clean break with his prodigy past, afforded him the opportunity to explore music at leisure, released him from the circumscribed routine of a touring virtuoso. When he descended from his Swiss mountain retreat in 1917, Szigeti went to the Conservatoire de Genève as head of violin master classes—a startling change in role. Lacking in musical stimulus these classes may have been, for talented students strayed only occasionally to Geneva, but they provided a steady source of income in Europe's most valued currency. With his bread-and-butter of existence thus assured, Szigeti for the first time in his life could give concerts to make music rather than to make money.

What the "new" Szigeti was like—Joseph now, not Joska—can be surmised from a series of Geneva recitals that he gave in 1919. Devoted to the ten violin sonatas of Beethoven, these programs were a far cry from what Szigeti had offered a decade before. No longer did his taste run to Goldmark, Ernst, or Poldini; no longer did he struggle to out-Elman Elman with the suave concertos of Wieniawski and Glazunov. He had found his own musical personality. Even before the end of World War I, all Switzerland and most of Central Europe had come to know that personality. His fastidious taste appealed so strongly to the discriminating Swiss public that he gave as many as forty-five recitals a year, an astronomical figure for so small a country. Eugene Ysaÿe, a man not given to indiscriminate praise, has left this testimony of Szigeti's art as it appeared in the years immediately after World War I: "I found in Szigeti that rare combination of musician and virtuoso. As an artist he seemed conscious of a high mission into which he put all his faith, and he placed technique entirely at the service of musical expression."

With a growing bank account in good Swiss francs, Szigeti began to rehabilitate his name throughout Europe. Financial means were a requisite in the years following World War I, for inflation had so cheapened most European currencies that a musician's fee would not even cover expenses, much less provide a profit. While maintaining his home in tidy, prosperous Geneva, Szigeti began to journey farther and farther afield. Those were the years when he became inextricably involved with contemporary music. In Berlin he was heard in the Busoni Violin Concerto with the composer conducting. In Warsaw he ripened his acquaintance with Szymanowski, the man and his music. In Paris he met Albert Roussel and thereafter proselytized for his Second Violin Sonata on both sides of the Atlantic. At the festivals of the newly formed International Society for Contemporary Music Szigeti was a frequent participant. Perhaps his most memorable ISCM appearance occurred during the 1924 festival in Prague, when he performed Prokofiev's Concerto in D with an orchestra conducted by Fritz Reiner, thereby establishing himself as the almost predestined interpreter of this sprightly, bittersweet composition. These scattered examples give only an inkling of his commerce with contemporary musicians. A full account would include mention of Milhaud, Bloch, Ravel, Berg, Stravinsky, Bartók, and Hindemith, to say nothing of those lesser composers whose music Szigeti has expounded in order—as Ansermet would put it—"to make known the document."

Leopold Stokowski, a modern-music propagandist fully equal to Szigeti, brought the violinist to this country in the season of 1925–6. Following his debut with the Philadelphia Orchestra came a recital in New York and solo appearances with the Boston and Chicago orchestras. Annually thereafter he returned to the United States, and always he adhered to the high standards that he had set for himself in Europe. With the Friends of Music and Bodanzky he performed the Busoni Concerto; he introduced the Ravel Sonata to New York, the composer assisting; there were sonata recitals with Cortot, Gieseking, and Gabrilowitsch; in Town Hall on successive Sunday afternoons he presented "A Survey of Three Centuries of Violin Music." No other violinist dwelled so consistently on such rarefied heights. But the heady atmosphere did not intoxicate the masses; except for those few cities where a "connoisseur audience" could be tapped, Szigeti's name did not draw.

Because of this relative lack of popularity and also because Szigeti is a confirmed Continental, he continued to base his activities in Europe. In 1925, following his resignation from the Geneva Conservatory, he moved his household to Paris; later he assumed French citizenship. There he lived until the outbreak of World War II. When the fall of France put return out of the question, Szigeti settled in Palos Verdes, California; in 1951 he became an American citizen. But Europe did not lose its hold. He was one of the first "expatriates" to resume tours of the Continent and Great Britain. In 1947, Szigeti joined with Artur Schnabel, Pierre Fournier, and William Primrose to lavish on the British public a series of eleven recitals that offered the major chamber music of Brahms and Schubert.

Szigeti's activity in the recording studio comes close to antedating that of any musician alive today. His 1909 waxings still turn up occasionally in secondhand shops—much to Szigeti's chagrin, though he admits to an "uncanny pleasure" when a phonograph repeats to him something he played long ago. With the introduction of electrical recording in 1926 Szigeti began building a recorded repertoire unequaled in quality and quantity by that of any other violinist. Long before he had "arrived" as a musical celebrity in this country, record-collectors were enlarging the sales of his many notable albums. During the first years of electrical recording he was often in the studio. In deference to the commercial reasoning of English Columbia he committed to wax such untypical encore pieces as Kreisler's *Tambourin Chinois* and Hubay's *Zephyr*, but to atone for these he insisted on recording also Milhaud's *Le Printemps* and the "*Nigun*" from Bloch's *Baal Shem.* In the late twenties and early thirties came the albums that spread his reputation throughout the world: the Brahms Concerto (with Sir Hamilton Harty conducting), the Beethoven Concerto (with Bruno Walter conducting), the Mozart D major, Mendelssohn, and Prokofiev concertos (all with Sir Thomas Beecham conducting), and two unaccompanied sonatas of Bach. Sated today with a luxuriance of fine recordings, we tend to forget how precious were these early examples of Szigeti's art.

"From my earliest manhood," the violinist once told me, "I have tried to avoid being objectionably national." The "Hungarian influence" that some commentators profess to discern in his playing is really nothing but a keen appreciation of the folk element (from whatever soil) that is to be found in all music. In this respect Szigeti is at one with Casals and Landowska. He descries peasant dances in the most unlikely places—the last movement of Mozart's G major Concerto, the *allegro assai* from Bach's unaccompanied Sonata in C, the "Dithyramb" from Stravinsky's *Duo Concertant.* Such hearty rhythmic propulsion is one of Szigeti's most creditable assets. He places his accents without reference to worn rhythmic clichés.

On Szigeti's tone—so different from the rich, honeyed sound cultivated by many violinists—opinion divides. Absence of excessive vibrato is its great virtue. Somebody once compared vibrato to the standard gravy that is administered in cheap restaurants indiscriminately to chicken, pork, and beef; Peter Yates has likened the tone of a vibrato-ridden violinist to "an interchangeable slip-cover patterned with large sleazy flowers which he slips over the original texture of any composition." Vibrato is a condiment. It bestows throbbing lusciousness on every musical phrase, but in the most emphatic way it is subject to the law of diminishing returns. The glowing patina of vibrato ends by robbing music of style. It takes the guts out of music, puts all violin literature on the level of the "Meditation" from *Thaïs*. Szigeti's tone substitutes variety for unremitting vibrato. He can play sweetly when the occasion demands (for example, in the opening phrases of Prokofiev's Concerto in D), but he can also play brusquely and huskily. He has learned that for music to go beyond mere sensation, sonority must be reckoned as a means, not an end.

Beyond tone there is Szigeti's mastery of musical rhetoric. You will not catch him arguing to redundancy the point of a musical work. He keeps a safe distance from the *éternelle effervescence* that Lucien Capet termed the bane of modern violin-playing. Szigeti has the instinct of an accomplished actor, understands when to throw away a line, appreciates the power of understatement.

I have limned the excesses that Szigeti avoids, and in so doing I run the danger of implying that what remains is dry and innocuous—careful but desiccated musicianship, with passion and personality excluded. It is exactly here that his genius shines, for patrician taste in his instance does not exclude the presence of emotion. "The striving to be effective easily leads into the error of exaggeration. But it by no means follows, as some persons seem to imply, that because exaggeration is a fault, tameness is a merit. Exaggeration is a fault because it is an untruth; but in art it is as easy to be untrue by falling below as by rising above." These words of G. H. Lewes, which refer to acting, hold true as well for musical interpretation. From avoidance of excess Szigeti does not fly to insipid whiteness. Free of vulgar hyperbole, he yet stamps every phrase he touches with the impress of a highly charged temperament.

How fortunate that Szigeti was not endowed with a transcendent technique! Had his exploits on the instrument aroused all auditors, had he been idolized from the start, he might still be Joska Szigeti, barricaded from introspection by the wall of his own brilliant success. But Szigeti's technical equipment has never been peerless. More than adequate to satisfy musical demands, it does not overwhelm audiences. Nature, having given him hands larger than ideal and a bow arm inclined to awkwardness, did not fit him for the role of violin prestidigitator. (A wag once quipped that Szigeti plays as if he were accustomed to practicing in a telephone booth.) Because other violinists could toss off Wieniawski with greater *éclat*, Szigeti was obliged to search elsewhere for musical fulfillment. We are all the gainers from the less-than-spectacular technique that denied him early fortune.

But too much can be and has been made of Szigeti's technical failings. He, too, might be tempted to bathe his listeners in silken reverie were it not that an exquisitely tailored style of playing all too often negates a composer's intent. "There is always," Szigeti believes, "a musical solution and an expedient solution." Steadfastly he chooses the musical solution and does not boggle at the technical pitfalls that lie in wait. One example must serve for a multitude: In the last movement of Beethoven's Opus 96 Sonata can be found a passage whose rhythmic pattern, Szigeti feels, demands the employment of open strings. To play it thus, which is "the musical solution," poses knotty problems of bowing and fingering. The left hand must make long skips while the bow jumps from string to string at a rapid pace. A much less taxing approach to this passage is possible, "the expedient solution," one in which fingers move in easy stages with the bow hugging the string. So performed, however, Beethoven's brusque thought becomes sicklied and pale. Szigeti prefers to take his chances with the open strings, no matter what technical problems must be overcome. "Better," he insists, "to fail gloriously than to conquer expediently. It is a question of ethics, of morality."

On Bernard Shaw's authority we are told that Eduard

Reményi refused to "sacrifice all other interests and activities to the cultivation of his violin-playing machinery." In this respect Szigeti emulates his famous Hungarian predecessor. The dazzling machinery he leaves to others. Szigeti illuminates music with knowledge and style, being careful not to scorch it with the flame of rampant virtuosity.

☼ Pablo *Casals*

THE VIRTUOSITY of Pablo Casals is of so transcendent an order and his musicianship so penetrating that the world would revere him no matter if he treated his fellow man with scorn, subscribed to the most retrogressive philosophy, and compromised at every turn to further his own well-being. But in this happy instance one need employ no blinkers. Surrounded by an artificial and devious society, Casals remains simple and ingenuous; in a climate veering ever more toward a belief in authority and the cult of bigness, he clings stubbornly to a respect for individual probity and a true faith in democracy; rather than establish a *modus vivendi* with a corrupt and imperfect world, he holds himself aloof; he prefers to achieve his ends through kindness and humility rather than through stratagem and despotism. In short, he is a Christian as well as a noble musician.

Like a profound theme and variations the life of Casals begins in simplicity, develops by stages into complex grandeur, and returns to a muted, resigned simplicity. He was born December 29, 1876, in Vendrell, a small town on the Mediterranean not far from Barcelona, where his father Carles served as church organist. Reared in a musical environment, Casals soon showed signs of amazing precocity. At four he joined the choir in his father's church; at six he was composing music; at eight he took up the violin; at ten he began to play the organ at church services. Energetic musical activity this, performed with the zest expected of a strong Catalan boy who could outjump and outrun his schoolmates, but lacking—nevertheless—in directed passion. Then, one day in 1886, Casals discovered "his" instrument. It is uncertain where he first encountered the cello. Was it in an itinerant circus as played by a clown? Was it in a local concert of chamber music as played by the Barcelona master José García? Accounts differ. Whatever the details, we are assured that it was a case of love at first sight. With a gourd and some strings he fashioned for himself a primitive instrument that made do until a few months later, when his father secured for him a cheap but authentic cello.

At eleven Casals was taken to Barcelona by his mother to further his musical education. The young boy, whose musical development had already attained a Mozartian level, threw himself into the life of Barcelona's Municipal School. To supplement the regular allowance from Vendrell, the student cellist entertained every night in a smoky café located in a Barcelona suburb. Conversation, card games, and the matching of dominoes are said to have halted as the twelve-year-old picked up his bow and began his absorbed, almost religious, playing. Isaac Albéniz, investigating enthusiastic rumor, paid the café a visit. Impressed beyond expectation, he responded with predictions of future fame and a letter of recommendation to a generous patron and musician in his own right, Count Guillermo Morphy, who lived in Madrid and was an intimate of the royal family. This Spanish aristocrat became a second father to Casals, obtaining a state grant for the boy and supervising his education closely. Royalty took an interest in the lad from Vendrell. He studied geography in the library of Alfonso XII, practiced foreign languages with the Infanta Isabella, played duets with the Queen Mother, María Cristina. His musical studies were dominated by Jesús de Monasterio, who aided Casals immeasurably with his comprehensive grasp of cello literature. Under the guidance of Tomás Bretón, composer of some forty operas and *zarzuelas*, Casals wrote chamber music. But as the months wore on, a conflict developed between Señora Casals, who wished her son to remain a performing cellist, and Count Morphy, who envisioned Casals as the revitalizer of Spanish music, indeed as the latent Verdi of Spanish opera. In the end the desire of Señora Casals prevailed. After two years in Madrid, Casals received a pension from the Queen enabling him to study his instrument at the famous Brussels Conservatory of Music.

One can well imagine the young artist's excitement as he crossed the Pyrenees for the first time. The centers of civilization were to nourish his soul, complete his education, and reward his talent. But Pablo's enthusiasm quickly curdled to disillusion. At Brussels he was directed to play for the head cello-teacher. Casals entered the classroom, sat in the last row, and listened to the students. What he heard did not impress him. Throughout the lesson he struggled against disappointment. Finally the professor took notice of the newcomer: "You are the little Spaniard? It seems you play the cello, and the director has asked me to hear you. What can you play?" "Anything that you choose, sir," was the confident reply. "Some Spanish dances?" the professor queried. Indignant at this condescension and annoyed at the students' mockery, Casals determined to hold his ground. "Yes, sir, some Spanish dances. But other things besides." Whereupon the professor enumerated several concertos and display pieces from the regular cello repertory. It seemed that Casals could play them all. The sarcastic pedant singled out one of the most difficult, *Souvenir de Spa*, a display piece by the Belgian composer Servais. "Now, young gentlemen," he announced, "we will hear something very surprising from this young man who plays everything."

The challenge imposed double difficulties, for to the technical hurdles of the piece was added the necessity of performing on a poor and unfamiliar instrument. It mattered not. The students' smirks faded as the brilliance of the Spaniard's playing gained their awed attention. Nonplused, the teacher drew Casals into his office. He offered elaborate apologies; he was laudatory to an extreme; he swore that Casals should receive without delay the Premier Prix du Conservatoire. But the teacher had not reckoned on the democrat who would one day abandon a career for the sake of a principle. "I do not like the atmosphere of your class," Casals said, and thereupon took his leave.

Two days later he departed for Paris, hoping to find there a more agreeable artistic climate. The wisdom of this move was not apparent to his sponsors in Madrid. The Brussels Conservatory inadequate? Impossible! Count Morphy urged Casals's return to Belgium; on being met with refusal, he canceled the pension. Pablo, stranded with his mother in the French capital, searched for work. For a while he earned a meager salary playing second cello in a vaudeville theater, the Folies-Marigny on the Champs-Élysées. But long hours, a frigid winter, and insufficient nourishment took their toll. Casals fell seriously ill. It was necessary to retreat to Barcelona.

On home soil his fortune was more encouraging. The Municipal School placed him in charge of its cello department. He played in many churches, was appointed first cellist at the opera, and organized local chamber-music recitals. Moreover, reconciliation was effected with Count Morphy and the royal family. Queen Cristina awarded him the order of Carlos III; somewhat more important, she gave him an excellent cello. In Madrid, Casals appeared for the first time as soloist with an orchestra, the "vehicle" being Lalo's Concerto in D minor. Gradually the prepossessing student gave way to the accomplished professional. After several years, and with a bank account sufficiently enlarged, Casals crossed the Pyrenees to try his luck once more in Paris.

It was the autumn of 1899. Casals, armed with a letter of introduction, auditioned for Charles Lamoureux. Like any conductor in his right mind, Lamoureux was wary of cellists, especially young cellists. He knew the rasping, ungainly sound of which the instrument is capable, and only grudgingly submitted to a fresh exhibition of its crudities. But as the twenty-three-year-old Spaniard struck up the first notes of Lalo's Concerto, Lamoureux shed his indifference, for here was cello-playing of an order heard previously only in the mind's ear.

In October 1899 Casals appeared at the Château d'Eau theater as soloist with the Lamoureux Orchestra. Paris responded ardently to the young artist. Within two months he had played again with Lamoureux. Eugene Ysaÿe, the Belgian violinist and conductor, invited the Spaniard to Brussels shortly after his Lamoureux debut. Acclaim followed acclaim. No career could have been launched more successfully. Casals began touring England, Germany, Scandinavia, Russia, Austria, Italy, and within a few years had established himself in Europe as the first cellist of his day. With his technical command of the instrument, he could easily have made his way playing *Souvenir de Spa* and like insipidities. Instead he preferred to concentrate on chamber music and the concerto literature. Early in his career the cellist shared recitals with the pianist Harold Bauer. England, France, Holland, Germany, and Russia, as well as North and South

America, heard them together. The year 1905 marked the birth of another renowned musical collaboration: the Cortot-Thibaud-Casals Trio. These three artists, wonderfully matched in stylistic refinement, continued their association for almost three decades, until ideological strains set them on differing paths. Happily their unsurpassed performances of Haydn, Beethoven, and Schubert trios have been preserved on records.

The United States heard Casals first in 1901, when he accompanied the American soprano Emma Nevada on a coast-to-coast tour—a tour that was interrupted in San Francisco when he injured his left hand. He came again in 1904, and was much applauded in the large Eastern cities. Elsewhere he met with a cold reception. By and large, America still equated musical merit with platform eccentricities or digital fireworks. According to either standard Casals appeared inadequate. It is not surprising that he looked askance for many years at subsequent offers from American concert-managers. Persuaded to return in 1915, he toured this country every winter thereafter, with one exception, until 1928. Illness forced him to cancel his 1929 tour, and European commitments—either musical or political—kept him on the other side of the Atlantic throughout the 1930's.

To chronicle in detail the two decades following Casals's Paris debut would be to take a grand tour of world concert-halls. However stimulating this itinerant life may be for the musician, it is unrewarding to the reader. Suffice it to note the musical development that these years encompassed, years when the cellist profited from fruitful intercourse with such representatives of Europe's musical elite as Saint-Saëns, Fauré, Nikisch, Richter, Casella, Enesco, and Ysaÿe. Music no longer served as the be-all and end-all of his existence. We are told that the Villa Molitor, Casals's home in the elegant Auteuil section of Paris, reverberated to the spirited inflections of philosophical and political discussion. Henri Bergson came often to visit, as did the painters Eugène Carrière and Degas. Casals became acquainted with Clemençeau and Briand, immersed himself in political and social questions. The writings of Marx interested him; social injustice troubled his conscience.

During those years the link with Barcelona was tenuous. Although Casals returned to his Catalan homeland every summer for a vacation, as a musician he belonged to Paris and to the artistic world of which it was the hub. Once a period of ten years went by without a single concert by Casals in Barcelona. Following the outbreak of World War I, his attention turned more and more southward. He gave up his Parisian villa and spent an increasing amount of time on home soil. It was a period of gestation for a cherished plan.

To conduct a great symphony orchestra had always been his ultimate goal. As a boy assisting his father in the church of Vendrell, Casals was ever eager to lead the choir. Midway in the first great tour following his Paris debut he wrote to a friend: "If I have been so happy up to now scratching the cello, think how happy I will be when I shall possess the finest of all instruments, the orchestra!" Virtuosity had never impressed him as the summit of endeavor. In 1901, when a mountain-climbing mishap crushed one of his fingers, his first comment is said to have been: "Thank God, I shall never have to play the cello again." He had his first taste of conducting at seventeen; the Barcelona Opera was preparing Granados's opera *María del Carmen*, and Casals, the orchestra's first cellist, was put in charge of rehearsals. Later he appeared often as guest conductor of the Lamoureux Orchestra. This experience served as apprenticeship for his ambitious plan, to found a permanent orchestra in Barcelona.

The city's symphonic history was not encouraging. Orchestras came into being, existed as long as the funds and energy of their organizers held out, and collapsed forthwith. Antonio Nicolau, Mathieu Crickboom, Granados, and Ricard

Lamote de Grignon had each labored to provide Barcelona with an orchestra, and each had been bested by the city's indifference. When Casals broached the project anew he was met with ridicule. Barcelona had neither the need nor the means to finance a permanent symphony orchestra, he was told. Realizing soon enough that the city's prominent men would offer only niggling support, the cellist attacked the job singlehanded. Presently word circulated in Barcelona about a new orchestra hired by Casals, paid by Casals, and rehearsed by Casals. Derision mounted; the press was openly antagonistic. What madness for this cellist to dissipate his fortune on a symphony orchestra! Shoemaker, stick to your last. To complicate matters Casals broke down from the strain of organizing so massive an enterprise. For weeks, while he was recuperating, the venture hung in perilous balance. Finally, on October 13, 1920, the first concert of the Pau* Casals Orchestra took place. As the seasons passed, the orchestra rose in public esteem. Subscriptions multiplied. Those who had scoffed now piped their reluctant approval. Casals was perhaps not entirely the fool. It took eight years, however, for the orchestra to become self-supporting, and in the interim the deficit was largely made up by Casals himself.

Those years during the twenties and early thirties were among the happiest and most fruitful of Casals's long career. In the spring and autumn he conducted his own orchestra. Winters he devoted to the cello and to chamber music. During the summer he rested (which means for him hours of daily work on the cello) in the seaside town of San Salvador, a few miles south of Barcelona, where he had built an imposing villa in Catalan style, surrounded by a large, classically ordered garden. Added to these material satisfactions was Casals's gratification over the birth of the Spanish Republic. Despite the cellist's affection for the royal family, he suffered

* Pau is the Catalan equivalent of Pablo.

no illusions as to the efficiency and justice of the monarchist regime, knowing full well that in matters of land reform and labor legislation it lagged far behind other European governments. In 1931 a national election demonstrated such vigorous pro-republican sentiment that Alfonso XIII left the country precipitately. The Republic was formed, and an era of social and economic reform began for Spain. Church and state were separated, government schools founded, the land of large expropriated estates distributed to the peons. Catalonia was granted near-autonomy; its art and literature were encouraged. For Casals, who had long been aware of the need for reform, the new government was heartily welcome. He found the leaders of republican Spain eager to sponsor cultural activities. The Junta de Música, of which Casals was a member, laid out a long-range program of musical education. Symphony orchestras and choral groups were subsidized, plans drawn up for a national theater, contests organized to encourage Catalan composers.

July 18, 1936, marked the abrupt termination of this period. On that day the Spanish Army, under the command of General Franco, initiated an armed revolt against the legal or—as it came to be known—Loyalist government. Notwithstanding his dislike of its violent anarchistic minority, Casals supported the Republic with every means at his disposal. Outside of Spain he gave concerts to raise money. In Barcelona, while the city was under bombardment, he played in hospitals and theaters in aid of children and the aged. When it became clear in the spring of 1939 that Barcelona had neared the end of its power to resist, Casals fled—along with thousands—across the border to France and freedom.

After a few restless and unhappy months in Paris, Casals settled in Prades, a small town of five thousand nestled in the foothills of the Pyrenees some twenty-five miles west of the Mediterranean and twelve miles north of the Spanish frontier. There the cellist captured the illusion of home, for this province of Roussillon resembles Catalonia more than it does France. The warm, dry climate and the friendly Catalan population eased Casals of his melancholy. He plunged into a new and characteristically humanitarian endeavor. Near Prades the French government had constructed several tremendous concentration camps to house the refugees from Catalonia who had poured over the border. Casals applied himself to the immense task of ameliorating a wretched situation. He saw that food, clothes, and medicines were properly distributed to his unfortunate fellow Catalans, financing much of this work from his own pocket.

While Casals was thus occupied, France was invaded, the Third Republic tottered, and Nazi armed columns streamed southward. Italy entered the war; rumors circulated that Franco would soon involve Spain. At this point Casals was persuaded to seek safety in England. He managed to reach the hectic port of Bordeaux amid all the confusion of retreating armies, only to learn on arrival that his ship had been sunk by enemy action. There was nothing to do but return to Prades. Vichy succeeded the Third Republic. Wherever the slogan "Liberty, Fraternity, Equality" appeared it was replaced by Pétain's "Work, Family, Country." Communication between France and the outside world dwindled to near silence.

For the first year or so after the fall of France, friends from abroad were able to keep in contact with Casals. As Prades was in the unoccupied zone, mail—though tortuously slow and scrupulously censored—got through. Moreover, on two occasions Casals ventured into free territory. In 1941 and again in 1942 the cellist toured Switzerland, giving benefit concerts for the International Red Cross and replenishing his own bank account, denuded by the refugee expenses. However, from the moment late in 1942 when the Germans occupied all of France until the liberation two years later, nothing was heard of Casals. The long silence gave rise to gloomy speculation. It was rumored that the Gestapo had delivered the cellist to Franco, that Casals was either dead or starving in a Spanish jail. Indeed, it seemed impossible that so famous and outspoken an anti-Fascist could remain unmolested in Hitler's *Festung Europa*. But the miraculous occurred. In New York late in 1944, Maurice Eisenberg, one of Casals's oldest friends, received a letter in the familiar handwriting and bearing the postmark of Prades. From across the sea Casals wrote: "Now that the enemy has been forced to leave I have resumed my practicing, and you will be pleased to know that I feel that I am making daily progress." During the occupation, Casals's personal safety was often in jeopardy. The Gestapo searched his room in Prades several times, but when Casals's attitude seemed overly belligerent Señora Capdevila, his devoted housekeeper and companion, would draw the Gestapo men aside to confide pityingly that the poor old man was not quite in his right mind. Once a delegation of German officials arrived in Prades to "invite" Casals to play in Germany. They brought word that Hitler had himself requested the revered musician to play again for the German people. A special sleeping-car would be at the cellist's disposal to bear him directly from Prades to Berlin—a startling offer considering the chaotic state of Europe's wartime transportation system. Casals realized, of course, that the Nazis' gentle persuasion stemmed from the desire to use him for morale-shattering propaganda purposes. He expressed his regrets; unfortunately, a rheumatic shoulder had made it quite impossible for him to play. Threats emanated from the Vichy militia. Casals's name actually appeared on a list of men to be arrested; only the intercession of a friend and the precipitate collapse of the Vichy government prevented the arrest.

With the ending of European warfare in May 1945 free

travel once more became possible. Casals chose England as the scene for his re-entry into international musical life. A lifelong respect and affection for this nation had been strengthened by Britain's conduct in the face of aggression. In Prades during the long years of the occupation Casals's main source of encouragement and hope had been the BBC news. On arriving in England on June 25, 1945, he published a communication to the English people:

> I feel more than happy and privileged to have this opportunity of assuring not only my fellow musicians in this country but the entire British public of the solicitude with which I have followed all that has befallen them during these six terrible years. . . . I am sure that history will always preserve the memory of how the British people kept alive the flame of civilization in wartime, and I am glad that I have lived to see that such things are possible. I was old enough when this war started and I am older still today, but let me say that I have lived fully during these years: I have survived all these great changes throughout the world. I have seen the collapse of the two most hateful forms of dictatorship, and having lived through them has given me renewed strength.

No artist has ever received a more fervent welcome than that accorded Casals on this tour of England. For the British to hear an artist of his superlative stature after years of musical isolation was as intoxicating as it was for Casals to be received by the drab and battered metropolis that had endured in the cause of freedom and that he now termed "the Capital of Hope." British Airways flew the cellist to London, refusing payment for his passage; His Majesty's Customs waived all baggage examination. This musician was received as an esteemed representative of free mankind. On June 27 took place the great concert in the Albert Hall, where twelve thousand listeners heard him play the Schumann and Elgar concertos (with the BBC Symphony under Sir Adrian Boult) and, as an encore, one of the unaccompanied suites of Bach. The tumultuous ovation of this concert was echoed many times that summer as Casals toured England. Enthusiasm took on still greater intensity in the autumn when he made another tour for the benefit of the RAF's Benevolent Fund—"my small contribution to the cause of this nation I so much admire." Everywhere the musician and the man met with fervent acclaim.

Despite the exaltation of these appearances in England, Casals became increasingly discouraged over the trend of international affairs. Broadcasting to Spain over the BBC in July he had said:

> I have come to England from my retirement in the shadow of Canigou, the other side of the Pyrenees, and first want to convey my gratitude to the English people for the cordial and enthusiastic way in which I have been received, these British people who have shown such civic conscience and heroism in meeting the sufferings of the war, even during those difficult hours when they were alone in the fight. They merit the admiration and love of all men who care for liberty and justice, and we continue to expect from them the consolidation of the peace and the moral reconstruction of Europe.

That consolidation and reconstruction did not materialize according to Casals's expectations. In British newspapers of conservative tendency he read encomiums of the Franco regime. Official British policy seemed to take a similarly favorable view of the Spanish dictatorship. In the view of the Spanish democrats, Franco's regime rested on a fragile foundation. A little pressure and it would tumble. Why was it, then, being shamelessly bolstered? Casals, as his autumn tour of England progressed, became more and more disturbed at the anomalous position in which he found himself. Oxford and Cambridge both wished to present him with honorary degrees. Casals was impelled under the circumstances to decline. "If in these moments I should accept honors in England," he explained, "it would appear to my compatriots that I was indifferent to their unhappiness, when the contrary is the case: I associate myself with them *completely*." At the conclusion of his tour, early in November 1945, the cellist canceled his plans for appearances in England the following spring. He called a halt to an extensive program that had been arranged by His Master's Voice, leaving a recording of the Haydn Cello Concerto half completed. Reiterating his admiration for the British people, Casals nevertheless insisted that he and countless other Spanish democrats felt cruelly deceived by Britain's "policy of turning a deaf ear to our just protests, by this method of ignoring our sufferings, or damping down any magnanimous impulse to help us, and of systematically postponing the solution of a problem which troubles the conscience of millions of democrats."

He left England to return to Prades, stopping in Paris on the way to give a gala concert in the Salle Pleyel. The date was November 13, 1945—the last time (as of present writing) that Casals appeared in one of the great musical capitals. Believing that "the life of an artist is inseparable from his ideals," Casals imposed silence upon himself. He refused offers from all quarters to play, for everywhere there was an inclination among governments in power to maintain the Franco regime. Casals's abdication connoted more than a protest against one dictatorship in one country. It was a protest against worldwide expediency and callousness and compromise—against all the moral backsliding that the man of high ideals could not countenance. Casals muted his cello because he felt that he and his kind had lost the war. There were those who labeled his action a feeble and futile gesture, who said that one man's silence would accomplish nothing, that Casals could achieve much more by playing for the benefit of those who needed help, by propagandizing actively for his cause. The cellist turned a deaf ear to all arguments. When the New Friends of Music invited him to New York for the 1946–7 season he could only reply: "Please understand that the policies of your country are against my ideas for my country. I love America, but I could not go to a country which I should criticize." From every quarter came requests for him to relent. Refusal was not easy. Casals admitted: "It is the greatest sacrifice of my life I am making. But someone must remember. Someone."

The world's greatest cellist, the intimate of royalty and statesmen, the man who knew on equal terms the outstanding writers and artists of his day, became the recluse of Prades. Six years of anonymity during the war had been followed by six months of glorious re-emergence. Now he returned to anonymity and to an almost monastic simplicity.

The postwar years dragged on. By December 1949 the silence had extended to four years. Memory once green began to wither. To a new generation Casals was more legend than actuality—a name on some prized phonograph records and an old man living in retirement somewhere in France. Then the name came suddenly to life. Word arrived from Prades that Casals would play and conduct for three weeks in June 1950 to commemorate the 200th anniversary of Bach's death. Had the artist broken his vow? Did he recognize that his individual protest was powerless against the forces supporting Franco? Casals took pains to set the world right on this matter. "I am not coming out of retirement," he announced. "I decided to play in the town of my exile this once, in spite of my retirement." This time Casals would not journey to New York or

London or Paris. If the musical world wished to hear him it would have to seek him out in Prades. Perhaps he felt that to appear in public on this occasion would strengthen the moral effect of his retirement. For the world had begun to forget him, and opinions circulated that the cellist had ceased to play not because of any political boycott but because his fingers no longer moved with their former ease. To show that his musicianship, far from deteriorating, had actually improved during the years of silence would be to emphasize the magnitude of his sacrifice.

Whatever the underlying motives, Casals's decision to play "this once" electrified the musical world. Soloists of the highest stature volunteered their services. The violinist Alexander Schneider, who had conceived the idea of a Bach festival in Prades, recruited an orchestra of thirty-five musicians, most of them from the United States. Tourist agencies attacked the protean task of transporting and garrisoning an army of music-lovers. As inquiries began to arrive by the hundreds it became apparent that Prades, with its single hotel of twenty-seven rooms, could not cope with so alarming an influx of visitors. Hotels in several thermal resorts near Prades consented to open earlier in the season than usual, and arrangements were made with local bus lines to transport people from these resorts (some of them twenty miles distant) to Prades for each evening's concert.

I belonged to that large company for whom Casals had been a personality purely phonographic, and with hundreds of other Americans I crossed the ocean in 1950 to hear the great cellist in person. Getting to Prades was no simple journey. It seemed as if the French railway system had set up special hurdles to test the zeal of the Casals pilgrims. One left Paris before breakfast on a Thursday morning and arrived in Prades on Friday afternoon. En route there were three changes of trains and a night's stopover in Toulouse. But the slow journey had its advantages: it prepared one for the startlingly new environment in which this festival took place. As the train threaded its way southward, the cool grace of classical France slipped imperceptibly away until, surrounded by the hot severity of austere Catalonia, one was suddenly made aware that civilizations had changed. The milieu of Prades is almost blatantly medieval. Abandoned forts dot the landscape of Roussillon, and its hamlets—most of them off the railroad and many accessible only to the adventurous motorist—have been unchanged by the centuries.

June 2, 1950, was for Prades a day of bizarre excitement and heady contrasts. In the noisy, dusty streets of that plain town could be seen a remarkable number of the world's eminent musicians. Newspaper and magazine reporters crowded the post office demanding telephone and cable facilities. A special postmark had been authorized to signal the day's importance, and the thousand-odd visitors to Prades managed to post that day some fifteen thousand letters or cards. Plans called for the opening concert to begin at nine o'clock. At eight thirty a bus for Prades left my hotel at the near-by village of Vernet-les-Bains, and wound its way down a steep mountain road, past gaunt Catalan villages bathed in a russet sunset glow. At the entrance to Prades a banner strung across the road proclaimed "*Bienvenue*—Welcome." Scores of automobiles parked along the narrow streets made it almost impossible for the bus driver to navigate his clumsy vehicle. After crawling through Prades at something like two miles per hour, the bus reached the square in front of the Église Saint-Pierre, a medieval edifice part Gothic, part Romanesque, which the Archbishop of Perpignan had put at the disposal of the festival. The square was brilliantly illuminated for the occasion, and in every inch of space the people of Prades—heedless of traffic—gathered to gape at the milling, many-tongued assemblage.

In the church confusion mounted as twelve hundred ticket-holders searched for their seats. Delman pumps and straw-soled espadrilles ambled down the aisle; the atmosphere was redolent of Chanel and garlic. The element of dull conformity attendant on most concerts was strikingly absent. And the widest-eyed were not the foreigners from across the sea, who would presumably be overwhelmed by the exotic surroundings, but the people of Prades. They were amazed, dumbfounded, incredulous. Already they had formed what seemed a liberal estimate of the eminence of their short, bald neighbor. But that these hundreds of rich people should bother to come all the way to Prades to hear him play, that was truly *formidable*.

A notation on the program reminded heathens that the sacred precincts of a church forbid clapping. When Casals appeared carrying his cello, the entire assemblage sprang to its feet in silent homage. The cellist, peering at the vast audience from behind his spectacles, motioned for the gathering to be seated. Then he took his own seat in front of the orchestra, closed his eyes for a few seconds, and began the Suite in G major (No. 1) for unaccompanied cello. Casals was playing in public again.

It is impossible to convey the reward of those first few notes. The phonograph records of Casals had, of course, prepared one for the wonders of Prades. But for me, at least, there had lurked always a suspicion that electronic enhancement partially explained the Spaniard's brilliance. Could the tortuous, rasping instrument really sound as resonant and buoyant as the phonograph intimated? One could not be sure. Yet no more than three measures of the Bach suite sufficed to prove that, if anything, the famous discs had borne inadequate witness. The singing amplitude of tone, the verve and lightness of bowing, the imaginative, architectural phrasing, the extraordinary purity of intonation—all justified in full measure the reputation of Casals.

It required determination, time, and money to hear Casals in his secluded habitat. Fortunately, a recording company was on hand to capture the Prades music-making for those who could not attend. I had the good fortune to witness the session at which Casals and the Swiss pianist Paul Baumgarten recorded Bach's Sonata in G minor (originally scored for viola da gamba and harpsichord). Several times that afternoon it was necessary, because of outside noises (the studio was improvised and inadequately soundproofed) or because of a slight musical imperfection, to remake a section of the recording. No matter how often Casals was called upon to repeat a portion in the midst of a movement, he was able always to re-create the intensity and fervor of his musical conception. Temperament in the pejorative sense seemed completely foreign to him. Indeed, watching Casals in the studio one would hardly have imagined him to be the fulcrum of the enterprise. While engineers and recording advisers bustled about—conferring with each other, moving microphones and shifting wires, studying the score—Casals remained quietly in his chair, puffing at his pipe, awaiting orders. When the hubbub had subsided and the signal to record once more was flashed, he picked up his bow and began to play with ethereal absorption, transporting the hectic workshop to the ordered slopes of Parnassus.

If the recording studio gave some indication of the simplicity and kindliness so often mentioned as characteristic of Casals, the rehearsals with the festival orchestra threw these qualities into triumphant relief. It is the prerogative of conductors to outdo Robespierre in severity—or so, at least, they often assume. Standing on the podium at rehearsals they can easily consider themselves exempt from normal rules of tolerant and democratic behavior. Here they may ruthlessly insist on their superior judgment, indulge in pointed and searing sarcasm, abuse an errant individual before his fellow musicians. Temper can run riot. Casals, however, will not buy perfection at this price. His respect for the individual, so apparent in private life, does not diminish when he mounts the podium. At the Prades rehearsals one sensed an unmistakable aura of gaiety and camaraderie. He did not act on the theory that all musical wisdom was concentrated in his head: he stood ever ready to heed suggestions from the players. In one instance a particular phrase would not come right, no matter how many times repeated. "I don't know enough about this yet," Casals confessed. "Let me try to work it out when I go home this afternoon."

Having said so much, it is necessary to add that at Prades Casals the conductor scarcely measured up to Casals the cellist. By an odd working of musical justice, his instrumental virtues often seem to breed orchestral failings. Only the most hidebound purist could object to Casals's rubatos or to his highly imaginative phrasing when he plays the cello. But when he conducts an orchestra the end effect is not always so persuasive. Magnified thirty times, the once-cogent intuition appears as a stylistic lapse, so that what was for the cellist a subtle freedom becomes the conductor's fall from grace. The control so marked in Casals's own playing is less apparent in his conducting, though the deficiency is more evident on the phonograph records than it was at the actual performances in Prades. The "Brandenburg" Concerto No. 2 is an example. At Prades one was conscious of an impelling tempo, a zest that made this music skip along irresistibly. On the recording one finds the speed manifestly too fast for comfort; a nervous and hectic quality obtrudes in the playing, and the ensemble, which seemed beyond reproach at Prades, sometimes frays around the edges.

How explain this inconsistency between memory and recorded evidence? Much can be attributed to the insufficiencies of an improvised recording-studio and the inexorable schedule set for the project. But some blame must surely be laid to the objective microphone. Alone among the devotees at Prades the microphone remained intransigently objective. Its pulse did not quicken as a thousand spectators filed into the Église Saint-Pierre; it experienced no wave of exhilaration at its first sight of Casals; it was not influenced by the rapt, fanatical attention bestowed on *le maître* by an adoring orchestra. At Prades the exaltation of the occasion and the personal magnetism of Casals contrived to close all ears to defects—all ears, that is, except the microphone's. Defects there were, and the microphone heard them.

Whatever Casals's preferences in the matter, it is as a cellist that the world venerates him. The cello can hardly be termed the most lovable of instruments. Bernard Shaw echoed a general opinion when he wrote: "I am not fond of the violoncello: ordinarily I had as soon hear a bee buzzing in a stone jug." The full justice of this widely shared view can be comprehended only by those who, like Shaw, have had occasion at some time or other to ply the trade of criticism. In the hands of an untalented performer a cello recital represents the nadir of auditory experience. The sound is trying—rasping, squeaky, seldom in tune, with wide variations in quality between lower and upper registers—and the musical logic is slight, most phrases coming to grief with a jerk, a bump, or a swoop. If for nothing else, Casals's name would figure in the bright lexicon of music as having given the cello respectability. When you listen to him, you are convinced that the execrable instrument is really a glorious agent of musical expression.

That Casals achieved this was owing in large measure to his revolutionary improvements of cello technique. The nineteenth century viewed the cello as a heavy instrument; it was played like the double bass, with many slides and undisguised effort. Not that nineteenth-century cellists were incapable of virtuosity. On the contrary, players of the first rank—such as

Julius Klengel and David Popper—indulged inordinately in pyrotechnics. But because of rigid canons of cello technique, to which all performers essentially subscribed, this virtuosic wizardry was purchased at the price of poor intonation and unmusical phrasing. Hence, the pre-Casals fraternity of cellists emphasized such works as were rich in flashy effects and poor in musical substance. Here is Shaw on this state of affairs, the date of his comment being March 4, 1891:

> Goltermann and Popper are all very well; but they are not Mozart and Beethoven. What with Hollmann, Klengel, and Gérardy, I have heard that *Mazurka Caprice* of Popper's not less than fourteen thousand times within two seasons. It has been encored each time; and the encore piece has always been Popper's *Papillons*—a pleasing title, but one which now strikes terror into me. *Kol Nidrei* is quite a novelty after Popper; but even *Kol Nidrei* palls as the years roll on.

It is altogether possible that Shaw never heard Beethoven's five sonatas or Bach's six suites; not once did he mention them in six years of music reviewing. Although cellists of the 1890's outdid each other in scintillating fireworks, they were unwilling to come to terms with the musical difficulties of Bach and Beethoven.

Casals approached the instrument with unprejudiced curiosity. His apprenticeship avoided all the established schools; when offered the opportunity of immersing himself in Belgian orthodoxy he luckily declined the privilege. Casals's technique, worked out by his own experimental efforts, is completely pragmatic, every device representing the solution of certain musical problems. A general and erroneous view pictures Casals as revealing that the cello can be played like a violin. Actually, he evolved a technique that was purely cellistic, though many instruments influenced his innovations. The traditional style of cello fingering demanded a constant shifting of position, which made for repeated "scoopings" and more often than not stood in the way of proper phrasing. Casals jettisoned the established "positions" and developed a new system of fingering—adapted, it is true, in some particulars from violin technique—in which the reach of the left hand was materially extended. The use of this so-called extension system made it possible for the left hand to follow much more closely the natural movement of each phrase. The playing became cleaner and the intonation truer. Hugo Becker, in his book on cello-playing, summarized the general view of Casals's predecessors in one fundamental area of technique. He maintained that phrasing and tone production, the domain of expression, are solely the province of the bow arm, the left hand simply providing the "frets" or changes of pitch. Casals believed otherwise, and achieved in his technique a much closer co-ordination of left and right hands. From his experience with keyboard instruments Casals worked out the means (involving both fingering and bowing) whereby certain notes seemed to be hammered out—a basic element in his mastery of rhythm. And from his observation of the voice came a method of bowing in which the varying amplitude and quality of a sustained note bore a close relation to the shadings employed by well-trained singers.

These several departures were already a feature of Casals's playing when, aged twenty-two, he made his Paris debut in 1899. It is true that his early appearances met with widespread acclaim. But like most victories, this one was gained over entrenched opposition. The professionals in his audience carped at the young Spaniard's "amateurish" technique. Cant, the bane of all professions, infects music with particular virulence, and cant flowed forth in all its woeful stupidity as the die-hards attacked Casals in an orgy of self-justification. The very simplicity of his methods provoked dissension. Even the lay audience found this disturbing. Their image of a cello virtuoso involved the tossing of arms and jerking of hands; mastery of this instrument was expected to afford a prime demonstration of the triumph of mind over matter. Casals upset these preconceptions. He made the cello appear too easy. Where was the show? The show, for Casals, lay not in the instrument but in the music.

The eminent pedagogue Diran Alexanian, an intimate associate of Casals for fifty years and his Boswell in the exegesis of cello technique, has set down for this book some recollections of the young cellist's working habits in the early years of the century:

> He would practice long and with an amazing degree of concentration. I remember well one afternoon in Paris during the summer of 1909. It was about two o'clock in the afternoon, and he was at work on one phrase in the last movement of the Beethoven E flat Trio (Opus 70, No. 2). As he worked I could observe his every move and almost read his thoughts as he would repeat a single note over and over, correcting intonation, altering the vibrato, experimenting with this or that fingering, molding his powers of expression.
>
> He would play the first note in the phrase, a G. The tone quality was not completely satisfactory. He tried it again and again, stopping for a moment to light his pipe and to reflect on the mental ideal that he was striving to reproduce. Then again he attempted to realize his ideal, saying to himself, half conscious of my presence: "No, that hasn't the singing quality which I want," or simply: "How difficult, how difficult." At length he was satisfied; then he went on, playing the grace note and the dotted eighth-note following. The attack on the grace note was not satisfactory to him. The finger struck from too high,

the articulation was too strong. He repeated with the finger closer to the string. Then the interval with A flat was not perfectly pure, and the speed of the grace note was too fast, then too slow. When he was satisfied with these two he went back to the G and worked on the three notes together. He often put down his cello to play the piano part, singing his own along with it. Then he would repeat it on the cello, thinking of the other parts as well.

In the next measure the skip from G to C caused him much concern. He felt the need for a slight portamento but also for a light attack on the consonant C. To achieve the effect he found necessary he extended the finger to a fraction below the pitch, then corrected it upwards giving just a suggestion of glissando. From a fast hammer to the softest touch of the string he would always find the articulation best suited to express the musical emphasis. Once he turned to me and said: "When I perform this, people will say I play as easily as a bird sings. If they only knew how much effort their bird has put into his song!"

With such concentration did Casals forge his technique. But technical achievement counts for little if allied to a mundane, shallow, unimaginative musical soul. The history of performance overflows with the record of virtuosos whose digital accomplishments eclipsed mental and spiritual intensity. "A first-rate technique put to third-rate uses." Critics have rung the changes on this phrase since quality of performance first became a matter of public concern. It sometimes seems that musicianship and technique appear in inverse ratio, so often is the one quality denigrated while the other is praised. Fortunately, Casals gives heartening proof that the virtuoso and the musician can walk side by side, inextricable and coequal. Yet when it comes to defining accomplishment, the musician is considerably more elusive than the virtuoso. Casals is the least didactic of interpreters. His reluctance to commit himself to a published fingering of Bach's unaccompanied suites is symptomatic of a fundamental distaste for interpretative rigidity. "There is not only one interpretation," he has said; "like nature it changes always, but the base—the sense of it—remains. There has to be each time a fresh insight; one changes constantly without meaning or planning to: only a real artist can understand and do this. It must always give the impression that the listener is hearing it for the first time, and the artist himself must feel that too, or he grows stale." This freshness of approach abides in everything he touches. Casals combines exalted improvisation with an astounding perfection of technical means.

While leafing through a scrapbook on Casals one day, I came across the following bit of criticism: "Everything was finished, perfect, wonderful, but it was not a soul's voice appealing to other souls." Did the critic for the *Boston Advertiser* in 1915 hear with different ears from ours or has the cellist undergone so remarkable a development since that review was written? If ever there was a man who ennobled the printed note with every fibre of his being, that man is Casals. To the stature of Bach he adds the stature of Casals. What else shall we make of the infinite serenity and breadth with which the cellist incants a slow sarabande? The conception belongs originally to Bach, but the realization is indebted in no small degree to Casals, who can express in those few simple notes the quiet resignation that is the legacy of a life filled with great disappointments; in the succeeding gavotte, too, the master of Leipzig and the master of Prades walk arm in arm, as Casals communicates with irresistible rhythmic propulsion the buoyancy and fortitude they hold in common.

As the subject has come up, it would be well to say a few words here on Casals's reassessment of Bach. Casals and Landowska, concurrently but not conjointly, revolutionized the interpretative approach to Bach. They liberated this composer from a rigid Teutonic mold in which he had all but suffocated, irradiating and Latinizing his music. To each the name of Bach conjures the word "dance." To each, also, fell the task of restoring to Bach one of his sovereign instruments. Although some had dabbled at the harpsichord just as others had made a try at the unaccompanied cello, it was in the hands of Landowska and Casals that these instruments assumed the grandeur and dignity that Bach's writing exacts.

"A strong claim to greatness is to be made for any artist who can do without masterpieces," remarked James Agate when confronted with Bernhardt's addiction to Sardou and Irving's to Leopold Lewis. One can go a step farther and interpose the query whether great artistry is not the more striking just when much has been made from little. Olivier's Œdipus is almost outdazzled by his Mr. Puff; Toscanini's "*Eroica*," for all its noble grandeur, is no finer a testament of orchestral artistry than his *Danse macabre*. So it is with Casals. His mastery is not deployed only on the peaks of musical endeavor. He lends himself with fervor to Boccherini and Bach, to Bruch and Beethoven. Through the sheer force of his ardor and genius the second-rate becomes in his hands a masterpiece. Despite effusive praise from Brahms, Dvořák's Cello Concerto does not ascend to the highest rung of the musical ladder—for proof whereof listen to any workaday, "scratch" performance. But Casals, with the art of a benign conjurer, will convince you momentarily otherwise. From that first magnificent thwack of the opening theme, a miracle of virile bowing, this interpretation sets an impeccable standard. To hear Casals arching the intervals of the second theme is to experience the almost unbelievable—a theme that could easily sound vulgar and commonplace, but which under his transmuting caress takes on an aspect of vaulting nobility. One could comment on the gentle, introspective lyricism of the middle movement or the bite of the march that follows, but it is useless to detail the wonders of this recording, for they are patent throughout, to the last long-held notes in the epilogue where Casals shivers the spine by the trueness of his intonation.

In 1951, and again in 1952, Casals performed in festivals. There is every expectation that the cellist will continue to break his "retirement" once yearly in this region of his self-imposed exile and every reason to hope that he will play thus for many years to come. It is unlikely, however, that he will ever set foot again in the Royal Albert Hall, the Salle Pleyel, or Carnegie Hall, unlikely—indeed—that he will ever venture far beyond the vicinity of Prades. And perhaps it is just as well. For Casals belongs to and complements the ancient province of Roussillon. The cellist admits his lack of rapport with modern times. He terms the present century "the century of shock and rupture." "One could almost believe," he says, "that God has checked the tireless offering that brought into being a Ninth Symphony." Certainly he has not gone out of his way to proselytize for contemporary music. He has turned his back on our high-powered civilization. Who has not at some time wished for the courage and tenacity to do likewise?

On the subject of Spain he has not been inhibited by the hobgoblin of consistency—nor, for that matter, has the present Spanish regime. No person has been more articulate than he in condemnation of the Franco government, in retaliation for which his statue was removed from Barcelona and the Avinguda Pau Casals renamed. However, his brother Enric, who is the present conductor of the Barcelona orchestra, was permitted to take part in the recent festivals in Prades and Perpignan. It is said that Pablo Casals could return to Spain whenever he wished and be greeted with highest favor. He will not set foot across the border, of course, until a new government is in power. What government? Here it is impossible to be specific. Lillian Littlehales, in her excellent biography of the cellist, outlined a three-step program for Spain that must have been his considered view when she visited him in the fall of 1947. By 1950 his opinions had altered. He is an apolitical person who owes allegiance to no party or faction. He seems to be "for" neither the exiled republican government nor the exiled pretender to the throne. What he seeks is justice for his country—a government that will guarantee certain essential freedoms and that will keep the opposition out of jail.

Casals will probably die waiting for the Spanish liberation of which he dreams. His protests have not caused Franco's flag to be furled. But who can conclude that his course was quixotic? He has showed that one need not temporize or compromise or avert the eyes. He has burnished a sordid age with the rare luster of nobility.

Budapest String Quartet

THE PHONOGRAPH record has put us under the spell of that illusory phenomenon, the "best performance." That there are absolutes in musical interpretation, models of perfection beyond cavil, is a proposition no performer—not even the most vain—would defend. A best performance is as impossible of attainment as a squared circle. But the exigencies of our phonograph-minded times would have it otherwise. Consider the lot of a tyro record-collector who steps into a music shop, makes his way to the record counter, and asks for the Beethoven Fifth Symphony. If the shop is well stocked, he will be required to choose from among seven or eight interpretations. This largess perplexes, for records are costly and one expects them to furnish long-standing pleasure. What is more natural than that the canny buyer, wary of inferior merchandise, should demand to know which interpretation is "best"?

He turns to the record critics for advice, and here the difficulty begins. Responding to the buyer's concern, record criticism has adopted the dangerous convention of the "best performance," has attempted to establish a hierarchy for the accomplishments of such men as Toscanini, Furtwängler, Walter, Koussevitzky, and Mengelberg. Admittedly, each of these interpreters views the exercise of his métier from a different coign of vantage, each varying in his regard for the letter of the composer's law. But it is a dubious service to play their several interpretations, say of a Beethoven symphony, in succession and then to pronounce one the "best." The making of music is beset with so many variables, so many imponderables, as to discourage such general use of the superlative.

More than two paragraphs are due this subject. I introduce it here apropos of the Budapest String Quartet only because this ensemble, by virtue of its many fine recordings, has been proclaimed from time to time "the best quartet." Lovers of chamber music are wont to be partisan in their affections; they tend to overestimate the difference between one good ensemble and another. I grant a basic tonal distinction between quartets in the French tradition and those in the Central European tradition, but otherwise find the vaunted diversities somewhat exaggerated. It is an expert ear that can identify in a "blindfold test" the Griller, the Paganini, the Pascal, or the Budapest ensembles. I would ascribe to the latter group no monopoly on musical virtue. It is a good quartet, one of many excellent ensembles now before the public, and better known than most.

The rumor that none of the four players has ever set eyes on the city of Budapest seems too good to be true. If not literally true, however, it holds good in essence. The "Budapesters" are Russian in origin, German in training, and American in domicile and citizenship. The oldest member in point of service is Josef Roisman, who completed a quarter century with the quartet in 1952. Roisman was born at the turn of the century in Odessa, fertile spawning-ground for violinists, and studied for several years in Berlin with Alexander Fiedemann as the protégé of a wealthy Crimean patroness. The boy's training with Fiedemann was halted by the outbreak of World War I, which emptied Berlin of all Russian nationals, but it sufficed to orient young Roisman in the direction of his life work; Herr Fiedemann—leader of a string quartet bearing his name—had implanted in his pupil an abiding affection for chamber music. Upon his return to Russia, Roisman began playing in quartets with similarly minded fellow students. But he did not remain there for long. Following the Bolshevik Revolution he made his way to Prague, where he played for some time in the Czech Philharmonic Orchestra; then he moved on to Berlin and his subsequent career with the Budapest Quartet.

This ensemble had been formed in Budapest, shortly after World War I, of musicians native to that city. It was not an especially cohesive group. The initial defection occurred in 1927, when Imre Poganyi, second violinist, resigned from the quartet to accept a job with the Cincinnati Orchestra. His post was taken by Josef Roisman, who was in Berlin looking for a chamber-music opening just when the remaining Budapest associates were looking for an experienced replacement. In 1930 the original cellist, Harry Son, was succeeded by Mischa Schneider, born in Vilna and educated in Germany. Two years later, the first violinist, Emil Hauser, gave up his post in order to tour with a harpsichordist. Roisman took over as leader of the quartet and has been its mainstay ever since. The desk of second fiddle which he vacated fell to Mischa Schneider's younger brother, Alexander. In 1936 the last Hungarian member, Istvan Ipolyi, was obliged to retire for reasons of health. To the viola desk went Boris Kroyt, another Odessa prodigy and a fellow student of Roisman's in prewar Berlin. Upon Kroyt's advent, Russian replaced German as the language spoken at rehearsals. Within nine years the Budapest Quartet had evolved into an institution no more Magyar than the Daughters of the American Revolution.

Subsequent changes in personnel have all centered on the transient position of second violin, which, if so corporate a body as a string quartet can be said to have a foot, would seem to be its Achilles heel. When Alexander Schneider decided to pursue a solo career in the early 1940's his post went to Edgar Ortenberg, also of Russia. This player in turn resigned after five years. The job then passed to Odessa-born Jac Gorodetzky, at which time the quartet's official language again switched, on this occasion to English. Brought to America as a child, Gorodetzky had never mastered Russian.

So much for the change in personnel. What of the change of venue? Until 1931 the Budapest Quartet ventured no farther west than London. It toured principally in Central Europe and Scandinavia, with occasional forays to England for concerts and recordings. When the group first came to America in 1931 chamber-music collectors were already conversant with its recordings of Schubert's "*Der Tod und das Mädchen*" Quartet and Mozart's "Hunt" Quartet, K.458. The field tilled by these recordings, however, was still relatively arid. On that first visit the Budapest Quartet played a mere dozen concerts. Such ensembles as the Kneisel and Flonzaley quartets had pioneered in the development of an American audience for chamber music, but that audience was to be found only in the largest cities. Roisman remembers playing in the East and in San Francisco on the Budapest's first tour, but recalls that "there wasn't much in between."

When Hitler came to power, the "non-Aryan" Budapesters were forced to give up their Berlin homes and their largest audience. For five years they led a nomadic life, then settled in the United States, where the public for chamber music had been steadily increasing, thanks to a rapid augmentation in sales of recorded chamber music and to the magnificent patronage of Mrs. Elizabeth Sprague Coolidge. Like most newly arrived musicians from Europe, the four set up headquarters in New York City. Later, the efforts of another chamber-music benefactress, Gertrude Clarke Whittall, induced them to move to Washington, D.C. Mrs. Whittall had donated four Stradivari instruments to the Library of Congress, together with funds sufficient to finance about twenty concerts in the Library each season. The one condition attending her bequest stipulated that the performers should use the Stradivaris both in concert and in rehearsal. In 1940 the Library of Congress approached the Budapest Quartet with an offer for exclusive use of the instruments and a contract for the annual series of concerts—a contract still in force as of this writing.

In the space of twenty years the Budapest Quartet had altered in personnel and had found a new audience. Did this betoken a change too in its way of making music? Was there a significant difference between the "primordial" Budapest Quartet and the ensemble as it evolved with new Russian blood? In answer Roisman concedes that the founding players were inclined to a scholarly approach. When the Russians took over they brought "more life." "Perhaps too much life," Roisman reflects. "We had the over-exuberance of youth. But in its own way it was good. Although we sometimes played too fast, there was a fine spirit." With years of experience, Roisman and his colleagues have learned to temper high spirits without lapsing into stodginess. They have attained sobriety and avoided pedantry.

In arriving at interpretative policy the Budapest Quartet adheres staunchly to the principle of majority rule. On matters of phrasing, tempo, tone, and repertoire a vote of three to one is decisive. Should the vote on a point of interpretation be deadlocked, the musical score decides. In other words, the opinion prevails that stands closest to the composer's markings. As scores can mean different things to different men, this would still seem to leave considerable room for discord. Roisman avows that a player in the minority can have a difficult time of it. "If you have to keep to a tempo that you feel is wrong, it goes against the grain." Especially is it onerous for Roisman, who as first violinist must lead the ensemble. In some quartets this difficulty is obviated by allowing the first violinist to issue interpretative edicts, though such a procedure hardly conforms to the ideal of four musical protagonists in amiable discourse. In the Budapest Quartet each member has a voice; however, the views of Roisman, by virtue of his position, carry somewhat more weight.

A maxim of quartet procedure requires that "during the rehearsal everything must be said; during the performance everything must be forgiven." The Budapest members keep this counsel ever in mind. They may gnaw endlessly over a dispute during the course of an afternoon, but at the evening concert they play as one. That phrase "as one" is not to be underestimated. For more than fifteen years the three old-timers in the quartet have played together without interruption, rehearsing daily for an average of three hours. Such familiarity knits an ensemble wondrously. So cohesive is this string quartet that the extempore deviation of one player is transfused intuitively through all. Often at a concert performance the foursome will depart slightly from the rehearsed interpretation, taking a rubato in one place, bowing a phrase differently in another, always with unconcerned aplomb.

Usually for love, sometimes from a sense of duty, the Budapest Quartet endeavors to play one modern work at every concert. Roisman is reticent when it comes to revealing which composers are a duty and which a passion, allowing merely that Béla Bartók and Paul Hindemith are special favorites. There have been those who reproved the Budapesters for neglecting contemporary music. With these players, it has been charged, music begins with Mozart and ends with Brahms. In truth, for many years the Budapest Quartet followed a markedly conservative line. This stress on the past, however, was not solely of its own making. To offset a prevailingly modern emphasis in the concerts subsidized by Mrs. Coolidge, the Whittall Foundation had stipulated that the Budapest Quartet specialize in eighteenth- and nineteenth-century repertoire. That condition has since been abandoned, with a noticeably modernizing effect on the Budapest's offerings. Lukas Foss, Quincy Porter, Walter Piston, and Samuel Barber have each been the recipients of Budapest attention in recent concerts. The Quartet's most spectacular venture into the contemporary idiom, however, took place not in the concert hall, but in the recording studio, when the four players accounted for a score by Darius Milhaud composed in eight parts. Two of Milhaud's quartets (Nos. 14 and 15) are so written that when played simultaneously they form an octet. In a Columbia recording studio the ensemble began by recording the Quartet No. 14, then put on earphones and recorded Quartet No. 15 while listening to the playback of the former. Afterwards, the engineers superimposed the two recordings so as to produce an octet played by four instrumentalists—an impressive stunt, even though it is generally agreed that a composition in eight parts is most successfully performed in normal fashion by a full-fledged octet.

A ripe, rich-hued tone commends the Budapest Quartet to its many admirers. Only occasionally does its luscious, warm sound become excessive. Spread on too thickly, especially when the composer is Brahms, its tonal sirocco can jade the ear. I have sometimes wished that the Budapest Quartet would set its musical thermostat at a lower reading, especially when it essays the French repertoire, but this is a small defect, easily counterbalanced by the ensemble's cohesion, vitality, and dependable taste. "A phrase played in turn by four instruments," Alfred Pochon once said, "may be compared to four portraits of the same person by four different painters. Although, on comparison, the portraits differ, yet each should resemble the original." The brush strokes of the four Budapesters may vary, but there is never any doubt that each delineates the same subject. If over the years one grows dimly aware of these players' separate musical traits—Roisman's delicate shading of pitch, Kroyt's caressing viola tone, Mischa Schneider's insinuating rhythmic support—individual impressions remain shadowy; it is always the ensemble that dominates the memory, an ensemble of stylistic dependability and intellectual distinction which has afforded countless listeners, myself included, a precious introduction to the chamber-music literature.

IV.

A *Clarinetist* AND A *Guitarist*

☼ Reginald *Kell*

TRADITION had encumbered the clarinet with vows of chastity. In tone the catechism of this instrument dictated undefiled purity; in dynamics, seemly moderation; in phrasing, cool precision. Reginald Kell, risking excommunication, turned clarinet renegade at the age of twenty-five. Sitting at the first-clarinet desks of the London Philharmonic and Royal Opera (Covent Garden) orchestras, young Kell had observed at close quarters all the great instrumentalists and singers of the world. Noting that passion and a personal involvement with music were traits common to every first-rate soloist or opera star, he was forced to the conclusion that the clarinet suffered from too confining a respectability. The demure, virgin estate to which this instrument had been relegated appeared more and more intolerable. "If Heifetz could let fly at the stuff, I decided I could too," Kell explains, and forthwith he stopped treating the clarinet as though it were the pipe organ's vox angelica. By so doing he precipitated a revolution in clarinet-playing and became acknowledged as an outstanding exponent of the instrument.

Reginald Kell was born in 1906 in the cathedral town of York. His father, musical director of a theater, handed Reginald a violin at seven. But young Kell hated the instrument, and when his father went off to war in 1914 he saw a fine opportunity "to chuck the violin under the bed." At fourteen he left school (the legal age in England at that time) and got a job as a machinist in York making dustguards for train axles. On weekends Reginald began to drop in on rehearsals of his father's band; he took a fancy to the clarinet and borrowed an instrument. With a book on "clarinet method" as guide, he started practicing in earnest. Despite this tardy initiation, Kell picked up facility with enchanting speed. Within a month he was performing in his father's band, and a year later—realizing that music was easier to make than dustguards—he went off to a job with a theater orchestra in near-by Harrogate.

To the musically ambitious, Yorkshire's provincialism can be pretty dispiriting. So Kell, aged twenty, set out for London and a position with a cinema orchestra. On one of his first days off he descended upon the Royal Academy of Music to inquire after the possibilities of a scholarship. To his dismay he learned that the only scholarship available was a competitive one open to all instruments—from piccolo to piano. Filled with bravado, but empty of confidence, Kell entered his name on the list of applicants. A fortunate presentiment warned him that a medley from *Rose Marie* might be inappropriate for a Royal Academy competition. What should he play? Mozart's Concerto for Clarinet was suggested. The school might just as well have mentioned a motet by Okeghem. Kell had never heard of the music, but thought he would have a go at it anyway. Much to his surprise he won the scholarship. "They must have wanted a clarinetist," Kell comments. "I'm sure I played the Mozart all wrong."

The new student was soon ushered into the principal's

office and admonished: "You must realize that the Academy intends to make you a good musician, not a good clarinet-player." Kell found himself wrestling with the piano, harmony, counterpoint, and score-reading, to say nothing of intensive study on his own instrument. It did not take long for these several chores to conflict with his orchestra job. Kell got the sack. "Those were some pretty lean times for me," he reflects. But there were compensations, such as a Queen's Hall appearance as soloist in Busoni's Clarinet Concertino.

After two of the scholarship's three years, Kell deserted the Academy in favor of playing first clarinet with the Royal Philharmonic Orchestra. When Sir Thomas Beecham formed the London Philharmonic in 1932, Kell sat at the first-clarinet desk. It was at about this time that the clarinetist determined to cut adrift from the prevailing "white" style of playing in favor of more expressive freedom. At first his colleagues viewed this departure with undisguised misgivings, deeming it showmanship in dubious taste. Kell observed, however, that when he played solo or in chamber music his audiences took notice as never before. In due course other British woodwind-players fell into step with Kell's stylistic innovations.

A financial disagreement with Beecham eventually occasioned the clarinetist's resignation from the London Philharmonic; thereafter, from 1937 until the outbreak of war, he limited his activities to solo work and occasional free-lancing with various British orchestras. August 1939 found Kell in Lucerne, playing first clarinet under Toscanini at the International Festival of Music. The Maestro would have liked to lure Kell to New York and a first desk in the NBC Symphony, but war and a BBC commitment intervened. A year before, when the Munich crisis had been festering, the BBC had singled out sixteen accomplished British instrumentalists and contracted for their services to begin the day war broke out.

Fearing that London's Broadcasting House might be demolished within twenty-four hours after the onset of hostilities, the BBC took no chances on an interruption of radio service. The sixteen musicians, of whom Kell was one, were to be sequestered in an obscure spot in England, ready to broadcast should any emergency arise. Kell's orders were to proceed to a certain secret studio one hundred miles from London when a declaration of war seemed imminent. One morning he picked up a Lucerne newspaper to read that Ribbentrop and Molotov had signed a nonaggression treaty. Kell decided it was time to bid Toscanini a hurried farewell and get back to Blighty.

Anyone who has strolled down Portland Place since the war will know that Broadcasting House was not disintegrated into a heap of rubble. But it received some nasty hits during the mass air attacks on London and lost much of its usefulness for purposes of broadcasting. In those days Kell and his fifteen associates were kept on a busy schedule in their country hideaway, helping to provide BBC listeners with "radio as usual." By the end of 1943, when it seemed that large-scale bombing was a thing of the past, this unit of star instrumentalists was disbanded. Kell, along with several other outstanding British players, joined the Liverpool Philharmonic, which was then enjoying a brief period of glory under Sir Malcolm Sargent's direction. This turned out to be his last assignment as an orchestral musician. As Kell puts it in his blunt Yorkshire way: "When you have to play the same Beethoven symphony six different ways under six different conductors it gets to be pretty trying. Conductors as a whole are more incompetent than orchestral musicians—and that's saying something. There came a time when I could no longer play in an orchestra and keep my self-respect." As a footnote to this stricture it should be observed that Kell himself later took a turn at conducting. He has directed a group of wind-players in some Mozart serenades recorded by Decca.

Late in 1948 the clarinetist came to this country and announced his intention of becoming an American citizen. He lives modestly in a New York suburb with his wife and son, tours a good deal, and teaches. His students have ranged from a sheer beginner (a member of *The New Yorker*'s staff who interviewed Kell for the magazine) to the most accomplished of professionals (Benny Goodman). That such a master as Goodman should come to Kell for instruction bears impressive witness to the Britisher's individual interpretative conceptions.

Kell likes to say that he introduced "vibrato" into clarinet playing. The term is somewhat misleading, for vibrato usually brings to mind the image of a violinist bathing music in tonal treacle. In Kell's usage vibrato connotes no more than the injection of imagination and personality into playing. "I use vibrato," he explains, "as a form of self-expression. I do not play the clarinet, I play music on it. I use it to express my personal feelings in sound." If this sounds excessively subjective, be assured that Kell's interpretations want nothing in the matter of taste or musicianship. His Mozart is the essence of grace and sweetness, his Brahms partakes of a glowing softness, his Weber skips joyously and lightly. This player exploits to the utmost the clarinet's wide dynamic range. One moment his tone will be muted and silvery, the next it will turn explosively sonorous. Abetting this lusty sense of dynamics are Kell's skill in coloring the clarinet's tone and his ability to give shape and contour to a phrase.

To talk to this plain, stolid Yorkshireman you would never guess him to be a musician of such sensibility. Yet his performances, in stature and impact, are of a Casals standard. His sincerity and absorption, his musical imagination, his mastery of instrumental technique all prompt the proposition that Kell's exploits on the clarinet are analogous to the great Spaniard's achievements on the cello.

If Reginald Kell as yet commands neither the prestige of a

Casals nor the fees of a Rubinstein, put this down mainly to public unawareness of the clarinet. That the instrument has any solo standing at all can be credited to missionary work by the phonograph. Even so, most of us are familiar with only a fraction of the total clarinet literature. Two concertos by Weber (as distinct from his Concertino) are reckoned by Kell as superior in interest to Mozart's. Aaron Copland and Paul Hindemith have recently enriched the repertoire with clarinet concertos, while in the domain of chamber music there exist little-known works by Mendelssohn and Milhaud, Schumann and Saint-Saëns, Bartók and Brahms, Bax and Beethoven. Kell's ambition today is to put as much as possible of this varied repertoire on public view.

☼ Andrés *Segovia*

SOUTH of the Pyrenees the man is rare who cannot coax from the guitar's soft-spoken jangle some few simple tunes. The crackle of its thrummed harmonies sounds at bullfights and street festivals, in cafés and over the radio. Never since the twelfth century has the guitar's hold on Spain relaxed. But in speaking of this instrument it is necessary to distinguish two sides of a split personality. One side of its nature is earthy, homespun, uncomplicated, high-spirited, and sometimes a bit raffish—the guitar of the flamencos. The other is aloof, complex, sophisticated—the so-called "classic guitar," the guitar of Andrés Segovia.

It is the reserved, the "classic," guitar that has served as a medium for serious composition, albeit a medium most fitfully employed. In the sixteenth and seventeenth centuries the guitar—or its near relative, the *vihuela*—found strong favor with Iberian composers, who elevated its standing in Spain to an eminence akin to the violin's in Italy or the harpsichord's in France. Toward the middle of the eighteenth century the guitar vogue spread northward to the rest of Europe, in particular to England. On the crest of this billowing interest came Fernando Sor (1778–1839), an outstanding figure in guitar annals both as virtuoso and composer, whom Fétis styled "the Beethoven of the guitar." As the description implies, Sor extended the expressive range of the instrument and greatly enriched its repertoire. Unfortunately, his forward strides went for naught; no sooner had he died than the guitar began to lose ground as a serious musical instrument. England tired of its charms, and in Spain its musical prestige declined quickly. For many decades it kept the stage only in its "popular" role, as an accompanying instrument idly strummed.

Under another adept virtuoso-composer, Francisco Tárrega (1854–1909), the guitar bade fair to blossom again as a reputable solo-instrument. But Tárrega was a shy man who disliked playing in public and who journeyed from Spain only once in his life. Such blossoming as there was yielded little fruit. It remained for Andrés Segovia to restore the guitar to the concert platform. Thanks mainly to his missionary work, the instrument has regained, indeed surpassed, the esteem and popularity that it enjoyed 150 years ago.

The Segovia audience is composed in part of people who venture inside a concert hall only when this guitarist gives his annual recital. They comprise the guitar cult, for whom no other instrument exists, a group at one with Berlioz in his belief that "the guitar is a miniature orchestra." These zealots find in the playing of Segovia sheer physical delight. Each time that his deft fingers pick out a tricky melodic configuration, they lean forward with an almost personal sense of achievement. Balancing this segment of the Segovia audience are others who care less about his mastery of guitar acrobatics and more about his mastery of musical declamation. For Segovia is no mere prestidigitator. He is endowed bounteously with what the French call *musicalité*, that is to say with a powerful instinct for making music speak winningly and cogently.

Of the musicians who figure in this book, Andrés Segovia alone seems fully entitled to the description "self-taught." Such instruction as he received was of the most elementary nature, and inadequate even at that level. The guitarist was born February 18, 1894, in Linares, a dingy Andalusian mining center. The burden of a large family proving too great for his parents, Segovia at an early age was adopted by a more comfortably situated aunt and uncle who lived in Granada. In that city, with its imprint of Moorish civilization, there was much to quicken the appreciation of a sensitive boy. Musically, however, Granada was a backwater. Segovia tried in turn the piano, violin, and cello in an effort to satisfy his early musical leanings, but the local teachers of these accepted concert instruments appeared to him so pettifogging and dull that he revolted, confining his musical efforts thereafter to the guitar. It was then an instrument of no serious pretensions; for some time, in fact, Segovia's affair with the guitar had to be kept clandestine for fear of his guardians' ridicule and disapproval. He started off by learning the technique of flamenco players (which he had afterwards to unlearn). Next, he came upon some music by Sor and Tárrega; then he addressed himself to the problem of sight reading, which he mastered with the aid of a solfeggio book and a manual of music theory.

During the boy's early teens his aunt and uncle died. With the small legacy that they had bequeathed he moved on to Córdoba. A train of acquaintances began to exercise significant influence on Segovia's musical development. An early inamorata initiated Andrés into the great domain that stretched from Beethoven to Brahms. It mattered not that her hands moved haltingly over the piano keyboard. However awkward the playing, music was communicated. This introduction to the piano repertoire was revealing in more than one way: "I realized," Segovia has related,* "what it meant to study with discipline so varied and complex an instrument as the piano. I understood then that the methods for studying the guitar were of a Franciscan poverty compared to the number, variety, and progressive order of the exercises contained in any book of piano technique, whether elementary or advanced. Far from discouraging me, however, this realization kindled in me a new interest in the problems of my own instrument. I carefully observed the efficacy of each study, how it made the fingers work, and what degree of independence, strength, and agility it developed in them. When I got back to my room, I would try to apply my observations to the technique of the guitar, and it brought me an indescribable joy to discover that the exercises I had worked out were also increasing the vigor, elasticity, and rapidity of my fingers." Segovia's principles of fingering have remained unchanged since that period. When today he prescribes exercises for advanced students they are the ones he evolved decades ago from a set of piano *études*.

Further friendships served to extend his musical awareness. A wealthy amateur guitarist, one Don Tomás Garrido, put at Segovia's disposal some unpublished manuscripts of Tárrega. This was probably the music that Segovia played when he began to perform in amateur concerts. At a Córdoba musicale he met Rafael de Montis, a young aristocrat who had heard many celebrated virtuosos during a protracted visit to Germany. De Montis was not the first person to find merit in Segovia's playing, but his praise was the first to give the guitarist real confidence. Previous commendation had come from provincials without the assurance of cosmopolitan standards; it had been blended, moreover, with skepticism concerning the guitar's station in life. Most Spaniards could not accept this household instrument as equal to the piano or violin. Rafael de Montis both appreciated Segovia's virtuosity and foresaw a

* In "The Guitar and Myself," *The Guitar Review* No. 4 (1947).

worthy future for the guitar. His encouragement emboldened Segovia to attempt a concert career.

Segovia's first professional recital took place in Granada, where—he reasoned—"old friends would make up with their affection for my failure, if such it should be." The date was 1910 (Segovia being then sixteen years old) and the recital was not a failure. Still, there was much to learn before he could enter his name on major musical lists. For six more years the guitarist labored unremittingly to increase the level of his technique and the scope of his repertoire. He gave occasional concerts in small halls. In time he moved to Madrid, where he heard for the first time musical interpreters of international stature. He was particularly moved by Alfred Cortot and Pablo Casals.

What Segovia calls his "real debut" took place in the Madrid Ateneo in 1916. During the preceding six years he had given concerts in several Spanish towns and in the smaller auditoriums of Madrid. But those were more in the nature of shakedown cruises than of a maiden voyage. The Ateneo is Spain's Carnegie Hall, and Segovia did not risk an encounter with its discriminating audience until he felt fully equal to the occasion. That "real debut" laid the foundation for Segovia's great success in Spain, a success owed in large measure to his unprecedented agility with the guitar, but also to the imagination and taste revealed in his choice of programs. The efflorescence of Spanish music in the sixteenth century, especially music written for the obsolete *vihuela,* was then a phenomenon to be appreciated rather more in the library than in the concert hall. Segovia mined this bountiful deposit of unplayed music, reviving the works of Luis Milan, Anrequez de Valderrábano, Alonso de Mudarra, and other sixteenth-century *vihuelists.* The groundwork had been laid over a decade earlier by Count Guillermo Morphy, the man who so decisively furthered the early career of Pablo Casals. Morphy had rummaged through the royal archives and edited a modern edition of *vihuela* music (*Les luthistes espagnols du XVIe siècle*, Leipzig, 1902), but it was Segovia who breathed life into his researches by adapting these compositions to the guitar and introducing them to audiences the world over.

Within a few years of the Ateneo debut Segovia's repertoire could boast of some music that was "tailored to his own measurements." The first composer to honor him so was Moreno Torroba, followed soon by Joaquín Turina and Manuel de Falla. In the years since, a considerable body of guitar literature has been composed for Segovia. I should not like to vouch for the quality of all this music. In at least one instance, Falla's gaunt *Homenaje: pour le tombeau de Debussy*, the Segovia guitar has inspired a minor masterpiece; in a few other instances—Turina's *Fantasia*, to take one example—it has provided a medium for first-rate "effect music." Some pieces with the superscription "Dedicated to Andrés Segovia" impress this listener as belonging to a fairly low echelon of contemporary composition. For this the guitarist himself is partly to blame. He looks askance at most modern art—whether it comes from the hand of Stravinsky, Joyce, or Picasso—and has thus isolated his instrument from many first-rate talents of our day.

Until 1923 Segovia confined his activity to Spain and the large Spanish-speaking cities of Latin America. There he could be sure of an audience predisposed to his instrument. But he did not know whether the guitar would appeal to listeners who did not have it in their blood. A season in Paris sufficed to dispel any insecurity that Segovia may have harbored. He made his *entrée* in the house of Henri Prunières, eminent French musicologist, who invited a group of high-placed musicians (Maurice Ravel among them) to hear the amazing young Spaniard and his adaptations of the old *vihuela* literature. Thanks to their accolade, Segovia's first Paris concert attracted a capacity audience. Thereafter, he embarked on extensive concert tours that took him to England, Germany, Scandinavia, Soviet Russia, and eventually the United States, which he first visited in 1928 through the good offices of Pablo Casals, who persuaded his own manager to import the guitarist for a New York debut.

Two by-products of Segovia's German tours are worth mentioning. It was during the early years of the Weimar Republic that he came across Hans Dagobert Bruger's complete edition of Bach's compositions for lute. Soon these works, transcribed for the guitar, began to appear on Segovia's programs. He has always taken care to adapt only such music as fits the potentialities of his instrument, which means keeping mainly to music written for the guitar's close relations—in Bach's case, the lute. One seeming exception would appear to be the guitarist's transcription of Bach's Chaconne, a pillar of the violin repertoire. When I asked Segovia why he had trespassed into this alien territory, he explained: "It is not so alien as it appears. The Chaconne is perfectly suited to the guitar. In fact, I am almost persuaded that Bach wrote it originally for the lute and later adapted it for violin, although it is only in the latter form that the work has come down to us. It is written in D, the best key for guitar, and the harmonic pattern of the variations bears a strong resemblance to Andalusian folk music." Whether or not Bach originally intended this work to be played on a guitar-like instrument I leave to judgment more expert than my own. As regards its effectiveness in the Segovia version I am on safer ground. In his interpretation the work is dry, sunlit, transparent, as ordered as a garden of Le Nôtre. The Chaconne bulks less formidably on the guitar, ceases to be an interpretative problem child—particularly because of the guitar's ability to play chords, so laboriously "double-stopped" by violinists and so easily dispatched with one stroke of the guitarist's hand.

Germany also provided Segovia with his favorite instrument.

On a trip to Munich in the early twenties he met a *luthier* who desired to fashion a new guitar for him. The first attempt, Segovia says, "had no soul," even though it was an exact reproduction of the Spanish guitar on which he then played. Each year this artisan submitted another instrument for Segovia's approval until finally, in 1935, he produced a guitar that was deemed perfect in every respect. Although it is of modern manufacture, its ingredients are ancient, for this guitar is constructed of wood taken from a seventeenth-century harpsichord. To Segovia's way of thinking, the harpsichord serves its best purpose when it is sawed up to provide wood for a guitar. He does not care at all for the harpsichord's "metallic jangle" and quotes approvingly Debussy's description of the guitar as "an *expressive* harpsichord." Segovia still uses the 1935 Munich instrument in his concerts. He receives guitars from three continents, but none can compare to the German product in tone and volume.

With the Spanish Civil War in full spate Segovia was forced in 1937 to give up his Barcelona home. He has not returned since to his native land. Following his removal, the guitarist settled in Uruguay. In 1943, after an absence of five years, he returned to the United States, where he has been a yearly visitor since. His old-fashioned apartment in New York, furnished with massive Spanish antiques, well reflects Segovia's old-fashioned personality. He is truly "a gentleman of the old school," mild, relaxed, courtly. His conversation may embrace music, literature, painting, or world affairs, but he does not wax polemical or fail to apprehend what another says. A disciplined calm permeates his home, his conversation, his playing. To Segovia, clarity is an article of faith. He knows of no more damaging epithet than the adjective "chaotic."

I have mentioned the guitar cult that helps to swell Segovia's audience. Its fervor is not for me, even though I am sensible of the instrument's perils and of how disarmingly Segovia transcends them. He manages to coax an amazing variety of sounds from the guitar. What is more, he works solely to the best interest of music and does not avail himself of crude effects calculated to gammon the easily impressed listener. Yet, granting these digital and artistic accomplishments, it is hard for me to rivet my attention on the guitar's soft tinkle for much more than an hour; I find myself applauding Segovia with more enthusiasm just before the intermission than just after the final encore. Fortunately, it is during the first half—while the ear is yet receptive—that Segovia plays the early lute and guitar music of which he is one of the rare exponents: the sweet modal *Pavanes* by Luis Milan, the elegant suites of Robert de Visée (guitarist to Louis XV), or the charming *galant* sonatinas of Mauro Giuliani. More than merely exhuming this music, Segovia re-creates it as only a master can. His feeling for tempos, his employment of rubatos, and his delicate placement of accents are worth anybody's study.

Because of Segovia's faith in the instrument, the guitar is enjoying today its highest estate since the eighteenth century. Not only in the conservatories of Spain, but also in Geneva, Florence, and Brussels there are now regular classes in guitar technique and literature. An ever-increasing roster of students would seem to assure the instrument's future—until one remembers that a like popularity 150 years ago dissolved precipitously. Only a rash man would predict its place in the musical firmament fifty years hence. But one can be assured that so long as Andrés Segovia is present to argue its case the guitar will not want for supporters.

V ☼

Pianists AND A *Harpsichordist*

☼ Robert *Casadesus*

Robert Casadesus, born in Paris on April 7, 1899, claims musical antecedents of almost Bachian number. Grandfather Casadesus, a Catalan (hence the unusual name) who acquired French citizenship in the Franco-Prussian War, grew so enamored of the violin that he resolved to direct all his sons toward musical careers. In this he was eminently successful. Four of his sons appear in Grove's *Dictionary*: Francis, conductor, composer, and founder of the American Conservatory at Fontainebleau; Henri-Gustave, founder of the Society of Ancient Instruments; Marius, violinist; and Marcel, cellist. The fifth son, Robert Casadesus *père*, was a renegade in this family of musicians. He preferred the stage, where he achieved success under the simplified name of Robert Casa. New Yorkers of the older generation may remember him from World War I days, when he was dispatched by his government to direct the New York Théâtre Français. The predilection for greasepaint on the part of Robert *père* did not pass on to Robert *fils*. His mother died in childbirth, and young Robert's upbringing was entrusted to his Aunt Rose, who carried on the family profession by teaching piano. This musical environment, together with grandfatherly promptings, more than sufficed to start him on the expected career. At ten years of age he was a member of the solfège class at the Paris Conservatoire. Three years later he began serious piano studies with one of the Conservatoire's most illustrious teachers, Louis Diémer, among whose former pupils were Edouard Risler and Alfred Cortot. By 1913 Casadesus rated the *premier prix de piano*. When his father entered government service a year later, the fledgling decided it was time to earn his own living. There followed a few years in the Opéra-Comique orchestra, where he played the celesta, gongs, and bells until he was drafted toward the end of the war. Before he saw active service the Armistice was signed. In 1920, having re-entered the Conservatoire the year before, Casadesus received another coveted award, the Prix Diémer, which brought with it not only a sum of money, but concert engagements as well. Meanwhile the pianist had commenced an ancillary career as composer. For the moment one need merely note the significant role that his Opus 2, Six Pieces for Two Pianos, played in shaping Casadesus's future life. He showed the work in manuscript to Professor Diémer. It was at this meeting that the teacher introduced Casadesus to his latest (and, as it happened, his last) prize pupil, Gaby L'Hôte. Three years later, in 1922, Gaby became Mme Casadesus.

They settled for a short while in Fontainebleau, where Robert's Uncle Francis had recently established the American Conservatory. Robert taught piano until increasing concert-demands crowded out pedagogy. As scion of an eminent musical family and as a skillful pianist in his own right, he began to move in exalted circles. France's greatest living composer took a benevolent interest in him. Actually, Casadesus's first encounter with Maurice Ravel dated back to

1912, the occasion being the *première* of the ballet *Ma Mère l'Oye*, when the composer, on hand to supervise rehearsals, halted the orchestra to demand: "Celesta, play louder." The erring instrumentalist was Casadesus. When formally introduced to Ravel a decade later, he had outgrown the necessity to earn a few extra francs in theater orchestras. In 1922, at one of the weekly concerts of contemporary music organized by *La Revue musicale*, two works by Ravel were allotted to the young pianist: "*Le Gibet*" from *Gaspard de la nuit* and the Toccata from *Le Tombeau de Couperin.* The composer expressed a desire to hear Casadesus's interpretations, and is said to have commended him particularly for sustaining the slow tempo throughout the whole of "*Le Gibet*," in which Ricardo Viñes, "official" interpreter of Ravel's piano music, habitually accelerated the tempo for fear that attention might otherwise flag. Ravel, a meticulous indicator of tempos, was naturally gratified to discover in Casadesus a pianist who paid scrupulous heed to his markings.

The friendship thus initiated burgeoned a few months later, when Casadesus accompanied Ravel to London, where the composer was to record piano rolls for the Æolian Company. According to those who heard him, Ravel was an indifferent pianist. His hands stiffened at the instrument; his playing sounded taut and insecure. Because of these technical limitations, Ravel chose to record for Æolian only a few of his easier compositions—the Sonatine, *Pavanne pour une infante défunte*, *Menuet antique*—while such hurdles as *Jeux d'eau* and *Ondine* were left for Casadesus's more agile fingers. Later that year the two were heard in public in the original four-hand version of *Ma Mère l'Oye*. They performed together subsequently on many occasions. Lyon, Brussels, Barcelona, and Madrid were visited by the duo, and once (in 1930) they appeared in the tiny Basque town of Ciboure, where Ravel had been born.

Ravel's rather ineffectual piano-playing influenced Casadesus little; Debussy's playing, on the other hand, created a deep impression. Casadesus describes Debussy as the most relaxed, supple, softly nuanced pianist he has ever heard. "Listening to Debussy," he says, "was for me a lesson of immeasurable significance. It taught me the extraordinary importance of understatement as a means to musical expression." Casadesus found a strong resemblance between Debussy's pianism and the descriptions of Chopin's. In interpreting music by the Polish master he frankly endeavors to emulate Debussy. He agrees, moreover, with André Gide that Chopin must be interpreted in such a way that his music seems almost to be improvised; for this pianist, as for Gide, Chopin never fully reveals himself in a high-strung, virtuosic performance.

During the twenties and early thirties Casadesus toured Europe, North Africa, and South America. In 1935 he made his United States debut, playing Mozart's "Coronation" Concerto with the New York Philharmonic under Hans Lange. No one seemed to take much notice of the French pianist except Arturo Toscanini, who was prompted to engage him as soloist for one of his own programs the following season. When Casadesus performed the Brahms B-flat Concerto on January 30, 1936, he occasioned much more comment—not all of it favorable. Critical opinion allowed the pianist an excess of vigor and muscular drive, complained of a deficiency in poetry and nuance (a condition fairly common among Toscanini soloists). Although subsequent recitals elicited greater enthusiasm, the pianist's first years in this country did not follow a pattern of unquestionable triumph. Walter Gieseking, whose mastery of French music had won him a devoted following, bulked as a formidable rival.

When Hitler overran Europe, Gieseking decided to stay in Germany. Casadesus managed to reach the United States, whereupon the office of French pianistic plenipotentiary devolved upon him. His tours grew, and he was engaged by numerous symphony orchestras as a soloist. Columbia Records contracted for a variety of recordings, and by the war's end the Telephone Hour had bestowed its accolade. Meanwhile Casadesus had done yeoman duty for the American Conservatory of Fontainebleau. When the Germans invaded France, Fontainebleau alumni in this country resolved that their school should carry on in America for the duration. Casadesus devoted each summer to directing this institution, which set up shop first in Newport, Rhode Island, and later in the Berkshires. One year after V-E day, Casadesus returned to France and re-established—with aid from the French government—the American Conservatory in its old home at Fontainebleau.

It is a source of considerable vexation to Casadesus that the public views him as a pianist who happens to compose. For him it is just the other way around. He enjoys playing, but his mission in life he takes to be composing. In view of the depredations, in time and energy, of a concert career, Casadesus's three symphonies, six concertos, nine sonatas, and the several other works comprising his forty-odd opus numbers add up to an impressive total. Some composers (Poulenc is one) like to note on the printed score the locale of the music's gestation. For Casadesus such geographical limitation would often be impossible. He usually composes on the wing: a work may be conceived in his winter home in Princeton, develop on trains and in hotel rooms throughout the United States, come to fruition on a transatlantic steamer, and be finally revised in his Paris home on the rue Vaneau.

Casadesus's music is mildly modern in language, but classic in form and content (Mozart could not have believed more heartily in the tonic-dominant relationship). His style seems to derive most appreciably from Albert Roussel, though at times one can trace in it the unmistakable influence of Gabriel

Fauré. Debussy and Ravel, for all the pianist's mastery of their music, seem to have affected his composing little, if at all. Casadesus feels keenly the disadvantage under which music from a performer's pen generally suffers. When he plays it, his music gets a hearing. Otherwise, it receives scant attention and less praise. When Charles Munch conducted Casadesus's Symphony No. 1 in Paris shortly after the war, the critics viewed the music sourly. A few weeks later Casadesus and his wife appeared as soloists in his Concerto for Two Pianos. This time the same critics overflowed with gentle approbation. The composer refuses to believe that these two works are of such unequal merit. He threatens to launch his next nonpianistic work under a name other than Robert Casadesus, on the theory that its chances for a critical imprimatur will thus be greatly enhanced. For keyboard music he is his own best proselytizer. Indeed, the only contemporary music that this pianist plays in public is his own. He recognizes a certain imbalance here, but pleads lack of time as validating excuse. Working on his regular repertoire, touring the world, and composing music leaves no time, he claims, for the addition of other contemporary works to his programs.

"It has been considered as the misfortune of first-rate talents for the stage that they leave no record behind them except that of vague rumor, and that the genius of a great actor perishes with him, 'leaving the world no copy.'" Hazlitt's dictum of 1817 applies today with far less force. The interpreter of words or music has now the means to perpetuate his art. Even so, the copy left to the world may not be perfect (until recently Casadesus often fared poorly in the recording studio). Records, too, have a way of disappearing from the catalogues once the performer is no longer on hand to command box-office prestige. Many of the discs made by Rachmaninoff have already become collector's items; Rachmaninoff's music, on the other hand, gains yearly in popularity. Perhaps it is the desire to leave behind something more substantial than "vague rumor" that impels Casadesus to concentrate on composition. It is for the future to decide whether he has been an important composer who also played the piano or an eminent pianist who also composed.

☼ Walter *Gieseking*

"THE MOST tragic thing in the world," says Bernard Shaw's bedside *raisonneur*, "is a man of genius who is not also a man of honor." When genius expresses itself through art, the tragedy of which Shaw wrote becomes that much more burdensome, and the dilemma quickly arises whether to accept the artist on purely æsthetic terms and let the acting man slumber in the oblivion of easy forgetfulness, or to hold honor high and dispense with genius at no matter what the loss. The case of Walter Gieseking can serve to clothe this philosophical predicament with musical substance.

One may question how important were the transgressions of Gieseking, but that he is suspect of a certain political flabbiness would seem undeniable. He belonged to that large class of German citizens who appear to have acquiesced to Nazism without ever signing on the dotted line. Expediency ruled his conduct. He ended his letters with "*Heil Hitler*," not because he dearly esteemed the *Führer*, but because that was the normal valediction. He admired the music of Debussy and Ravel, though not so much that he would break a law when performance of their works was forbidden in Germany. He deplored the racial bigotry imposed on the magazine *Musikerziehrer*, but did not withdraw his name from the masthead. He was fond of his Jewish manager in Germany, but quickly dispensed with his services when to do so seemed advisable. He denies any sympathy with Hitler's New Order ("this is so silly that it would make me laugh if it wasn't so stupid and insulting to me"), yet he made no move to sever his connection with the Nazi State.

This latter is probably the most damaging fact against him. Along with other German citizens of world renown, Gieseking was in a favored position to protest against the political autocracy and moral barbarism that had descended upon his country. A large non-German income and an extensive international reputation presumably rendered him immune to financial and personal constraint, and as beckoning examples there were such other "good Aryans" as Thomas Mann, Fritz Busch, and Toscanini. Gieseking declined to join this distinguished roster of expatriates who put political morality above the flag.

Readers who have persevered thus far will know that my concern in this book is not with the involutions of personality. These are musical, not psychological, essays. Some of the musicians discussed herein may be avaricious and unpleasantly self-centered, they may be unfaithful husbands and tyrannical fathers, but in so far as these characteristics have no concern with art, they have been ignored. I introduce the matter of Gieseking's political behavior only because of the position he holds in the musical hierarchy. It is a question of *noblesse oblige*.

If anyone can claim musical nobility, it is Walter Gieseking. On the basis of his prewar concerts and postwar records, I would rate Gieseking as the most accomplished of living pianists, a performer of rare technical facility who is unapproached in encompassing mastery of musical style. He plays with like perception Bach and Scriabin, Beethoven and Debussy, Schumann and Ravel. His specialty, if he could be said to have one, is music by the so-called French Impressionist composers. Here the variety of his tonal chiaroscuro, the delicacy of his melodic tracery, is unique. In the *Images* and *Préludes* of Debussy or the *Gaspard de la nuit* of Ravel he has set a standard just as surely as Toscanini has with the Verdi Requiem or Casals with unaccompanied Bach. But it is misleading to talk of specialties in connection with an interpreter of Gieseking's catholic taste. The touchstone that he provides for the interpretation of Debussy is by no means his only achievement. He plays Bach with strength and clarity, Schumann with radiant poetry, Mozart and early Beethoven with gentle grace. His reading of late Beethoven sonatas is remarkable for cogency of expression and wealth of tone. He has one blind spot, the music of Chopin—doubtless a major lapse, but not sufficient, in my opinion, to challenge his pre-eminence in the fraternity of contemporary pianists. One expects much from a musician of this stature. One expects him, as a human being, to set the same kind of example as his musical peers Toscanini and Casals. But in the crucial decade after 1933 Gieseking did not live up to these expectations.

He was born November 5, 1895, in Lyon, where his father—a German doctor—was then practicing. Aside from musical training, he was never exposed to formal schooling, perhaps because his parents did not wish their son to attend a French-speaking school. Fortunately, there was a piano in the Gieseking home in Lyon, and Walter seems to have picked up a serviceable technique by himself. When the Giesekings moved back to Germany in 1911, the boy entered the Hanover Conservatory, where he studied for three years with Karl Leimer.

"At the conservatory," he recalls, "I worked on nothing but technique. After that it was there, and I could forget about it."

Gieseking's Berlin debut was scheduled for the season of 1914–15, but war and the requirements of the German Army intervened, and the debut did not take place until 1920, when he played a program featuring the works of Debussy and Ravel. This predilection for French music is not traceable to his boyhood in Lyon, for it was only upon studying in Germany, he says, that he came into contact with French music. The inclusion of Debussy and Ravel in his first Berlin recital was intended mainly to attract those newspaper critics obliged to choose from among three or four simultaneous concerts. Gieseking's bait—an all-modern program heavily larded with music that was still considered *avant-garde*—snared his prey. The critics came and lavished such praise that Gieseking had to give seven Berlin recitals during his first season. Desirous of repeating his initial success, he kept to the modern French repertoire in subsequent recitals. Thus it was that he became established early in his career as an exponent of the Debussy-Ravel idiom.

In 1923 he ventured across the Rhine, in 1926 across the Atlantic, and wherever he played he was expected to perform contemporary music. To master this repertoire Gieseking and his former teacher, Karl Leimer, developed a method of memorization and a technique for working out musical interpretation away from the piano. According to this method, one should never touch the piano until every note of a composition is memorized, until all questions of fingering, pedaling, and the like are decided in abstract. A pianist of the Gieseking-Leimer persuasion intellectualizes an interpretation before he muscularizes it; once he has a piece of music thoroughly in mind, the actual playing is said to come easily. Gieseking inveighs against the concept that practice makes perfect. "It is necessary to enter into the mood of a piece, to retain one's spontaneity, and this is impossible," he insists, "if one practices incessantly."

Gieseking's New York debut (January 10, 1926) set off a volley of critical praise which resounded across the country. He returned to the United States annually thereafter until 1938, made increasingly long tours, and became one of the most potent of box-office attractions. Early in 1939, with Austria and Czechoslovakia already overtaken by the first flood of Nazi aggression, Gieseking completed his thirteenth season in the United States, and sailed for Germany and his Wiesbaden home. Plans had been made for his usual American tour to begin late in 1939, but the 145 concerts that were booked never materialized. Inability to obtain transportation was given as the reason for Gieseking's remaining in Germany —an explanation that has never seemed fully convincing. In December 1939, when the pianist was due to depart, the war was still in its "phony" stage and egress from Germany (via Lisbon or the Trans-Siberian Railway) posed no insurmountable problem. Inasmuch as many German nationals managed to travel to this country by means of regular public transportation as late as the spring of 1941, it would seem fairly plausible that considerations other than Britain's blockade influenced the cancellation of Gieseking's 1939–40 American tour. Reasons of personal safety (the fear of becoming an enemy alien through United States involvement in the war) may have been persuasive.

As it turned out, Hitler's *festung Europa* proved to be a fertile field for Gieseking's musical activities. During five years of total war he toured the Continent—Germany, the occupied countries, and the few neutrals spared by the *Wehrmacht*. Altogether he gave 196 recitals outside the borders of Germany, the great majority of which were arranged through regular concert-management channels. Such bookings, it seems, were endorsed but not instigated by Berlin authorities. However, Gieseking has admitted to performing in a few foreign countries at the direct behest of Goebbels's henchmen. Paramount among his foreign propaganda-missions was a series of recitals given in Turkey in 1944. "The Propaganda Ministry was most insistent," he explained later on.

With the fall of the Third Reich in May 1945, Gieseking kept close to his home in Wiesbaden. That autumn he was blacklisted and denied further public appearance by the American Military Government on the charge that "he was under suspicion of having given concerts during the Nazi regime in foreign countries"—a suspicion that subsequent investigation proved to have been founded on fact. But Gieseking's case has never yielded to fact or strict legal interpretation; æsthetic predilections and philosophical dialectic have a way of creeping in. It soon became obvious that the silencing of this artist was extremely unpopular with the British and French occupation authorities; further, that even within the U. S. Army's Information Control Division considerable difference of opinion existed. Matters simmered for a year until, in December 1946, the blacklisting was repealed, though the charges on which it was predicated had never been controverted.

Having been formally "cleared" by the Military Government, Gieseking began to resume his prewar career. Throughout 1947 the pianist gave concerts in all occupation zones of Germany, as well as in Switzerland and Italy. In December of that year he appeared on what was presumably unfriendly soil, playing concertos by Mozart and Liszt with the Colonne Orchestra in Paris, and evoking "a delirious reception." Three weeks later more than a thousand would-be listeners were turned away from Gieseking's sold-out recital in the mammoth Palais de Chaillot. Paris having bestowed its valued accolade, the rest of Europe came easily. Soon there were appearances in Holland (a country notoriously hostile to its own Nazi collaborators) and in London, where the pianist made his first postwar recordings. In the summer of 1948 he reconquered South America. Nothing then remained but for him to reinstate his reputation with the North American public, and to that end he set up plans for his fourteenth United States tour, to begin in New York on January 24, 1949.

But at this juncture something happened to interrupt his rehabilitation in international musical society. Gieseking arrived at New York's La Guardia Airport one day before the scheduled recital. During the afternoon preceding his concert he went to Carnegie Hall to reacquaint himself with this auditorium's acoustics. Passing through the stage door, Gieseking undoubtedly noticed with satisfaction the words "Sold Out" overprinted on placards announcing the concert. It looked as though New York were to follow a pattern set in Paris, London, and Buenos Aires. But late that afternoon the pattern was broken. At the last minute the Department of Justice ordered Gieseking's concert canceled and requested the pianist's immediate removal from the country. This news was broadcast in the early evening, too late to save several hundred ticket-holders from a fruitless trip to Carnegie Hall. The pianist flew back to Paris the following morning, and as of this writing he has not attempted another North American tour.

Even those who were opposed to Gieseking's renewed participation in our musical life regretted the high-handed manner in which his New York recital was prohibited. It was generally felt that a decision should have been made long before Gieseking left Europe, and that if national policy forbade the appearance of a musician suspected of Nazi sympathies, it should have been so stated weeks in advance and not three hours before a sold-out concert. In this as in several other postwar instances (the Austrian conductor Josef Krips underwent a similar experience) the State Department, which issues visas, and the Justice Department, which has jurisdiction over aliens, seem to have been in basic disagreement.

Since the *contretemps* of January 1949 the complexion of international affairs has shifted radically. Germany is being revived, and the canker of Nazism is receding in the face of a new danger. Everywhere but in North America, Gieseking is welcomed and extolled, and even here his recordings sell well and receive critical praise. Doubtless this pianist, who is now at the height of his interpretative powers, will return before too long. Despite the rebuff of 1949, I believe that he would welcome the opportunity to tour again in the United States, which is still the world's most profitable area for concerts. Nowadays Gieseking is trying to rebuild the fortune that he lost after the war when the Russians reportedly confiscated his Berlin bank account. He wants now to fill the largest auditoriums, which means that he plays the type of program a mass audience will relish. Gone are the days when Gieseking stood in the vanguard of the latest musical fashions, when his name was attached to programs compounded entirely of contemporary works. Whatever missionary zeal he once had seems to have vanished. Today he is full of reservations about contemporary piano music. He believes that the best of present-day composition is not for piano; he knows of no pianistic counterpart to the quality of a score like Stravinsky's *Orpheus*.

A detailed consideration of this musician *qua* musician should await the day when he picks up the thread of his interrupted American career. More needs to be said of his technique, with its incredible lightness, its impalpable *pianissimi*, its gossamer magic (in such contrast to the effortful movements of his hulking body); and the boundaries of his stylistic skill need to be more precisely charted: Gieseking, though catholic, is not omniscient. It is risky, however, to pinpoint the characteristics of a musician *in absentia*. This chapter can attempt no more than to sketch the details of a career that, in its political ramifications, has been a disappointment to those of us who are prone (mistakenly, I fear) to equate artistic sensibility with human goodness.

☼ Myra *Hess*

"ALL-BRITISH Manufacture" could be stamped on Myra Hess's passport. She was born on February 25, 1890, in Hampstead, a north London suburb redolent with memories of Keats and Constable. Progress under various piano teachers led to a scholarship at the Royal Academy of Music when she was thirteen. There she studied with Tobias Matthay, a pioneer in the "science" of piano technique, sometimes dubbed "the English Leschetitzky." Previously, her training had been wanting in organization and discipline; there was, as Matthay's wife reported years later, considerable "scrimmaging and bolting" in her playing before "Uncle Toby" took her in hand. Under his guidance she acquired a poised and consistent artistry. Dame Myra insists that her success is directly owing to Matthay. "He developed my mind, which very much needed developing." He developed also rhythmic control and bodily relaxation, two Matthay legacies persuasively evidenced in her playing. Disciplined rubato, whereby time taken from one measure is restored to another, amounted to an article of faith with Matthay.

To him time could be "bent but not broken"; rubato existed to bestow life and shape to music, but was not to be an end in itself, perceptible as such. He was of a meticulously scientific disposition, believing that the "mystery" of good piano-playing was reducible to rational analysis and verbal explanation. "What made him a great man and a great teacher," according to Dame Myra, "is that he never once lost sight of music despite his scientific leanings." Precepts that with him were never categorical, she says, have since been crudely exaggerated. For instance, Matthay emphasized a relaxed wrist—this in reaction to the Clementi-inspired dogma of playing with a hand so stiff that a penny would remain neatly balanced thereon—but, says Dame Myra, he would never have endorsed the flabbiness so often prescribed in his name.

Myra Hess studied with Matthay until he died, in 1945, aged eighty-seven. Her intensive work with him, however, ended in 1907. During that year she made her first professional appearance in London, playing Beethoven's G major Concerto with a young English conductor named Thomas Beecham. The reviews were complimentary to a degree, as they were again a few months later when she gave a first solo-recital in Æolian Hall. But, like most young artists, she had to learn that a few cordial notices in the press do not butter bread. There was nothing "sensational" about this serious, sincere young woman; it could hardly be said that her manager was flooded with offers of engagements. For over a decade she earned her living in large part by teaching, many of the students being routed in her direction by Matthay. Those virtuosos who spring from a debut recital into international prominence do not overly excite Dame Myra's envy. She has found her years of teaching beneficial in many ways, and recommends a similar course of action for any aspiring concert artist.

With each succeeding musical season the number of her public appearances increased. In 1914 Willem Mengelberg invited her to appear with the Amsterdam Concertgebouw Orchestra, a coveted engagement that helped to establish her reputation. By 1922 an American manager was willing to book her for a few recitals. That first visit caught the fancy of critics and public alike. Of her debut recital Richard Aldrich wrote in the *New York Times*:

> An extraordinary artist made her appearance in New York yesterday afternoon without preliminary heralding. . . . She is a true interpreter and makes her interpretations deeply engrossing through their vitality, their finesse and subtle qualities, their intensity and glowing warmth.

Aldrich continued in this approving vein for several paragraphs, and he was seconded by equally enthusiastic comments from W. J. Henderson of the *Sun*. Hats were thrown into the air, with the predictable result: another New York recital and an extended tour of the country. When she returned to England in the summer, Myra Hess cut rather more of a figure than when she had left.

For sixteen subsequent seasons she returned to America. From the outset she refused to trifle with audiences in this country; over the protests of her manager she played the same program in Lincoln, Nebraska, as she had in New York. This respect for her art and her listeners, allied to a rare understanding of nineteenth-century music, enabled Miss Hess to hold her own against such meteoric rivals as Vladimir Horowitz and Walter Gieseking. Certain music—the Schumann Concerto, for example—was said to be hers alone.

The season of 1939–40 promised to repeat more or less the preceding seventeen, the first half given to England, the second to America. But Great Britain's declaration of war on September 3, 1939, changed everything. War was declared on a Sunday. The following morning British newspapers were freighted with emergency orders from the government, among them a decree shutting down all theaters, movie houses, and concert halls. While London was growing acclimated to the blackout and to other wartime disruptions, there was wisdom in so drastic a measure, but as the opening days of the "phony war" grew into weeks it became plain that London could not subsist entirely on whatever cultural fare emanated from the BBC. It was toward the end of September that Myra Hess put forward the idea of chamber-music concerts in the National Gallery, the century-old building on Trafalgar Square which had already been emptied of its art treasures. Situated in what the guide books call "the heart of the British Empire," the National Gallery seemed an ideal spot for midday concerts. Miss Hess began negotiations. Within a matter of days the trustees of the Gallery gave their consent and the Home Office relaxed its ban on public gatherings. On October 6 it was announced that lunchtime concerts would be featured in the National Gallery every day from Monday to Friday, with an admission charge of one shilling.

Because no one knew how London's public would respond, Miss Hess shouldered the responsibility of the first concert herself. Although at most two hundred people were expected, close to one thousand came to hear her play the "*Appassionata*" Sonata, Brahms intermezzos, and Schubert waltzes. Obviously, London craved musical activity, war or no. Having demonstrated this, Myra Hess might easily have exclaimed "I told you so," and—dumping the National Gallery project in the lap of a committee—have taken the next boat to America. But a cable went off to her manager in New York canceling the tour that had already been arranged for the early months of 1940. America was advised that she would remain in England for the duration.

Now came the task of rounding up talent for five concerts a

week, and of maintaining musical standards. How well she succeeded can be seen from the collected programs of five and one-half years of National Gallery concerts, where can be found listed the complete chamber music of Beethoven (including several cycles of the string quartets and violin sonatas); the complete chamber music of Brahms; all twenty-one piano concertos of Mozart; all thirty-two piano sonatas of Beethoven; both books of *The Well-Tempered Clavier*; forty-five string quartets by Haydn; the six quartets of Béla Bartók. Schumann's *Dichterliebe* was sung nine times, Schubert's *Die Schöne Müllerin* six. Bach's *Musikalische Opfer* and *Kunst der Fuge* were each presented three times. It would be idle to maintain that these performances were invariably of the highest order. Balancing gala occasions, as when Elena Gerhardt and Miss Hess collaborated in songs of Schumann, were concerts of a far less exalted nature. But the well of first-rate talent was far from dry: it included Harriet Cohen, Mark Hambourg, Louis Kentner, Moura Lympany, Denis Matthews, Benno Moiseiwitsch, and Solomon among the pianists; Yelly d'Aranyi, Isolde Menges, and Albert Sammons among the violinists; Astra Desmond, Kathleen Ferrier, and Peter Pears among the singers; and the Griller Quartet and the Boyd Neel Orchestra among the ensembles.

For a year after V-E Day, or until April 10, 1946, the concerts continued without interruption. Londoners came to depend on this regular lunchtime music. For many it offered an initiation to serious music, an initiation without the usual drawbacks. These concerts were inexpensive, less costly than any other form of entertainment. They had an air of informality; one dressed as one pleased, one could even bring along a sandwich and eat it in the interval between two works. The concerts formed a part of life, like feeding the pigeons in Trafalgar Square outside.

A total of 1,698 concerts was given, and at a majority of

them Miss Hess was on hand. Besides supervising the project from start to finish, she played in 130 concerts herself. For this war work George VI conferred on her the title, Dame Commander of the British Empire. There is no doubt that the National Gallery concerts bolstered London morale. In E. M. Forster's memorable phrase, they promised the "continuity of civilization, a return to the sane." Yet Myra Hess anticipated more from these concerts than a mere wartime palliative. She had always disliked the formality and the social pretentions of prewar concert-giving. To her mind the atmosphere of the National Gallery concerts seemed more wholesome. Here, she felt, was an institution to be nurtured. Others did not share her conviction. The National Gallery served notice that the building had to be closed for extensive repairs, and—despite the strongest appeals—no other home for the concerts was offered. Defeated in her plan to make the National Gallery concerts a permanent institution, Myra Hess resumed the career that the war had interrupted seven years before.

Her return recital in New York—October 12, 1946—sold out the house. In the years since, her drawing-power has showed no signs of abating. To fill Carnegie Hall with paying customers is an achievement vouchsafed to no more than half a dozen pianists. Just why Dame Myra should be among this select company may seem at first glance a bit puzzling. It can no longer be laid to the aura of her wartime activity. As a curiosity of the blitz she now holds scant interest. It cannot be ascribed to dazzling technical brilliance. Her hands are small; in a massive Brahmsian chord she may even be forced to leave out the least-significant component. It is not owing to artful program-making. She neither plays down to the audience that devours short musical sweetmeats nor up to the audience that craves the esoteric. It cannot have much to do with temperament. Hers is not the personality to galvanize listeners.

What remains to account for Miss Hess's popularity is her honesty and absorption, her intelligently directed talent. Her manner on the platform is simple and unostentatious. She has the friendly idiosyncrasy of darting a glance at the audience—a pleased, almost triumphant look, as if to say: "It turned out beautifully, that phrase!" Yet in this little quirk there is nothing of the exhibitionist. Indeed, a Hess recital is the very antithesis of Music at an Exhibition. She induces the listener to forget that he is only one of three thousand. Such is her warmth and good-spirited calm that one accepts easily the role of guest rather than that of awed spectator.

Her repertoire, though large, is somewhat restricted in style. The music of France lies outside her bailiwick; so does almost all contemporary composition. Although twenty years ago she played Debussy and Ravel at almost every recital, today she leaves them to others. "Their works are the shrimp cocktails of music," she says. "Every now and then I, too, like shrimp cocktails. But for a steady diet I prefer roast beef." "Roast beef" to Miss Hess means the piano music of Mozart, Beethoven, Schubert, Schumann, and Brahms. In fairness it must be owned that she is not restricted to the usual cuts; Mozart's twenty-one concertos and the dances of Schubert are not to be found in every butcher shop. Bach, Scarlatti, Chopin, and Liszt are also served on her programs, but they garnish rather than sustain. Despite these patent restrictions Miss Hess would not like to be dismissed as a musical reactionary. "I enjoy hearing Prokofiev and Bartók—but at the concerts of others."

With the composers that please her (and with whose music, as she puts it, she can grow) Dame Myra is on eminently good terms. She plays Schumann as few can, with relaxation, comfortable cheer, and tender nostalgia. Excitement never works itself into frenzy, nor does tonal emphasis degenerate into pounding. Her approach to the Romantics is gentle. You will not find her sentimentalizing their sentiment, treating Schumann or Brahms as if they were Germanic equivalents of Rachmaninoff. Her way of making music is relaxed and noble; like Sir Thomas Beecham, she exemplifies all that is best in the English tradition of amateurism in the arts.

On two points Myra Hess is crotchety. She has no use for the shibboleth that requires a performer to play from memory. A musician can comprehend the architecture of a score, she maintains, without having to store every sixteenth-note in his brain. Several years ago a Canadian conservatory failed some students whose memorization was faulty. This vexed her so that on principle she has ever since made a point of playing from music. Whether she does so at every recital, I do not know; at those which I have attended she has always had a score on the rack for at least one work. Her other vagary concerns her recordings. She is never satisfied with her playing as it comes from the loudspeaker. Compromise, she claims, attends any recording session. A microphone and the baleful image of an engineer twirling dials are no adequate substitutes, she feels, for the warmth of an audience. This attitude explains why the admirers of Myra Hess have had to content themselves with so few records. It is not the fault of His Master's Voice, with whom the pianist has long been under contract. This company would gladly record her in a large repertoire, if only the lady were willing. It is possible that recording on magnetic tape may partially overcome her objections. HMV hopes to install a tape recorder in her home so that she may play for the microphone amid surroundings more congenial than the functional studio.

When Wilhelm Furtwängler conducted his first concert in London after the war, many people—in the United States especially—were surprised to see that Miss Hess had consented to appear with him as soloist. Furtwängler, despite a few tentative gestures toward independence, had served as a valuable musical exhibit of the Third Reich. Dame Myra not only came from a Jewish home, but also labored throughout the war to maintain the morale that Hitler struggled to shatter. Yet she was among the first to extend her hand to Furtwängler. To those who protested she countered: "Who am I to judge?" Furtwängler, she contends, may have felt, just as she did, the urge to offer what musical sustenance he could to his countrymen. And this she refuses to find despicable. Again, she cannot bring herself to censure an artist who, like Alfred Cortot, collaborated with the occupying enemy in matters pertaining to his art. What would have happened, she asks herself, if the Germans had occupied England and she had been allowed to continue the National Gallery concerts? Would she have refused, knowing that to do so would have deprived Londoners of music? Dame Myra hesitates to say. And in this uncertainty lies her compassion for fellow musicians who chose to play in Hitler's Europe. Woolly thinking? Misplaced chivalry? Perhaps. But there are affection and good will in her attitude, the warmth that endears Myra Hess to her large and faithful audience.

This audience knows that a Hess recital carries the assurance of quality. Technique, musicianship, choice of repertoire will be first class. She always delights. But does she, to borrow Doctor Johnson's antithesis, ravish? It depends, I suppose, on what meaning is lent to that torridly ambiguous word. I take it to imply incandescence, a leap to rarefied altitudes, the drawing aside of curtains hitherto closed. In this sense I find Myra Hess earthbound. Her strength lies more in presentation than in illumination. She lays music before you—and in so orderly and rounded a manner, with such personal grace and warmth, that you barely miss the element of afflatus. Sturdy craftsmanship and dependable taste form the foundation on which Dame Myra has risen to eminence.

☼ Vladimir *Horowitz*

"MUSIC in these days," wrote Voltaire, "is no more than the art of performing the difficult; and that which is merely difficult, and nothing else, cannot please for long." This impatience with virtuosity for virtuosity's sake has a familiar, an almost classic, ring. It is the fashion today to rebuke the virtuoso for his pyrotechnics. But, like any fashion, this one has been parroted to excess; it has been carried by some to an inordinate extreme. The bravura technique so often scorned can be a powerful ally of musical expression. Like money in the bank, technique provides a backlog for any enterprise and furnishes the means for an occasional splurge. Only by squandering it indiscriminately do some virtuosos turn themselves into artistic paupers; lavishing technical largess, they risk musical insolvency.

Vladimir Horowitz does not belong to the company of spendthrifts. As a master of the pianistic wallop he is imposing —indeed, unique—but his overwhelming dexterity has not been emphasized to the exclusion of all else. Music other than the narrowly virtuosic lies within his competence. Nevertheless, the sum total of his artistic achievement is disappointing. A consummate technique, a keen intelligence, and a great reservoir of temperament have thus far yielded dividends incommensurate with his resources.

To explain this phenomenon we must look at Horowitz's career, relatively uneventful in itself, yet by its rocketing success of profound effect in the shaping of his musical personality. He was born in Kiev on October 1, 1904, the son of a prosperous electrical engineer. His mother, an amateur pianist, began to teach him music when he was six. At twelve he entered the Kiev Conservatory, where he remained for six years while Russia endured revolution and civil war. His chief mentor was Felix Blumenfeld, a onetime pupil of Anton Rubinstein. Blumenfeld found Horowitz technically adept and musically illiterate. The boy possessed an intuitive technique and had already solved his basic digital problems; but aside from piano showpieces he was in large measure ignorant of musical literature. Blumenfeld made Horowitz conscious of the full range of music. He gave valuable counsel on details of interpretation, though on the mechanics of playing he offered little advice. "Blumenfeld," says Horowitz, "taught me music rather than execution. He guided me as a conductor guides an orchestra."

Until Horowitz was eighteen, his efforts were divided between piano and composition. As a student he preferred the latter pursuit. He might never have undertaken a concert career but for the consequences of the Bolshevik revolution, which cost his parents their savings and their home. In 1922, faced with the necessity for recruiting the purse, Horowitz began to give piano recitals. He has pursued this lucrative vocation ever since, though not to the utter exclusion of composition. He is author of many works for piano—as yet unplayed beyond the walls of his home. He composes every summer. "Some day," he says, "I may be satisfied enough with my music to play it in public."

An uncle who was a music critic in Kharkov arranged for Horowitz's debut in that city. A small audience attended, but those few carried away such admiring reports that a repeat performance quickly followed. In all, Horowitz was called upon to give fifteen recitals to satisfy Kharkov's demands. Kiev, Moscow, and Leningrad heard him thereafter. By the end of his last season in Russia (1924–5) he had climbed to first place among Soviet pianists. At this period of his career he played in small halls and favored concentrated programs of a more intimate nature than those he now espouses. He would devote one evening to keyboard works by Bach, another to Mozart, a third to Medtner. His repertoire was immense. One year Horowitz gave twenty-four recitals in Leningrad alone, never repeating the same composition more than once. He played chamber music and sometimes joined other pianists in two-piano recitals.

In the autumn of 1925 Horowitz left Russia for a concert tour of Germany. He carried a Soviet passport, and his intention was to return. In Berlin his debut loosed a spate of adulation. Soon Paris and London were bidding for his presence. He canceled plans for his return to the U.S.S.R., and responded instead to the demands of Europe's capitals. The size of his audiences and the extent of his acclaim grew. His fame reached across the Atlantic to New York, where—on January 12, 1928—he made his American debut playing the Tchaikovsky B-flat minor Concerto with the New York Philharmonic under Beecham. On this occasion the critics did not respond with high praise. Pitts Sanborn went on record: "Rarely, if ever, have I heard another piano so unashamedly banged as was his in the grandiose prelude of the concerto." Olin Downes took a more charitable view: "His treatment of the work was a whirlwind of virtuoso interpretation. Mr.

Horowitz has amazing strength, irresistible youth, and temperament." Whatever the reservations of New York's critics, audiences throughout the country found this musician's flair much to their liking. He soon became the most sought-after of pianists, and he has remained so ever since, save for the period from 1936 to 1940, when illness forced his temporary retirement.

As Horowitz's audiences grew, his style altered. Although success did not freeze him into a state of perpetual adolescence, it appreciably restricted the scope of his endeavor. Whereas at one time he had devoted an evening to Bach or Mozart, he now put emphasis on the brilliance of Chopin and the glitter of Liszt. "My own career," Horowitz explains, "forced me to change my style. Today my smallest audience is in Carnegie Hall;* more usually I play to five or six thousand people. I must program music that will be communicated." This means pianistic music, the kind of music that exploits the full keyboard and calls for coloristic pedaling and manifold varieties of dynamics, the kind of music that captures and holds attention. Does it mean as well descending to the lowest common denominator of taste? Horowitz would deny this. In his view it merely means performing music appropriate to the physical circumstances. You do not raise musical standards, he contends, by playing to five thousand people music that was intended for the intimacy of a small room. As an example he cites Schubert's Sonata in B-flat. Horowitz speaks of this work with reverent enthusiasm. He often plays it for himself or for a gathering of friends, but he would hesitate to perform it in public. "It is too long, too introspective. You cannot keep the attention of five thousand people through four long movements of Schubert. It would be a wasted effort. The music would not carry."

As with Schubert, so with late Beethoven: Horowitz sees

* Capacity: three thousand.

no service to music in requiring a large audience to pick its way through the intricacies of the "*Hammerklavier*" Sonata. The piano works of Beethoven's third period he regards as "primarily of value for connoisseurs." He finds a parallel in painting: "Late Beethoven is like late Cézanne. You know it is just a beginning, the groping toward a new style. The paintings of Cézanne's old age paved the way for Seurat and Picasso and Rouault. In themselves they are incomplete. I do not mean to criticize. I would give anything to own a late Cézanne, but I would recognize it for what it is." The same applies to Beethoven, whose last-period piano works are pointers to the future, but not—says Horowitz—of sufficient listening-value to recommend them for recitals in large auditoriums. For public performance Horowitz prefers early Beethoven, where the writing is "less problematic, healthier." Yet the preference is only relative. In general, Horowitz feels that Beethoven's piano works are far inferior to the orchestral works as expressions of the composer's creative personality. "It's not that Beethoven's piano writing doesn't sound the way *I* want it to; it's because his writing doesn't sound the way *he* wanted it to." Today, except for an occasional early sonata or the Thirty-Two Variations, Beethoven appears rarely on Horowitz's programs.

Horowitz is likewise disinclined to exhibit eighteenth-century music in a large hall, though he does so—notwithstanding his convictions—in an effort to balance his programs. Classic delicacy, he holds, is not to be appreciated under usual concert conditions. The harmonic and dynamic range of the writing is too circumscribed, and the modern concert grand is badly miscast for the assignment. "If you play classic music in correct style on a big piano and in a big hall, it will bore most of the audience. This is not the listeners' shortcoming," Horowitz insists. "It just demonstrates that classic music was written for small pianos and small rooms." He gives as the one exception Scarlatti, whose sonatas are effective under modern concert conditions "because they are short." Horowitz reasons that an audience can adjust to tiny dimensions and understated playing for three or four minutes, but that listeners begin to lose contact when subjected to classic music for a quarter of an hour (as in a Mozart or Haydn sonata). Certainly, Scarlatti comes off better than Mozart in a Horowitz recital, though to admit this does not necessarily endorse Horowitz's explanation. It could well be argued that he understands Scarlatti and thus presents his music with conviction, whereas he misconstrues Mozart and transmits his misunderstanding to the audience.

This pianist's philosophy of what constitutes inappropriate recital fare has its own validity once you grant the basic premise on which it is formed—that the performing musician should reach the largest possible audience with the most effective music. The premise is certainly open to dispute. Artur Schnabel, holding a viewpoint diametrically opposed to Horowitz's, practiced a philosophy of program-making which made room for the very works Horowitz excludes. Each philosophy can claim its own cogency. But to say as much does not allay one's regret that the Horowitz *modus operandi* rules out so many introspective masterpieces of piano literature. For this pianist is not the simple virtuoso that many people take him to be. The Horowitz who thunders so persuasively through the rhetoric of Liszt is capable as well of whispering the fragile poetry of a Scarlatti sonata. He can steer his course through the driving rapids of Prokofiev and can navigate just as surely the undulating waters of Schumann. Horowitz has dropped enough crumbs to establish his affinity for small-scaled music. Any pianist who can play the *Kinderscenen* with his subtle comprehension ought to do it more often. Does Horowitz boggle at the prospect of playing intimate music to a mammoth gathering? Then he should be induced to play for the phonograph what he deems inappropriate for the concert hall. To date he has seen fit to record only the repertoire that he exhibits in public. Perhaps in the future he may record for *our* pleasure what he now plays in private for his.

Meanwhile Horowitz keeps us more than reasonably content with fireworks. In music that deliberately exploits the piano's resources he sets his own standards. His ringing metallic tone, his incredibly agile fingers, his driving sense of rhythm, and his acute control of dynamics combine to make him the exponent *par excellence* of Liszt and Liszt's musical progeny. He plays this kind of music so convincingly as to wring pleasure from the most reluctant listener. He gives a breadth to *Funérailles*, a delicacy to the *Valse oubliée*, and a rollicking sense of pandemonium let loose in the *Rakoczy March*, that are irresistible. A temperamental antipathy to the music of Liszt prompts me to pass over these triumphs, however, and to nominate the Mussorgsky *Pictures at an Exhibition* as Horowitz's interpretative masterpiece—a work that allows him to give full rein to his cyclonic and poetic humors. He has made his own arrangement of this score on the principle (hardly to be controverted) that Mussorgsky did not understand the piano's full potentialities. To Horowitz, Mussorgsky's score of the *Pictures* resembles nothing so much as a *Klavierauszug*—that is, a reduction of symphonic music to keyboard dimensions. In his reworking of the *Pictures*, Horowitz addresses himself to details of scoring. He has left unchanged the basic musical structure, altering only the clumsy pianistic realization. (For example, he inserts effective rhythmic patterns to replace Mussorgsky's stale *tremolandos*, but the harmonies remain the same.) Occasionally he lowers or raises the pitch by an octave. Only in one place has he tampered with the composer's thought. In the closing measures of "The Great Gate at Kiev" Horowitz has augmented Mussorgsky's writing with a clanging-bell motif. It would take a more Spartan purist than I to cavil at this interpolation. Horowitz's finale to this work is overpowering in sheer sonorous impact: that so much music can pour from one instrument or that two hands can manage so many notes seems scarcely credible.

Horowitz's agility and intensity of temperament combine to raise an audience to a state of hypnotic exhilaration. "No artist to a like degree possesses this power of subjecting the public, of lifting it, sustaining it, and letting it fall again." What Schumann wrote of the young Franz Liszt applies with equal justice to Liszt's twentieth-century counterpart. Horowitz has a fantastic power of charging an auditorium with temperamental static. This quality draws listeners: even the tone-deaf respond to personal magnetism; but it has served, I think, to obscure the range of his capabilities and potentialities. Subjected to the mesmeric atmosphere of a Horowitz recital, one is led to the generalization that this performer is more acrobat than musician. Responsible criticism has voiced this opinion, if not quite so baldly. Horowitz has been sketched as a virtuoso beyond redemption, distorting music willy-nilly and relying solely upon the "wow" technique to propagate his interpretations. This portrait, though accurate in many details, is too simple. It ignores those instances when Horowitz interprets nonacrobatic music with searching insight—the *Kinderscenen*, a Scarlatti sonata, a Brahms intermezzo. It ignores his championing of contemporary music, substantial sonatas by Prokofiev and Samuel Barber, which can hardly be dismissed as easy obeisance to modern art. It ignores his sense of artistic propriety, which has kept him a total stranger to those media—the movies and television—which he considers inimical to serious musical endeavor. It ignores his insistence upon never playing more than two concerts a week, on the principle that too much repetition would stale his responses.

Finally, the portrait ignores Horowitz's offstage personality. In conversation with him you encounter no mad necromancer of the keyboard, but an objective, analytical craftsman, a musician aware of his shortcomings and in search of further knowledge, a man concerned with his artistic responsibilities and determined to fulfill them as best he can. Horowitz listens to his own records with rare severity. No one, for instance, feels the limitations of the Tchaikovsky Piano Concerto recording (with Toscanini) more acutely than the soloist himself. And this is only one example wherein Horowitz acknowledges a past failing with the pledge of future amelioration. He senses, too, the deficiencies in his playing of Mozart, is interested in the problem of ornamentation (filling in "improvised" melodic sequences where Mozart has indicated only the outline), and searches for the proper means to cope with eighteenth-century style on a twentieth-century instrument. The man, modest and self-critical, creates a quite different impression from the performer in the supercharged atmosphere of a crowded auditorium. Will the private and public Horowitz ever merge completely into one rounded musical personality? There are many grounds for hope.

☼ Artur *Rubinstein*

FROM the moment that Artur Rubinstein walks out on stage—a brisk, jaunty walk, exultant with professional confidence—you are aware that for this artist the show is the thing. Whether he has really to fly up from his bench in order to give weight to a Brahms *forte*, whether his hands must bounce quite so high in the "*Ritual Fire Dance*" are matters on which at least some doubt may be expressed. Necessary or not, these platform gambits present an engaging spectacle. It would be a churlish critic who held this showmanship to Rubinstein's discredit. Were his performing all show, one might have occasion to carp; but this pianist offers more than ornate façade. To platform spectacle he weds musical probity. In truth, nothing less should be expected from an artist of Rubinstein's background. He was extremely fortunate in the influences—Joachim, Paderewski, Dukas, among them—that bore on his formative years. With such mentors it is not surprising that Rubinstein matured into a musician as well as a virtuoso.

According to his own testimony, the pianist was born in Lodz, Poland, on January 28, 1889. By the age of two he is said to have manifested unmistakable signs of musical talent. To his infant ears "every voice was a melody." This was the more remarkable in that the Rubinstein family had shown no musical aptitude whatever. His forebears, both immediate and distant, inclined to business, not to the arts. It is true that his older sisters went through the formality of piano lessons, but mainly because such lessons were considered proper for children of good bourgeois parents. Rubinstein's father and mother occasionally set foot in the Warsaw opera house—again, for social standing rather than musical delight. Being thus amusical, the Rubinsteins were at a loss to know what should be done with their precocious youngster. And precocious he certainly was. Rubinstein says he could identify by ear the notes in a complicated chord and repeat long melodies without a falter. Such feats were easy for him. "I was much prouder," he recollects, "of being able to jump down the stairs three steps at a time."

An uncle who boasted of an accomplished German literary style offered a suggestion. He would write to Berlin, to the most eminent musician in that musical capital, and ask his advice. Although Joseph Joachim, to whom the letter was addressed, knew nothing of his correspondent in Lodz, the story of young Artur aroused his interest. Joachim advised strongly against early musical instruction, recommending only that the boy be allowed to hear as much good singing as possible. The renowned violinst concluded with an offer to see Artur, should an opportunity be found to bring him to Berlin.

Thus it came about that when one of Rubinstein's sisters journeyed to Berlin to buy a trousseau, her four-year-old brother was taken along. Joachim kept his word about the audition. Suspecting that Artur might be a "trained seal" taught to do a few musical tricks by rote, he tested the boy carefully. "He sang a theme from Schubert's 'Unfinished,'" Rubinstein recalls, "and then asked me to pick out the melody on his piano. I not only played the melody, but harmonized it correctly. Joachim was flabbergasted." He urged that the youngster be allowed to remain in Berlin, and offered to take full responsibility for his education. But Rubinstein's parents—well-to-do people with a comfortable home—would not consign their youngest child to the care of strangers, and back he went to Lodz. For two years he dabbled at the piano on his own; then he began commuting to near-by Warsaw for instruction with a private teacher named Rozycki. Toward this pedagogue his sentiments remain cool. "He would fall fast asleep," Rubinstein complains, "whenever I played."

"Fortunately for me, my father went bankrupt while I was studying in Warsaw." "Fortunately" because his parents, no longer in a position to finance their son's musical instruction, grew more amenable to Joachim's offer. Although by this time Rubinstein's flair for the piano was evident, Joachim still wished to supervise his education—even if, as a violinist, he could not contribute to it directly. He went so far as to donate one quarter of the expenses, with three Berlin bankers contributing the rest. Only one condition accompanied Joachim's largess: Rubinstein's parents were to promise not to exploit their child as a prodigy. In later years the pianist was to acknowledge a great debt to Joachim, not the least for this "priceless condition" imposed upon his parents.

Joachim insisted on Artur's attendance during rehearsals of his quartet. "Sometimes I would sleep through long adagios (for I was only a boy of ten, not a hero), but an impression was made just the same. Joachim introduced me to associates and pupils of Brahms, Schumann, and Mendelssohn. I bathed in the tradition of their music." In time this atmosphere began to weigh on him. The boy had "too many ghosts" about him.

His piano teacher, Heinrich Barth, contributed to this sense of oppression. Barth belonged to that company of despots whose tyranny is suffered because of their irreplaceable talent. He gave to his pupils a solid technique and a disinclination to cross his least injunction. Even in youth Rubinstein was an individualist: seeds of revolt sprouted. "I started to live a double life. For Barth I would play Mendelssohn, but I would go home immediately after my lesson and play *verboten* Wagner."

Meanwhile, Artur Rubinstein had made his debut in Berlin, at the age of eleven, playing Mozart's Concerto in A, K.488. It was a curious "vehicle," considering the circumstances and the era. Chopin, Schumann, and Liszt in man-sized doses then provided usual prodigy fare, but Joachim very wisely proscribed such ambitious enterprises for his young ward. For years he insisted that Artur avoid taxing public appearances. The choice of this particular Mozart concerto, however, was Rubinstein's own. (In passing it may be noted that the A major Concerto has always been a favorite of Rubinstein's; he recorded it in London during the early thirties and again in St. Louis in 1950.) As a result of his debut, young Rubinstein became known as a Mozart player, appearing during those years of tutelage with several German orchestras as soloist in Mozart concertos.

His dissatisfaction with the Barth regimen festered. Finally it reached a point at which he was emboldened to speak to Joachim. The violinist understood the situation, and acknowledged that Rubinstein needed a change. A letter went off to Paderewski, requesting that he hear the boy. Rubinstein was fifteen when he set off for Morges, the town on Lac Leman where Paderewski owned an elaborate mansion. He had been invited to lunch with his exalted compatriot, but even before they sat down to table he was asked to play. Rubinstein says that he felt ill at ease in Paderewski's presence and as a result performed very badly. "But Paderewski could smell talent behind all the finger slips, and I was given another chance. He invited me to come back that evening for a dinner party. It was a typically lavish affair, with lobster and pink champagne. After dinner Paderewski charmingly asked if I would play for his guests. Thanks to the champagne, I was not quite so much in awe. I played well."

The outcome was an invitation to spend the coming summer months with Paderewski in his Swiss château. Rubinstein accepted blithely, without considering the effect his decision would have back in Berlin. When the young man returned to Germany with news of his summer plans, his teacher flew into a temper. Heinrich Barth appears to have been an almost pathologically jealous person who operated on the principle that "all pupils are traitors." Barth gave Rubinstein to understand that if he so much as took one lesson from Paderewski their relationship would be at an end. The boy was obliged to swear fidelity. However, he was allowed to spend the summer with Paderewski on the stipulation that no pedagogy would be involved. Instead they played two-piano music together every day. When Rubinstein told of all this, I observed that he seemed to be splitting hairs. Were not those duo-piano sessions, I inquired, lessons in all but name? "Certainly not!" the pianist replied forcefully. "There were no lessons at all." So vehemently did he insist, that one might have thought Herr Barth was hiding behind the curtain, waiting for his former pupil to make a damaging admission.

Soon after Rubinstein's sixteenth birthday the bickering with Barth reached a point of no return. The break came over a purely personal matter. Herr Barth had strong misgivings about a certain young pianist with whom Rubinstein had become well acquainted. He demanded that the friendship be dissolved. Rubinstein refused, broke off relations with his teacher, and retreated to Poland—much to the chagrin of his family, who believed that a promising career had been jettisoned. He spent several months in the country working by himself. "I learned practically my whole repertoire then—the concertos of Brahms, Chopin, Schumann, Beethoven." It was at this time that he met Karol Szymanowski, six years his elder, who soon became a close friend and an estimable influence.

But he could not remain in the country and accept the hospitality of friends forever. At loose ends and with no ordered plan for the future, Rubinstein decided to give a concert in Warsaw. This, his first "virtuoso recital," was well received, but a career could not be built on the strength of Warsaw commendation. When acquaintances stopped him on the street to ask about his plans, Rubinstein announced that he would shortly leave for Paris. Actually this was only an exercise of his imagination. "I had no contacts and no money. But a good fairy has always watched over me. Just when a stroke of luck would be needed, it seemed to come my way." At this particular juncture the good fairy took the form of a Polish nobleman with whom Rubinstein was only slightly acquainted. Within a few weeks of the Warsaw recital, a letter arrived from this aristocrat inviting the pianist to visit him in his villa near Paris. With the invitation was enclosed money for the journey.

In Paris, Rubinstein was introduced to Gabriel Astruc, son-in-law of the publisher Enoch and organizer of a newly founded concert bureau called La Société Musicale. This impresario signed his first contracts with Wanda Landowska and Artur Rubinstein. For Rubinstein's Paris debut, Astruc engaged the Lamoureux Orchestra under Camille Chevillard's direction and rounded up a dressy, society audience. Rubinstein played concertos by Saint-Saëns and Chopin, and in the interval between concertos Mary Garden sang several songs by the then-controversial Debussy. His debut, Rubinstein admits, was not brilliant. "I was neither a *Wunderkind* nor a mature artist." But, Paris being Paris, he did not take his cool reception too much to heart. The beautiful city and its beautiful girls turned his head. The routine of faithful daily work, inculcated through the years in Berlin, fell into abeyance. He would often stay out all night, go to bed at nine in the morning, and eat breakfast at six while most of Paris was preparing for dinner. Fortunately, there were friends disposed to take him in hand. The composer Paul Dukas once met Rubinstein at one of those evening breakfasts and admonished him severely. "He did me a great service," Rubinstein acknowledges, "by showing me how I was ruining my health."

An appreciation of Paris attractions other than wine and women began to dawn on the pianist. He was introduced to the circle around Maurice Ravel, the so-called "*apaches*," an artistic brotherhood of such diversified talents as the poet Tristan Klingsor and the composer Manuel de Falla. He busied himself with the latest music—Ravel's *Jeux d'eau*, Debussy's *Estampes*, Dukas's Sonata in E-flat minor. But however much he began to accomplish artistically, Rubinstein only managed to tread water professionally. He was therefore quite puzzled when Bernard Ulrich, a representative of William A. Knabe, approached him in the summer of 1905 regarding appearances in America. His Paris recitals had hardly seemed to warrant transatlantic interest. The explanation was that the Boston critic William F. Apthorp had heard Rubinstein play at Paderewski's home and had urged Knabe to engage him.

Early in 1906, when he was seventeen years of age, Rubinstein arrived in America for a tour of forty-five concerts. About his playing, critics in New York were as little enthusiastic as their confreres in Paris. In the opinion of Richard Aldrich, Rubinstein was "full of the exuberance and exaggeration of youth . . . concerned chiefly with the exploitation of his dexterity and with impressing not only the ears but also the eyes of his hearers with his personality and the brilliancy of the effects he can produce." He further noted: "There is little warmth of beauty in Rubinstein's tone and little variety in his effects. All is meant for brilliancy and display; thus far he is highly successful. It would be interesting to know whether he can express some of the deeper things there are in music of deeper import. Until he can show this he is not likely to impress himself upon this public as a musician of influence." Aldrich's reference was to the pianist's debut appearance with the visiting Philadelphia Orchestra. A week later Rubinstein gave a solo recital, which "did nothing," said the critic of the *New York Herald*, "to better the impression at his recent debut. . . . His programs made demands upon him for something more than a firm touch, fleet fingers, and the other surface accomplishments of a virtuoso. It cannot be said that he disclosed the deeper qualities of musicianship to meet those demands." In Boston the *Transcript*'s critic complained that "his personality is yet without magnetism, and his playing had the effect of a tedious sermon, which set the wits to wandering or turned them at times to thoughts of the clock." Notices of this character served to postpone further American tours for thirteen years. Rubinstein acknowledges that he often played carelessly during his first American visit, though he feels that American critics were too harsh. "They didn't recognize my potential gift nor my underlying musicianship."

After the American tour, Rubinstein retired to Poland, his contract with Gabriel Astruc having lapsed. He characterizes the next decade as a transitional period in his life during which he underwent great "mental turmoil." He brooded over his apparent failure. No longer were managers interested in him. He feared that he might languish forevermore on musically barren Polish soil. Happily, another "good fairy" came along in the person of Prince Lubomirski, an old-school patron of the arts who subsidized the Warsaw Philharmonic. Hearing that Rubinstein was in need of financial sponsorship, Lubomirski offered to help. Gradually the pianist managed to rehabilitate his name. He appeared in Vienna, in the large cities of Russia, in Berlin, in Rome. In London he played in recitals with Casals and Jacques Thibaud. But in the consciousness of the mass European public his concerts made barely a ripple. It was still, he admits, "a struggling career."

In 1916 the struggle turned to triumph. Rubinstein had gone to Spain, his first visit to that country, and was scheduled to give four recitals. Before he left, the four appearances had ballooned to well over forty. Spanish audiences acclaimed Rubinstein with the gusto they usually reserved for a master bullfighter. For the first time he enjoyed the intoxication of great popular success. And it was a mutual infatuation. "I had a born instinct for Spanish culture. I loved everything about the country–Spanish food, Spanish dress, the Spanish language. When I was twelve I saw a Spanish ballerina in Berlin and fell in love with her. I invented excuses to get out at night and went to see her perform again and again. To me Spain had always seemed the most glamorous country of all." His mania for things Hispanic was allied to a rare comprehension of Spanish music. Back in the early days in Paris, Rubinstein had met Isaac Albéniz ("a little fat man who loved to tell jokes and dirty stories") and had been greatly attracted to his keyboard music. "It was the first Spanish music I had seen which was interestingly written for piano." On his tour south of the Pyrenees, Rubinstein delighted audiences with electrifying interpretations of Albéniz's *Iberia* and Falla's *Noches en los Jardines de España*. He aroused enthusiasm too for his efforts as plenipotentiary of contemporary music. During the 1916 season he gave eight concerts in Madrid alone, introducing such unfamiliar compositions as the Scriabin Sonata No. 5,

Medtner's Variations (Opus 10), and pieces by Szymanowski.

His reception in Spain paved the way for a successful tour to South America. With a special passport obtained through the good offices of Alfonso XIII, he made the Argentina-Uruguay-Brazil circuit—again to the profit both of his reputation and of his bank account. By 1919 Rubinstein's potency as a box-office personality was considered strong enough for a New York manager (R. E. Johnston) to risk sponsoring a return tour. This time the press treated him more kindly, though the tone of criticism could not be described as encomiastic. James Gibbons Huneker, reviewing the opening New York recital in Carnegie Hall, concluded that Rubinstein was a miniaturist. In telegraphic prose Huneker wrote: "He is a trifle old-fashioned in style; the Viennese school, with its light action keyboard, the lack of depth in his chord playing, the too rapid scales also superficial in tone"—a description which bears little resemblance to the Rubinstein we know today. The *New York Post* reported that "the general impression produced by his playing was one of mingled pleasure and displeasure. Pleasure, because of his mastery of the keyboard, his energy and enthusiasm. Displeasure, because of his tendency to blur rapid passages and harmonic changes by careless use of the pedal; because of an excess of storm and stress, and particularly because of a tendency to take the bit between his teeth and run away."

The pianist returned to the United States yearly until 1927, though with only indifferent success. His espousal of contemporary music may have militated against him, for in the twenties Rubinstein salted his programs with liberal amounts of Stravinsky, Prokofiev, Bloch, Szymanowski, and Milhaud. (In a 1920 recital for the Society of the Friends of Music he played Szymanowski's Sonata No. 2, Poulenc's *Mouvements perpétuels*, Ravel's *Valses nobles et sentimentales*, and a transcription of the final scene from Stravinsky's *The Firebird*—which seems considerably tamer today than it seemed then.) Another pertinent factor was his slipshod playing. These were Rubinstein's "café society years," when the Casino at Monte Carlo and elegant parties in Paris and London usurped much of his attention. He did not consider piano-playing a very important activity. It was more in the nature of a game, a by-product of life. He bothered little about technique, preferring to get by on temperament.

Following his marriage in 1932, Rubinstein "reformed." "For the first time in my life," he says, "I really worked hard." Testimony to his newly won prowess reached this country by way of recordings made in London of the complete Chopin scherzos and polonaises. When the impresario Sol Hurok brought Rubinstein back to America in 1937, the pianist was already well esteemed by those who had had access to these excellent recordings. This time there was no mistaking the enthusiasm of press and public. In twenty-eight concerts that year he laid the foundation for a great mass popularity that was to snowball in a few years to the point at which he would give 160 performances in one season. Rubinstein's advocacy of new music dwindled as his box-office receipts multiplied. Although he still admits easily digested Villa-Lobos and Poulenc to his programs, his bailiwick has otherwise contracted almost exclusively to the nineteenth century. All-Chopin evenings are a Rubinstein specialty. He is partial also to Schumann, Brahms, and "middle period" Beethoven. His erstwhile composer friends—Dukas, Szymanowski, Albéniz—rarely engage his attention, to say nothing of the more dissonant Stravinsky, Bloch, or Milhaud. Such composers, Rubinstein now feels, have "lost contact with the soul of the piano."

What he does play—the standard concertos, Chopin, intermezzos and rhapsodies of Brahms, the well-traveled Beethoven sonatas, impromptus by Schubert, the *Symphonic Études* of Schumann—is accomplished with extraordinary finish. Rubinstein resembles a veteran actor whose command of stagecraft is so adroit as to oil the most inconsequential performance. Many are the times when I have been tempted to cavil at a Rubinstein interpretation, only to find the barb of criticism blunted by his convincing surety and control of the instrument. He is a natural pianist, as some people are natural singers. Under his ministration the unruly piano yields such caressingly beautiful sounds that one is given to overlooking the stereotyped programs, the often obvious phrasing. He commands a variety and range of tone well within the symphonic orbit. It is round, resonant, and prismatically hued. It can thunder with brassy sonority or whisper with a fine-drawn aside *sul ponticello*. Always it is suave and rich. From some quarters comes the complaint that it is *too* rich. This is an opinion worth recording, and were the piano not so often abused I might share it. But exposure to more than a fair share of banging and jangling by steel-fingered pianists has left me inordinately susceptible to his dulcet playing.

Rubinstein's reputation, of course, does not repose solely on technical agility and tonal caress. He is a man of culture and discernment, and when the spirit moves him he plays with imagination and insight. His statement of the opening theme in Ravel's Trio (as recorded with Heifetz and Piatigorsky) is a miracle of sensitive pacing and inflection. In Chopin he can play with sinuous and subtle poetry (as witness such imposing legacies as the 1939 recording of the mazurkas and the 1952 recording of the polonaises). Occasionally he misses the point of a work (with Beethoven, for instance, he is sometimes inclined to prettify passages of brusque intent), but outright lapses intrude rarely. Rubinstein is too intelligent a musician to fall often into bald stylistic error. When he fails to give a full quota of musical satisfaction, it is not for obvious faults; rather it is because of his interpretative predictability. He usually does just what is expected. Like a writer who cannot resist adding "eagle" to "eye," Rubinstein is overly addicted to worn furrows of expression.

Doubtless this is the price the virtuoso must pay for repeating himself too often. André Gide complained of the "unbearable assurance," the lack of improvisation, in virtuosic playing. As well to complain that an ocean liner kicks up too many waves! The nature of the beast is to be so. Recognizing Rubinstein's conventional programs, his inclination to the musical cliché, one can yet appreciate his mastery of the instrument, his personal magnetism and—despite the blandishments of Hollywood—his continuing respect for music.

☼ Wanda *Landowska*

MAY we say, in the manner of Voltaire, that if there had been no Landowska it would have been necessary to invent her? The question is posed without levity. It fastens directly on that ever-fascinating speculation whether the Great Man is the actuator or the tool of history. Scholars may ruminate on it idly, just as they may ponder on the probable course of history had Creasy's fifteen decisive battles been won by the opposite side. They will never know for sure. Neither can we say with certitude whether the popular rehabilitation of Bach and his contemporaries is owing to Landowska or whether she serves rather as the most persuasive exponent of an inevitable *Zeitgeist*. That the question can be raised at all is indicative of the imposing position this performer commands in the musical history of our time.

Landowska has had the good fortune to witness the triumph of her principles. She has lived to see the cause become a commonplace. But do not for a moment assume that she views complacently this great renascence. Does the growing brood of harpsichordists fill her with parental satisfaction? To a degree, yes; but her pleasure is tempered with decided misgivings. The vast majority of these performers, you are given to understand, mistake the true character and capabilities of the instrument. Do the Bach festivals and the ambitious recording-projects give her the sense of a mission satisfactorily completed? Hardly. "They play Bach everywhere now," she complains, "but often the music is interpreted clumsily, with no knowledge of the proper style." For Landowska is an arbiter of uncompromising standards—and, as the truth will out, a prima donna as well. But approach her when she is in a benign humor, and you can detect a note of satisfaction in her words. The conversation will revolve about her early years in Paris, the quest for an instrument worthy of Bach, the problem of rediscovering a harpsichord technique, the trials of converting musicians and public alike to fresh interpretative conceptions. Then, remembering that she is talking to someone forty years her junior, Landowska will add: "Of course, you cannot begin to appreciate what has happened. Today there is no more struggle. The battle is won."

Wanda Landowska was born in Warsaw on July 5, 1879, and in coming into the world almost killed her mother. Amid the general consternation, Wanda was neglected. According to one of those "old family stories," her father appropriately deposited the newborn infant in the piano, where she remained, swaddled in blankets, until her mother was out of danger. The Landowskis belong to Warsaw's upper bourgeoisie. Of Jewish extraction, they had entered the Catholic Church. It was a household familiar with the arts. Wanda's mother was a gifted linguist, and her talent found an outlet in voluminous reading—in French, German, and English, as well as in the Slavic tongues. Wanda inherited this gift; her early forays into literature encompassed authors as diverse as Dickens, Anatole France, and Goethe. (Nor has she ever lost the habit of reading: her home is filled with books and her conversation with literary allusions.) Her father earned a living at the bar. In his home musicians invariably received a welcome. One of Landowska's earliest memories is of that master of *bel canto*, Mattia Battistini, performing at one of her father's informal musical parties.

In an atmosphere thus friendly to music, what more natural than that Wanda's first tentative ramblings over the piano keyboard should have been seized upon and made the pretext for early musical instruction? But do not conclude that the small girl plunged headlong into the Forty-eight Preludes and Fugues. The future apostle of Bach was born in an atmosphere of Chopin veneration. For the first two or three years she studied piano under Jan Kleczyński, a Chopin scholar of some reputation. Landowska was happy with this kind man who, despite his enthusiasm for Chopin, understood her adolescent love for Bach, Haydn, and Mozart. Even then the young girl felt a strong inclination toward the pre-Romantic idiom. It was an enthusiasm not shared by many. At the time of Wanda's childhood in Poland, Chopin was the ruling deity. Music of pre-1800 vintage was almost completely ignored, with the exception of Bach—a Bach heard mainly through transcriptions—and a little Haydn and Mozart. Only Anton Rubinstein, with his rare "Concerts Historiques," had dipped into the works of Rameau, Daquin, and the English virginalists. Otherwise, the entire musical civilization before and around Bach was unknown, unexplored, almost as if nonexistent.

Eventually, Wanda's mother decided that Kleczyński was too indulgent. Other teachers followed, uninteresting pedants who prescribed a rigorous diet of études and forbade Wanda to play Bach. Later, the girl was sent to the Warsaw Conservatory, where her master was Alexander Michalowski, a respected pedagogue and celebrated interpreter of Chopin. Pupil of Moscheles, Reinecke, and the school of Leipzig, Michalowski knew and revered Bach (though his knowledge was founded mostly on transcriptions). Having recognized Wanda's rapport with Bach, Michalowski allowed her to play his works in addition to Chopin and other conventional repertoire staples of the time. At her first concert in Warsaw—she was fourteen—she played the English Suite in E minor. Glimmerings there may have been of future insight; nevertheless, it is reasonable to assume that the Warsaw student played Bach with the misguided exaggerations to which that post-Romantic age was prone.

Were there visions during these formative years of a concert career? If the lady's hindsight is to be trusted, the examples of such dazzlers as Teresa Carreño and Sophie Menter held no great attraction. For many years, indeed, the voice claimed almost as much attention as the piano. It sent her to the opera regularly, impelled her to memorize the score of *Don Giovanni*. Zerlina, "her role," she performed many times before an imaginary audience. Fortunately, there was none of the frantic practicing and polishing that obtains when a family is hell-bent on grooming a prodigy for the public platform.

Wanda's nonmusical education was accomplished at home. "Home" meant equally the town house of her father and an estate of her aunt near Kielce, in the Polish hinterland many miles from Warsaw. It was in the country, far from the routine and restrictions of the city, that the young musician felt most happy. Even in the 1880's, Polish farm life persisted much as it had for centuries. Peasant customs and dress had altered little since feudal times. At harvest season peasants from the district would gather in the village square to dance to music handed down by rote for countless generations. Odd native instruments, unfamiliar rhythmic patterns, a wealth of haunting melody captivated the young Landowska's ear and provided native bricks from which she would later build an interpretative edifice. "It was then," she explains, "that I learned to play the true mazurka." This Polish heritage, so important to an understanding of Landowska's art, is not revealed solely on those few occasions when she essays the works of Chopin or his earlier compatriots. It is often to be sensed in her playing of Bach. Take, as the first example that comes to mind, her interpretation of the F major Prelude from Book I of *The Well-Tempered Clavier*. This rendition is surely one to call up fantasies of peasants gaily dancing, swirling embroidered skirts, and stamping wooden clogs. Its dynamic is referable, not to textual research in matters of eighteenth-century musical style, but to a temperament nurtured on the dances of Poland's peasantry.

For a Pole of the late nineteenth century Berlin figured as cultural mecca, and there Landowska was sent at the age of seventeen. In the domain of keyboard technique further tutelage would have been superfluous. Thenceforth she developed according to her own lights. But in another realm of endeavor she still required guidance. Her predilection for vocal music evidenced itself in an urge to compose songs—songs, as Landowska now wryly confesses, of a distinctly Romantic flavor. She took private lessons in composition with Heinrich Urban. A short "honeymoon" with this teacher terminated when she discovered, with disappointment, his condescension toward the music of Bach. The teen-aged musician took full advantage of Berlin's concerts and nightly opera performances, though she professes to have been "very critical" of what she heard. Above all, she never lost an opportunity to hear her beloved Bach. Such opportunities presented themselves rarely in that particular musical environment, but every winter the *Christmas Oratorio* was performed, and this Landowska considered "the great event of the year."

She composed many, many songs; she worked at the piano; she formulated one nebulous enterprise after another. It was a time of drifting.

A volatile compatriot a few years her senior, whom Landowska met just before the turn of the century, put a dramatic end to these undirected days in Berlin. Henry Lew was a student of Jewish folklore, a fervent Zionist, and—to quote Landowska—"a radical in every way." He quite dominated the irresolute pianist-composer with whom he had fallen in love. Within a matter of weeks Landowska was persuaded to turn her back on the stodgy routine of Berlin and follow him to Paris. But her allowance from home did not permit so lavish an expenditure as a railroad ticket to the French capital. Her landlady made up the deficit—which largess unfortunately killed the goose that laid the golden egg, for once the news got out of Wanda's subsidized defection the parents of the remaining boarders saw to it that their daughters were quickly removed to less generous and more respectable quarters.

Now life grew interesting. The two set up housekeeping on a frugal scale, for Lew was on a scholarship collating material on Jewish customs and habits, and the cash proceeds were scanty. Eventually the two legalized their relationship to satisfy parental scruples, but by then Mr. and Mrs. Lew were a well-domesticated couple, even to the point of owning a fine set of china that bore the initials "WL." A canard has it that this crockery was filched piecemeal from the Wagons-Lit dining-cars. Not so, counters Landowska. It appears that the Wagons-Lit Company had built a large hotel for the Exposition of 1900, and that, after the fair closed, everything in the hotel was sold. "Lew bought this much-discussed china because it was cheap. The initials," she insists, "were just a happy coincidence."

When Henry Lew heard the lieder that his young wife had composed in Berlin he begged her to stop wasting time over such "bourgeois" musical accomplishments. As antidote he prescribed a text entitled "*Die Weber*," which was strongly endowed with social significance. The song that resulted is the only one of her compositions which Landowska still values. Forty-five years later it did duty as thematic material for a Fanfare composed on the morrow of the liberation of France. The song reveals much, especially when sung by the composer with her own fiery ardor. Bold, incisive, soaringly rhythmical, this memento of her first year in Paris shows the germ of what Landowska was later to become.

Composing, however, soon lost its attraction. Providence had brought Landowska to Paris at a singularly fortunate moment. For anyone with curiosity about the music of the past, Paris in 1900 was the center of the world. Berlin had been engulfed in the heavy atmosphere of post-Romanticism. That city concentrated on Wagner, Brahms, and Bruckner, and their predecessors, Beethoven, Schubert, and Schumann. In Paris a decade earlier the horizon would have been similarly circumscribed. Pierre Lalo described it thus:*

> Those who were best educated had some knowledge of Beethoven, Berlioz, Gounod, Wagner, Italian and Meyerbeerian opera, some songs of Schubert and Schumann (always the same ones), some arias by Gluck and Mozart, a little Haydn, a smattering of Bach. And that was all. Beyond that yawned emptiness. It seemed as if music, and French music in particular, was an art without origins, without continuity, an art whose past was either of negligible interest or quite lost in obscurity, an art of which only the most recent period appeared worthy of interest.

By 1900, when Landowska arrived in Paris, all this was in process of change. A new ferment vastly widening the musical landscape had set in. Its guiding spirit was Charles Bordes. It is said on the basis of those few works he managed to complete that Bordes might have developed into one of France's most

* Pierre Lalo: *De Rameau à Ravel* (Paris: 1947).

renowned composers. But this talented student of César Franck became enchanted early in life by the unperformed and unappreciated music of the past. To its resuscitation he sacrificed such music as was imprisoned in himself.

Bordes's historical performances began in 1892, when he was twenty-nine years old, at the church of Saint-Gervais on the Île de la Cité. To a public familiar only with that part of the musical spectrum beginning with Haydn and ending with Saint-Saëns, these first revelations at Saint-Gervais gave brilliant illumination. The names of Palestrina, Lotti, and Josquin were only words—"sonorous words," writes Pierre Lalo, "but always unreal and devoid of sense." Their works were "dead matter, which may have been exhumed every now and then by some musical archeologist, but which immediately began gathering dust again in the library. It was Bordes who blew off the dust, who breathed life into these works, so that they were no longer buried in the past but blended into the present; he it was who introduced them into the current of our life and thoughts."

A year later, Bordes and his Chanteurs de Saint-Gervais shifted their attention to secular music of the fifteenth to seventeenth centuries. During the following season, 1894, Bordes presented six church cantatas of Bach. Paul Dukas, reviewing the latter for the *Revue hebdomadaire*, characterized the enterprise as "crowned with a most merited and incontestable success." "It is evident," he wrote, "that musical taste in France has undergone serious transformation; the interest that is aroused today by productions which just a little while ago would have seemed highly tedious furnishes irrefutable evidence." The success of these first offerings emboldened Bordes, D'Indy, and a third enthusiast, Alexandre Guilmant, to found the Schola Cantorum, an organization whose initial object was the propagation of pre-nineteenth-century music in France.

All of this took place in the years immediately preceding Landowska's removal to Paris. It can readily be seen how stimulating such an atmosphere must have been to a young musician in sympathy with the music of the past, especially when it is remembered that her only contact theretofore had been with persons whose attitude toward this music was either barely comprehending or frankly antagonistic. It can be seen why Landowska avows: "The atmosphere of France was a blessing to me," and why with all humility she adds: "Everything that I am I owe to France."

Landowska reveled in the performances at the Schola Cantorum. "Here," she says, "I learned what I could not have learned in Warsaw or Berlin: the surroundings and predecessors of Bach." Soon she was introduced to Charles Bordes. Finding himself confronted with what he supposed to be a typical budding *pianiste*, Bordes dutifully asked Landowska whether she might not like to play some Schumann for him. Landowska replied with no little diffidence that she preferred to play Bach. And with this exchange began a close and fruitful friendship. Landowska could not have found a finer mentor, for Bordes stood at the opposite pole from pedantry. Of him Pierre Lalo wrote:

> Others before him, and even at the same time, devoted their attention to old music. Excellent editions existed of sixteenth- and seventeenth-century music. Yet these publications exerted no influence. The majority of scholars lack taste; if a text is old they publish it without making any distinction between a worthwhile work and a dull one. . . . With Bordes, on the other hand, an infallible taste, a sort of divination, always directed his choices from among the works of the past; everything that he revealed was exquisite or sublime. And he was not content just to edit this music which he so loved; he believed

> nothing had been accomplished if the music remained immured in a book. He could not refrain from imparting it to us directly; bringing it to us, so to speak; making us hear it as he heard it himself. From this stemmed those extraordinary interpretations at the newly founded Schola. . . . No other conductor, even with infinitely more powerful resources, could ever have awakened in us comparable feelings.

This vital savant was only one of a brilliant group that helped to orient Landowska in the direction of her subsequent career. Through Bordes she met Jules Écorcheville, an erudite young man whose life work was tragically terminated in World War I. Écorcheville was then reviewing mountains of scores and documents in preparation for his treatise on musical æsthetics, *De Lulli à Rameau: 1690–1730*. His library was wonderfully complete and, says Landowska, "it was usually to be found in my home." Another member of this circle, one considerably older than Landowska, was Lionel de la Laurencie. Only a year before meeting Landowska he had given up a career at law to concentrate on music. La Laurencie's passion was for seventeenth- and eighteenth-century French music, and his books on French violin-music, on the creators of French opera, and on Lully and Rameau are still unsurpassed.

Yet another friend whom she met through Charles Bordes was André Pirro, a scholar intensely fond of Bach and engaged in amassing the great backlog of information that was to flower in his books *L'Orgue de Jean-Sebastien Bach* and *L'Esthétique de Jean-Sebastien Bach*. Pirro directed keyboard instruction at the Schola Cantorum. Although Landowska never studied with him in any "official" sense, he afforded her inestimable help in finding a way to the proper interpretation of Bach. "Through Pirro," she explains, "I discovered the beauty of Bach's cantatas, and it is in the cantatas that I find the key to my interpretation of the harpsichord works."

Drawn into this vortex of stimulating personalities, Landowska emerged quickly from her former irresolution. The spontaneous love that she had borne since childhood for the music of Bach now found sustenance in commerce with these savants. She had first to catch up with this heady milieu, to explore the history, the literature, the æsthetics of pre-nineteenth-century music. After that might come original thought and contribution. Thus in 1900 commenced the education of Wanda Landowska—a process still in operation.

Enthusiasm and ability soon secured Landowska's place in the affections of Bordes, Pirro, La Laurencie, and those other scholars and musicians who were reactivating the music of the past. Landowska appeared often on the programs at the Schola Cantorum, playing Bach or the French *clavecinistes*. Always she used the piano; but little by little the conviction grew upon her that the music of Bach and his predecessors could not be penetrated successfully with this instrument. In all honesty she had to admit to the method in the madness that had prompted a Liszt or a Tausig to encumber Bach's writing with anachronistic fireworks. For when one played Bach on the piano exactly as it appeared in the Gesellschaft edition, the music failed to "sound." The nineteenth century, in so far as it bothered with Bach's keyboard writing at all, had met this deficiency by grafting its own ideas of musical brilliance onto Bach's own bare structure. Landowska saw no lasting merit in this solution. There must surely be a way, she felt, to perform Bach's music both effectively and without treason to his style or thought.

At this juncture the harpsichord enters. It is inaccurate to say, as many do, that Landowska reclaimed the instrument from utter silence, that until she took hold the harpsichord had languished as a museum exhibit. In spirit this may be true, but not in detail. "Modern" harpsichords existed; indeed, one of Landowska's first impressions in Paris was the sight of a harpsichord in the Erard showrooms. Nor was this a solitary phenomenon; the firm of Pleyel had also produced a contemporary model of the instrument. These first reconstructions, however, could not render full justice to the works of the great harpsichord composers; rather were they quaint playthings, bought by wealthy amateurs for the performance of easy gavottes and minuets. No one considered the harpsichord a vehicle of genuine musical expression. On its rare public appearances the instrument is said to have been tinkled rather than played. It was viewed in the same light as a cherub by Watteau—engaging, deliciously rococo, but hardly worth the expenditure of much intellectual or expressive power.

This partially explains why even such enthusiasts of old music as Charles Bordes or André Pirro could be prejudiced against the harpsichord. For, amazing as it seems today, these far-ranging pioneers, who did so much to re-establish the music of Bach and his contemporaries, professed to dislike the instrument for which much of that very music was composed. However, the tinkling estate of the harpsichord as it existed in 1900 only begins to explain their opposition. More important was the notion, based on a firm nineteenth-century belief in material progress, that the piano represented advancement, a substantial improvement on an inadequate instrument. How nonsensical, it seemed to them, to revert to an "archaic" and "imperfect" mechanism. What is more, the spirit of the time did not encourage musical interpretation based on historical data. Had Bach died without ever setting eye on a piano? The answer did not seem to matter, for one was asked to ignore pedantic minutiæ in interpreting his music. "One can lay down a principle," wrote Paul Dukas in 1896, "that the more universal and profound a musical conception is, no matter from what era it dates, the less will its execution depend on archaic details. Historical accuracy with regard to interpretative fidelity is of little importance. . . . What matters is that we should be shown those aspects of a work that are directed to us across boundaries and through the years. To go further, under pretext of historical truthfulness, is to give undue emphasis to the transitory and perishable." There need, of course, be no conflict between the universal spirit of a composer's work and the interpretative letter of the law that his epoch obeyed. But Dukas, and here he spoke for most of his contemporaries, failed to see this. In 1896 the two elements seemed irreconcilable. Is it any wonder, then, that the harpsichord met with disfavor? To consign the profound and enduring musical expressions of Bach to the timid jangle of an "obsolete" instrument appeared to be the height of folly. Dukas reduced it to the absurd: "One might as well conclude that in order to increase interest in *Don Giovanni* each member of the audience should receive a wig at the box-office."

Landowska felt confident that in one respect her learned friends were mistaken. She knew that for Bach's music the modern piano did *not* represent progress. Quite the contrary. Far from representing an improvement over its plucked-string ancestor, the piano actually lacked certain sonorous resources to translate Bach's keyboard music. Armed with this conviction, and despite the pleas of friends who attempted to dissuade her from pursuing an *ignis fatuus*, Landowska threw in her lot with the harpsichord. She moved to the quiet of L'Hautil, a little village seventeen miles northwest of Paris, and there she began to work at the harpsichord that Pleyel had lent her. This meant exploring virgin territory. Those few people who played the instrument at that time treated it as an inferior piano. Landowska realized that she must first discard all that she had learned of piano technique and approach the harpsichord as an utterly different instrument. Ahead of her lay the rediscovery of a forgotten technique through painstaking research into historical documents, years of experimentation, and the designing of a larger and more variegated instrument.

But the accomplishment of all this lay in the future. Wanda Landowska's career as a harpsichordist began with her debut recital in Paris in 1903. On this occasion she played only one piece on the harpsichord. The remainder of the program she played on the piano. This may seem surprising, but Landowska, being then admired as a pianist, had to proceed slowly in imposing the harpsichord. The practice of introducing the harpsichord in a small, single dose was followed on the tours that she now began to make through France, Switzerland, and Belgium. Gradually, as audiences became accustomed to the new instrument and as Landowska progressed in her mastery of it, she increased the harpsichord content and decreased that of the piano. Even those programs with a preponderance of harpsichord over piano trod nimbly on the patience of audiences. The day when Landowska could offer a program consisting solely of the "Goldberg" Variations was yet many years away. On these early tours she played mostly short pieces or snatches from larger works—Daquin's *Le Coucou*, Rameau's *Le Tambourin*, Couperin's *Le Rossignol en amour*, Handel's "*Harmonious Blacksmith*," a gavotte or musette from one of Bach's English Suites. For friends, and occasionally in public, she would essay more daring material —a complete *Ordre* of Couperin or Bach's Chromatic Fantasy and Fugue. Slowly those who had seemed intractable began to take a kinder view of the harpsichord. As early as 1905 Albert Schweitzer had written in his great book on Bach:

> Anyone who has heard Wanda Landowska play the *Italian Concerto* on her wonderful Pleyel harpsichord finds it hard to understand how it could ever again be played on a modern piano.

When Landowska demonstrated the instrument to a congress of musicologists at Basle, the warmth of their reception astonished her. Slowly she was coaxing back to the harpsichord the respect it had lost over a century before.

As her reputation grew, the tours widened. Once in Russia she played for Tolstoy at his country home, Yasnaya Polyana, arriving there by sleigh at the height of a blizzard. Spain was added to her itinerary, as were Poland, Germany, and the British Isles. (An interesting footnote to these early travels can be found in Landowska's observation that those countries where plucked-string instruments were common accepted the harpsichord most readily. Thus, Russia and Spain—with their tradition, respectively, of the balalaika and guitar—were quicker to appreciate the harpsichord than Germany or England.) Her concerts in Paris became more concentrated. In February 1904 she gave her first all-Bach program, though only one work was performed on the harpsichord; and on March 11, 1905, at the inaugural concert of Gustave Bret's Bach Society, she played the G minor Concerto on the harpsichord. At home the experimentation and research progressed with increasing zeal. With her husband as collaborator Landowska wrote *Musique ancienne*,* a militant book that espoused the cause of old music through a graceful blend of erudition and ironic wit. Read today, more than forty years after publication, *Musique ancienne* may seem laden with the obvious. If so, that is because its battle has been won.

Along with this volume addressed to a lay audience came a stream of monographs written for specialists. Two of great

* Paris: 1909; English translation, *Music of the Past* (New York: 1926).

importance were "*Les Allemands et la musique française au XVIIIe siècle,*" published in the *Mercure de France* (1911), and "*Les Influences françaises chez Bach,*" which appeared in *Le Courier musical* (1912). They combated the general opinion that Bach had composed in an artistic vacuum, secure in his provincial German town against all outside influences. Paul Dukas had written in 1896:

> *The Well-Tempered Clavier* is a production of the eighteenth century. If one compares it with the preludes and fugues composed by other German organists before Bach or contemporary with him, one is forced to admit that it shows only the sketchiest relationship. Study of these other preludes and fugues will afford no help to the interpreter of Bach's *Well-Tempered Clavier.* To arrive at a proper interpretation one must rely on the expressive content of each prelude and fugue, paying no heed to such archaic clues as may be applicable to Rameau or to Handel.

Landowska's researches showed this image of Bach's isolation to be erroneous. Augmenting the work already done by Pirro on this subject, she demonstrated that Bach knew and admired the music of French and Italian harpsichordists. Then, turning to the works of Bach, she proclaimed the strength of this Latin influence. She instanced the striking similarity between the Courante of Bach's B flat Partita and Couperin's *Le Moucheron.* She showed how the D major Fugue from Book I of *The Well-Tempered Clavier* was in reality a typical "overture in the French style." This was more than the mere redress of a historical inaccuracy. It afforded innumerable clues to proper Bach tempos and rhythms. It showed that one way to the soul of Bach lay down the avenue of early French music.

The longer Landowska played on her original Pleyel harpsichord, the more surely she realized that it and the similar instruments produced by Pleyel's French competitors were inadequate to the demands of Bach's keyboard writing. Their volume of sound was too slight, their tonal gamut too diminutive. Most important, they lacked balance. The first Pleyel harpsichords were built with the eight-foot and four-foot registers (i.e., the normal octave and one octave higher), but they did not have the sixteen-foot register (one octave below normal) to provide the proper balance. It was plain to Landowska's ears that Bach's resounding masses of counterpoint (for instance, the G minor Fugue from Book I of "The Forty-Eight") called for an instrument of greater potentialities.

Landowska tracked down every document she could find pertaining to harpsichord construction; on her tours she never lost the opportunity of examining museum instruments. Especially valuable was the rich collection in the Heyer Museum at Cologne, where she saw fine examples of early eighteenth-century harpsichords whose capabilities far exceeded those of the "modern" Pleyel on which she performed. Small wonder that her little gavotte-player could not cope with Bach's sublime writing! But between this realization and the construction of an amplified contemporary harpsichord lay years of work, first in arriving at the proper specifications, and then in translating them to actuality in Pleyel's workshop. The new instrument finally made its debut in 1912 at a Bach festival in Breslau. Now, at last, Bach could be sounded with full majesty.

Not only had the sixteen-foot register added a deeper, more balanced tonal quality, but every sound produced by the instrument—even those from the less resounding four-foot and eight-foot registers—took on greater brilliance and volume. With an expanded set of pedal "stops," the performer could employ a much wider range of timbres. Yet these very refinements, the fruit of long research and planning, incurred from the outset harsh criticism–criticism, it should be noted, that echoes even today. Bach, the objections went, could not possibly have possessed a harpsichord with the mechanical perfection achieved by Pleyel's factory. Complaint centered on the "anachronisms" of Landowska's new instrument. It belonged, critics alleged, to the twentieth century rather than the eighteenth; it was too brilliant, too loud, too variegated. After forty years Landowska has learned to accept these rebukes philosophically. "I cannot sign a guarantee that this is how Bach wanted it," she will say, "but I *feel* that my harpsichord is right for his music." Who can dispute this matter with certitude? Bach's day did not enjoy the blessings of mass production. No standard harpsichord existed; every instrument-maker fashioned his own according to a different set of specifications. Landowska designed her harpsichord as a "symbol" of the early eighteenth-century instrument, a synthesis of many prototypes. To the best of her knowledge it is a faithful re-creation.

That the new harpsichord made its debut in Breslau betokened the increasing interest and respect that Landowska's work enjoyed in German musical circles. Hermann Kretzschmar, director of the Berlin Hochschule für Musik, decided in 1913 to found a class for the harpsichord in this important conservatory, and invited Landowska to conduct it. She accepted, and was caught in Germany at the outbreak of World War I. She was separated now from her friends and coworkers in Paris, for the Imperial German government held her, her husband, and her parents in Berlin as civil prisoners on parole. Years of isolation followed, yet years rich in musical satisfaction. Now there was nothing but time–time to become completely acquainted with the new instrument, time to learn the proper exploitation of its diverse resources. Now, too, was the time to study Bach manuscripts in the rich German libraries. At the end of World War I, just as the Landowska entourage was ready to return to Paris, Henry Lew was killed in an automobile accident. The loss of this volatile companion, invaluable collaborator, and knowing organizer of practical affairs was cruel and devastating. For the first time in Landowska's life she was confronted alone with the direction of her career. And that career pursued its own inexorable course. Ten days after Henry Lew's death she had to appear in Basle, where a performance of the *St. Matthew Passion* depended upon her participation.

With the end of the war, Landowska returned to Paris, to her friends and the intellectual atmosphere she had come to relish. Her homecoming recital evoked tumultuous enthusiasm. Five years earlier, she had left Paris as the chief representative of a cause still in contest. Now, in her forties, she returned as a welcome ambassador of old music and the harpsichord. The Landowska cult spread across Europe in the wake of her extensive tours. In 1923 its reverberations overseas were such that Arthur Judson booked her for a tour of several large American cities. She made her debut in this country with the Philadelphia Orchestra under Leopold Stokowski, playing concertos by Bach, Handel, and Mozart. The success of this and subsequent concerts impelled Judson to bring her back the next year. By 1925, when she came again not only to play in public but also to teach at Philadelphia's Curtis Institute, she had earned an impressive position in American musical life.

After her departure from Berlin in 1919, Landowska's life remained for some time preponderantly itinerant. She was an "attraction" continually in demand, and to satisfy the world's curiosity she traveled to Stockholm and Cairo, to Buenos Aires and Minneapolis, accompanied always by her faithful companion Elsa Schunicke. Trouping in this fashion offered its financial rewards; it offered, too, the satisfaction of displaying widely an entirely new artistic concept. But time brought an increasing discontent with a regime revolving constantly around timetables, hotels, and the careful transportation of a harpsichord. Besides, one aspect of the conquest was complete. The world had been taught to accept the harpsichord and to acknowledge the validity and beauty of interpreting Bach in the style of his day. Now even more ambitious projects beckoned, and for these Landowska required a headquarters.

In 1927 she established herself in Saint-Leu-la-Forêt, a little town ten miles north of Paris whose principal claim to eminence lies in Landowska's thirteen-year residence there. Like thousands of her admirers, I have made the pilgrimage to St.-Leu; but when I went—in the spring of 1950—no music had sounded within the walls of her house for a decade. Curiosity prompted me one sunny day when I was visiting Paris to take the half-hour railroad trip to St.-Leu. The town itself turned out to be a typical Paris suburb, centering around a wide main street of scant charm and a church quite accurately described by the *Guide Bleu* as "*sans intérêt.*" I walked into a café adjacent to the station and asked—without much hope of getting an answer—where the house of Madame Landowska would find itself. I had not reckoned on the strong memories that St.-Leu still treasured of its former "attraction." The directions were immediate and precise: just walk up the avenue Charles de Gaulle (that was certainly a new note!) until you reach No. 88. A five-minute walk up a hilly street brought me to the house. The view of all but the roof was obstructed by a high brick wall, and a strong metal door barred entrance. "*Sonnez,*" said the sign, but five minutes of patient ringing produced no response. A kind neighbor walking his dog volunteered the useful information that the bell had not worked for years. Much banging and shouting finally sufficed to attract attention from within the house. Landowska's former secretary, Diana Mathot, who has watched over the neglected property since the war, appeared at the gate. I explained the nature of my visit, that having heard so much of this house and its associations I wanted to see it at first hand, and the door was kindly opened.

From many prewar photographs I thought I knew what to expect. The gate would open onto a footpath leading past the house and through a neatly shrubbed garden to a trim, modern concert-hall. The path would be shaded by an arbor of luxuriant vines. But when the gate did open, a sadly different scene appeared—a garden overgrown with weeds, the grass a ragged six inches high, debris littering the ground, no arbor but a naked rusting trellis, the modern concert-hall now streaked with fissures, its windows agape with dirty, broken glass. Here was the legacy of the Nazis, who despoiled the place of all its musical treasures, billeted troops in the house, and loaded the concert hall with supplies.

I had to dismiss the present and call back yesterday. Here in this little hall, which Landowska had built especially for her concerts, took place some of the outstanding musical events of our century. From everywhere musicians came to hear her play, to attend her master classes, to examine the collection of old instruments, to consult a rich library of music and documents. Every Sunday from May to mid-July the two o'clock train from the Gare du Nord would carry some three hundred visitors to Saint-Leu-la-Forêt, nicknamed—quite inappropriately—"the French Bayreuth." They would walk up the avenue Charles de Gaulle (it was then the rue de Pontoise) and find their seats in the small hall. At three o'clock Landowska would appear, take her seat at the instrument, and begin to talk about the program for that afternoon's music.

A program ensued the like of which could be heard nowhere else, a program that made no concessions whatever to the conventions of concert-giving. It might, for instance, be occupied entirely with Bach's "Goldberg" Variations, which until their rehabilitation by Landowska had been known mainly in a two-piano transcription, and then only to amateurs, never to the musical public. At St.-Leu the Variations were on the program season after season, two or three times a year. On one occasion Landowska's program might be devoted entirely to sonatas by Scarlatti; on another it might be all-Couperin; a third program might be given over to works by Rameau. All this was unprecedented. Scarlatti, Couperin, and Rameau were often to be heard at the outset of a piano recital, offered by the artist as an aperitif, but never were they allowed to dominate a program. Landowska showed that all-Scarlatti made as much sense as all-Chopin or all-Beethoven. She showed, too, the treasures that had come from the pens of composers hitherto known only as names in history books: Chambonnières, Gaspard-le-Roux, Gauthier-le-Vieux, Pachelbel, Kuhnau, Fischer, Froberger, Marcello.

Only part of the activity at St.-Leu was accounted for by these concerts. A stream of students came and went. Some were content with two or three lessons, enough to go forth into the world with the impressive designation, "student of Wanda Landowska"; others—like Clifford Curzon, Ruggero Gerlin, Denise Restout, and Putnam Aldrich—stayed on for years, and continued afterwards to work in the spirit of the school. At St.-Leu, also, were made many of Landowska's great recordings. And always the research, the experimentation went on. The concerts in Paris and the tours throughout Europe continued as before, but it was in this town on the edge of the Montmorency Forest that Landowska found full scope for her ever-developing genius. Here she erected a temple of music to glorify the age of Bach.

Early in the morning of May 10, 1940, the Nazi *Wehrmacht* invaded France; three weeks later their cannon could be heard north of St.-Leu. The temple had to be abandoned.

Into a car put at Landowska's disposal by Diana Mathot went some rare scores and books, together with necessary clothing. Yet even when entirely filled the car contained only a fraction of Landowska's possessions. Left behind were dozens of instruments, thousands of books and scores, treasured letters, and memorabilia. At the time the loss did not seem permanent. Faced with disaster, we fortify ourselves with a grand show of optimism. After all, General Weygand would surely counterattack soon; then one could return to St.-Leu and resume life as before. Landowska, her companion Denise Restout, and Diana piled into the laden automobile and headed toward Blois, where a good friend and pupil had offered them sanctuary. Blois lay one hundred miles to the south, and they arrived there in a few hours. As soon as the trunks and boxes had been removed, Diana drove back to St.-Leu. That night the radio news report made clear their dangerous mistake. The French Army had all but collapsed, and Blois itself would shortly be threatened.

The next day Denise began a frantic search for a car to take them farther south. She hastened from garage to garage, only to be told that all forms of conveyance had been spoken for. In one garage she found a driver who had been hired to drive to Paris. "Would it not be more discreet to travel in the other direction?" Denise suggested. The logic of this, plus a healthy sum of money, did the trick. At four the next morning the Landowska entourage left Blois. And just in time. When they arrived that evening in Montauban, far to the south, the papers carried the report that Blois had been attacked by air during the day.

By July Landowska was settled in Banyuls-sur-Mer, a fishing village just north of the Spanish border, where her friend Aristide Maillol had his home. For several weeks melancholy and inertia overwhelmed her. This was a state of morale that could not long withstand Landowska's resilient temperament.

She discovered that her landlady had an old upright piano. Soon the harpsichordist was embarked on a typically Olympian project—nothing less than a complete restudying of Bach's *Well-Tempered Clavier.* On this battered upright Landowska worked out anew the entire harpsichord registration, and the results of her imaginative exertions are to be heard in the RCA Victor recording, for the interpretation heard on these records stems directly from the conception formulated at Banyuls.

In October 1940 a disturbing postcard came from St.-Leu. Without going into detail, it intimated that something very serious had happened to Landowska's property. By then the armistice had been signed, turning over the northern half of France to German occupation. It was decided that Denise had better risk a return to St.-Leu and investigate on the spot. What she discovered surpassed their worst fears. Shortly after the occupation of St.-Leu, Gestapo men had arrived with several large trucks and looted Landowska's house of all its instruments and music. Nothing was overlooked, for they came with a detailed catalogue of her possessions. To this day Landowska wonders how such a list was prepared. After the Gestapo had shipped off the booty to Germany, they turned the place over to some *Wehrmacht* officers, who proceeded to help themselves to her furniture. This was the situation as Denise found it. She appealed at once to the French authorities, but they were powerless to help. Landowska's Polish birth and Jewish ancestry combined to deprive her of any rights.

Landowska had meanwhile decided that the south of France was no place in which to remain indefinitely. A devoted Swiss pupil, Isabelle Nef, had lent her money to purchase the last harpsichord at Pleyel, and concerts were once more possible. Landowska tried to arrange a tour in Spain, but was refused permission. Next she tried to arrange some concert dates in Switzerland, and for this approval was granted. In October 1941 she left for Geneva accompanied by Denise, who had finally returned to Banyuls by illegally crossing the border between Occupied and Free France. On the way they stopped over at Marseille to obtain visas at the U.S. Consulate and to make reservations on an American ship sailing from Lisbon in six weeks. Early in November, Landowska, Denise, and the harpsichord set out on the arduous trip to Lisbon over dilapidated Spanish and Portugese railways.

When they sailed from Lisbon, the United States was a neutral. When they docked in New York City it was at war. In those first days after Pearl Harbor the immigration authorities were extremely wary of incoming aliens. Landowska and Denise were dispatched immediately to Ellis Island. It took a sheaf of letters from influential citizens testifying to Landowska's eminence in the world of art—rounded up by the basso Doda Conrad—to secure the release of the two from Ellis Island.

Unaware that it had decayed from its splendors of fifteen years before when last she had stayed there, the great harpsichordist took a room in a shabby Times Square hotel. And it was just as well that she chose modest accommodations, for her cash resources on arrival totaled less than three hundred dollars. She needed desperately to make money so that she could pay her debts for the harpsichord and the steamship passage to America; more than that, she needed to make music, to found a new temple to Bach, to compensate for what had been left behind at St.-Leu. A recital in Town Hall was announced. Friends counseled a varied program; Landowska insisted on *la spécialité de St.-Leu*—an afternoon devoted to the "Goldberg" Variations. The decision to gamble the reestablishment of a career on so recondite a work was eminently characteristic of this pioneering artist. She played on February 21, 1942, to a full house that was, Virgil Thomson reported, "virtually a social register of professional musicians." At the concert's end Landowska knew quite certainly that the spirit of St.-Leu could be revived in the New World.

History began to repeat itself. Just as in 1919, when she returned to Paris after several years' absence, so now in New York her reappearance generated fervent enthusiasm—most of it genuine, some of it artificial and snobbish. With the proceeds from her first concert she rented a sprawling apartment in an old building on Central Park West and began to hold master classes in its large living room. *Life* photographed her; the press interviewed her. When the Petrillo ban on recording ended in 1944, RCA Victor jumped on the Landowska bandwagon and signed her for a series of recordings. Though she had already recorded the "Goldberg" Variations in Europe before the war, RCA Victor persuaded her to do them again with the benefit of new recording techniques. The company anticipated a comfortable sale of four or five thousand sets. They were more than a little surprised when at the end of the first year it had reached fourteen thousand, and their amazement grew when at the end of six years the sale had climbed to thirty-five thousand.

With the war's end came the renewal of ties with France. From various corners of Hitler's defeated empire, remnants of the St.-Leu library came to light. The artist's favorite harpsichord turned up in Germany, found by the same Doda Conrad who had extricated Landowska from Ellis Island in 1941. (The instrument is now in Lakeville, Connecticut, and can be heard in the recording of *The Well-Tempered Clavier.*) As France came closer to normal life, Landowska's friends pleaded with her to return, or at least to give a series of European concerts. The temptation was great; tentative plans were drawn up for a three-month tour throughout France, England, and Switzerland. But in the end, despite her nostalgia for France, Landowska thought better of it. Having reached the age of seventy, she hesitated to dissipate her energies. All her strength was to be reserved for the greatest project she had yet attempted.

Landowska has called her recording of *The Well-Tempered Clavier* "my last will and testament." The expression is not to be taken in a purely valedictory sense. Her gusto, her buoyant spirit and physical well-being will never stomach the pale desuetude of retirement. She means, rather, that these discs represent a summation of her musical legacy. In them are embodied the result of study and experience spanning more than half a century. Never was a recording more carefully prepared. Landowska is taking four years to complete it, with eight preludes and fugues recorded per session, each "session" lasting three or four weeks. If necessary, she will record the same prelude or fugue five, six, seven, twenty times, until the interpretation accords with the standard she has set for herself. Between sessions stretch periods of four or five months during which she studies the next eight preludes and fugues to be recorded. Her *modus operandi* well illustrates Carlyle's contention that genius is the capacity for taking infinite pains.

The recording is a monument to patient care and rational planning. It is not a mausoleum. Infinite pains are all very well provided they do not kill vitality. An appreciation of this danger underlies Landowska's aversion to being called a perfectionist. Her interpretation of *The Well-Tempered Clavier* is anything but static. It is unpredictable, but never capricious. Instances abound where, in tempo, in accent, in phrasing, in timbre, she has upset all former notions of how the score should sound. In many instances she is bolstered by research, of which more anon. But the basic consideration is her attitude toward Bach and his "severe" contrapuntal writing. "Be not overawed by the stern appearance and heavy wig of Father Bach," she adjures. "Be not afraid of the supreme contrapuntal science of the fugues. Let us gather around him, feel the love, the noble goodness that flow from each one of his phrases and which invigorate and bind us by ties strong and warm." She is fond of saying: "Bach and I, we understand each other; we make a happy couple."

In 1950 Landowska gave up her New York apartment and moved to the house in Lakeville, Connecticut, which had previously served merely as a summer home. In this house RCA Victor makes recordings; here come a few fortunate students; here the harpsichordist is writing her commentaries on *The Well-Tempered Clavier*. Two or three times a year she journeys to New York to give recitals; occasionally she will venture as far afield as Boston or Washington. But if her immediate connection with the world of music is tenuous, in a less direct, more far-reaching sense she exerts a prodigious influence. With Toscanini and Casals she belongs to a triumvirate occupying an unassailable position among contemporary performers—a position owing to absolute technical mastery and an original interpretative temperament of revolutionary effect.

In what does her pre-eminence consist? There is, first of all, the command of her instrument. Like Casals, she forged a new technique that has largely been accepted as gospel. Indeed, Landowska's accomplishment transcends even that of Casals. He upset previous conceptions of fingering and bowing to such good effect that he has been widely emulated. Yet the previous conceptions *did* exist, the cello *was* played—so that Casals was able to profit from the mistakes of others. Landowska had to commit and undo her own mistakes. As the tradition of harpsichord-playing had withered a century before her time, she was obliged to work in a vacuum, to form a technique out of nothing. Pioneering has grave disadvantages; the less hardy retreat or perish at the frontier. Those who persevere long enough, however, are usually well recompensed. So it has been with Landowska. She who first attempted the rediscovery of harpsichord technique has been rewarded with unequaled mastery of the instrument.

Next, in defining Landowska's stature, would come her immense knowledge of musical literature and history. She bristles at the term "musicologist," with its usual reference to a narrow specialist who grubs among documents, dispassionately amassing information for its own sake. It is hard to strike sparks from the cold stone of musicology. Landowska's love of old music derives not from scholastic curiosity, but from its sheer beauty. "To me," she says, "research has only been a path to this beauty, an aid to its discovery." For half a century she has pursued and devoured documentary evidence on matters of interpretation and technique. Leather-bound tomes—mostly early musical treatises and encyclopedias—fill her library. Often a volume of eight hundred pages will have yielded only a single clue; but if one morsel of information was found, a bookmark will indicate the passage, with comments neatly penciled in the margin. Probably no one has a greater firsthand acquaintance with pre-Beethoven keyboard music. Farnaby, Peerson, Byrd, Sweelinck, Frescobaldi, Froberger, Chambonnières, Dandrieu, Francisque, Daquin, Kuhnau, Pachelbel, Telemann, to say nothing of Rameau, Couperin, Scarlatti, Bach, Handel, Haydn, and Mozart—these are the composers whose works have been Landowska's searching concern for more than fifty years. And she has not been content to experience them only on her own instrument. You will find her as conversant with Couperin's vocal *Tenebrae* as with his *pièces pour clavecin;* she can find her way among Handel's operas and oratorios as surely as among his keyboard suites; long ago she took André Pirro's advice and familiarized herself with Bach's two hundred-odd cantatas. I can think of no contemporary performer and few "musicologists" who can draw on so deep a well of knowledge.

Technical mastery and immense erudition—these are the

bricks of the Landowska musical edifice. The mortar that holds them together is the performer's vital, original musicianship. This ingredient has been neglected too often in generalizations applied to her. Thus, it is said that, steeped in musical and literary research, she eschews the promptings of instinct in favor of intellect; that she stands in the vanguard of a purist revolt against the romanticizing of Bach; that she propels whatever lies under her hands with a relentless, metronomic beat. All these statements carry the germ of truth; but push them too far and they collapse. She is intellectual, of course; but a divine intuitive sense commands her playing. A purist she is in the sense of striving always to play Bach "according to Bach"; but this endeavor often leads away from a literal rendition of the text to something claiming strong kinship with romanticism. Rhythmic drive she exhibits always; but it is compounded at times of demonstrably unmetronomic liberties. How fortunate that these contradictions exist! Without them Landowska would be a musician of consequence; with them she is a musician of genius.

One could memorize every word of *L'Art de toucher le clavecin*, read the complete works of Molière, and gaze perpetually at the ordered canvases of Largillière without anticipating the sinuous style, the dry wit, the pathetic tenderness, that Landowska can release from the works of Couperin. Her interpretation of *Les Folies françaises* is one of those rare pinnacles of musical achievement, an accomplishment to be ranked with Toscanini's "Manzoni" Requiem or Lehmann's Marschallin. Landowska lifted Couperin straight out of the Dresden china cupboard into which decades of tinkling had placed him; she demonstrated persuasively that his contemporaries had added "*le Grand*" to his surname with good reason. Agile fingers and copious research lie at the core of her accomplishment, but they would have made no odds had not Landowska brought her own fancy to bear, had her imagination not been able to hurdle the usual view of Couperin, *le petit maître*, and see instead a musician of subtle and profound poetry.

It is all very well to be familiar with the German, French, and Italian antecedents out of which Bach's keyboard music grew, to possess a working knowledge of the entire Bach canon, to translate his ornaments in conformity with historical research, to have reached the point of technical proficiency at which the independence of each hand is assured. Undoubtedly, these are essential factors in Landowska's interpretations of Bach; but without the catalysis of her audacious musical temperament they would have won no world conquest. It was the savant of seventeenth- and eighteenth-century music who discovered that Bach's D major Fugue (Book I, *The Well-Tempered Clavier*) should be performed in the manner of an *ouverture à la française;* it was the musician of genius who gave to this fugue's interpretation such coruscating sweep, such dazzling pomp. A similar coexistence of mind and spirit can be found in her playing of the prelude preceding this fugue. It was the erudite student who knew the propriety of embellishing the concluding chords; it was the creative master who saw embedded in the flow of sixteenth notes a vibrant horn-call that could act as focal point for the prelude.

A superficial hearing of a Landowska recording nets the impression of unflagging tempo, a steady drive from start to finish, like the ticking of a train over railroad ties. But get down to cases, subject it to the beat of a metronome, and you will realize that within the seemingly straightforward, rhythmic pulse there are minute liberties that inflect and animate the conception. In whatever she touches, be it the *Italian Concerto*, the "Goldberg" Variations, or any of the "Forty-Eight," a subtle tempo rubato lurks behind the rigid framework. Why do rhythmic liberties in lesser hands impinge on the music's argument, while in Landowska's they heighten its poetry? She answers with one of her articles of faith: "My playing is very free; but the more I am free, the more I am controlled." In other words, her liberties come *after* she has established perfect and rigid discipline.

Because Landowska is an *exécutante attitrée* of Couperin and Bach, she has earned the reputation in some quarters of being herself of an antique disposition. Her deportment on the concert platform certainly does not belie this general reputation. As she floats out onto the stage slowly and noiselessly in a medieval, red-velvet gown, sits in a high-backed baroque chair, and turns down the lamp by her harpsichord, she seems to have stolen into our midst from a distant century. But all this is to serve the exigencies of what Jules Lemaître used to call *l'optique du théâtre*. It helps the listener make the transition from the twentieth century outside the concert hall to the eighteenth century of Bach. In real life she exhibits nothing of the old fogy. "I have always been in revolt," she says with pardonable relish. And, indeed, there are still many conservative souls who refuse to accept her musical audacities. That the great figures of twentieth-century French music—Ravel, D'Indy, Dukas—were her close friends is symptomatic of the fresh vitality of her temperament. Manuel de Falla composed a harpsichord concerto for her and Francis Poulenc a *Concert champêtre*. She worked closely with both Falla and Poulenc, giving each the benefit of her experience with the instrument, and she has played these contemporary harpsichord works on numerous occasions. But most indicative of her modernity is her attitude toward old music. "The fact that this or that music is old," she avows, "never made it dearer to me. I love and play Bach, Mozart, and Couperin because they are young and beautiful."

Some virtuoso musicians are best encountered across the footlights. Face to face you may find them incorrigibly one-sided, vain, and of no great personal distinction or charm. Landowska is not of this ilk. She is wise and lovable. She has read voraciously and with understanding for sixty years. Tolstoy, Rilke, Rodin, Valéry were her good friends. You can talk with her to advantage about literature and about criticism (her "special love"). This rounded culture is reflected in her playing. There are in her person and her playing nobility, calm, and faith—faith not in any revealed religion, but in the Humanities, the world of art. Paraphrasing Louis Dubedat, Landowska could deliver this creed: "I believe in Couperin, Mozart, and Bach; in the might of design, the mystery of sound, the redemption of all things by Beauty everlasting, and the message of Art that has made these hands blessed."

Index

A Note on the Type

THIS BOOK *was set on the Linotype in* JANSON, *a recutting made direct from the type cast from matrices (now in possession of the Stempel foundry, Frankfurt am Main) made by Anton Janson some time between 1660 and 1687.*

Of Janson's origin nothing is known. He may have been a relative of Justus Janson, a printer of Danish birth who practiced in Leipzig from 1614 to 1635. Some time between 1657 and 1668 Anton Janson, a punch-cutter and type-founder, bought from the Leipzig printer Johann Erich Hahn the type-foundry that had formerly been a part of the printing house of M. Friedrich Lankisch. Janson's types were first shown in a specimen sheet issued at Leipzig about 1675. Janson's successor, and perhaps his son-in-law, Johann Karl Edling, issued a specimen sheet of Janson types in 1689. His heirs sold the Janson matrices in Holland to Wolffgang Dietrich Erhardt.

The book was composed, printed, and bound by THE PLIMPTON PRESS, *Norwood, Massachusetts. Designed by* HARRY FORD.